NEWT
Father of Michigan Men's Gymnastics

Colt Rosensweig

Colt Rosensweig

HURON
RIVER
PRESS

Huron River Press
P.O. Box 7797
Ann Arbor, MI 48197-7797
www.huronriverpress.com

HURON
RIVER
PRESS

LIBRARY OF CONGRESS CATALOGING-IN-PUBLICATION DATA

Rosensweig, Colt.
 Newt: the father of Michigan gymnastics / by Colt Rosensweig.
    p. cm.
 ISBN 978-1-932399-28-8
 1. Loken, Newton C. 2. Gymnastics coaches--Michigan--Biography. 3. University of Michigan--Gymnastic-sl--History. I. Title.
 GV460.2.L65R67 2012
 796.44092--dc23
 [B]
                                    2011052547

Table of Contents

Introduction

It all started with a small stuffed tiger.

I was six years old when my mom brought Tiger home. For three years, I carried him around under my left arm everywhere I went, until the only stuffing left was in his head, held there by a pair of faded scrunchies.

Tiger, and tigers, became an obsession. My dad saw an opening. A dedicated baseball fan, he had been trying in vain to interest me in the game on the field, as opposed to the vendors roaming the stands. Though he gleefully dressed me in tiny Dodgers uniforms, I never took to his team—or the local Giants or A's. "You know," Dad said to me one day, casting a glance at Tiger, "there's a baseball team called the Tigers."

My eyes got big. "Really?"

And with that, I was hooked. The Tigers immediately became my team. I had, it turned out, chosen a singularly unfortunate time to start following them, as they were mired in a twelve-year stretch of losing seasons. By the time I was fourteen, Dad and I were attending the entire Tigers-A's series in Oakland each year. As my attachment to the Tigers deepened, I began talking about going to see a game in Detroit, to "be among others of my kind."

And in 2000, the team's first year at Comerica Park, we finally attended a Tigers-A's series in Detroit.

It was amazing. Being surrounded by people wearing Tigers gear was a new and entirely delightful experience. I was about to start high school—and so I started thinking about college. What was the best school that was closest to my beloved Tigers?

The University of Michigan.

So began four years of dedicating myself entirely to that one goal: Getting Into Michigan. If not for my parents' urging, I wouldn't have applied to any other school. The day I received my acceptance letter was one of the happiest of my life.

Even so, it took a while for me to settle into Ann Arbor. Luckily, my friend Karl Stampfl dragged me to 420 Maynard, the offices of *The Michigan Daily*, and I had found my niche. Being a devout Tigers fan, I most wanted to cover Michigan baseball. But I discovered that in order to do that, I'd have to cover two small-sport beats and prove myself. As winter of my sophomore year approached, it was time to pick my second small sport. I put the question to my group of friends, who promised that if I covered men's gymnastics, they would accompany me to as many events as possible. I was sold.

After just a few weeks of covering my new team, I knew it wasn't just a stepping-stone to bigger things. I loved watching the guys practice and compete, loved the road trips to the meets, loved learning all I could about the sport. By my second year with the team, I was coming to practice at the Newt Loken Gymnastics Training Center nearly every day. And that's how I met Newt Loken himself.

I'd been hearing his name since I started covering the team—the award for best performance of the night, given out at every home meet, is called the Newt Loken Award. I was a little starstruck when I sat down one Monday by the pommel horse and found out the older gentleman next to me was *the* Newt

Loken. That quickly went away as we started talking. Newt told me stories of his career from the time we sat down every Monday till the time he headed home. I started telling my parents the stories when I talked to them.

In April of 2007, my mom and I were in State College, Pa., for the NCAA Championships. We were devouring a plate of stickies at The Diner when Mom said, "You should write a book about Newt." At first, I blew it off ... until I realized she was right. Newt's life is an amazing story, and no one yet had written it.

So began years of researching and interviewing. I spent a summer holed up in *The Daily* library reading through the bound volumes. I talked to any and all former gymnasts who answered my letters and e-mails. I recorded my long, rambling conversations with Newt in the gym and at the library. I spent about a week with Newt's Wonderful Book of Memories, lovingly constructed by his daughter Lani, poring over its detailed pages of photos, articles and letters. Once the manuscript began to take shape, Newt read it—over and over; any time I completed a new chapter, Newt wanted to read the entire thing again.

Before Newt passed away, I was able to talk with him one more time. I let him know that the big final edits on the book were finished, and that Steve and Shira Klein, the publishers at Huron River Press, were giving it its last review. After years of jokingly saying, "Well, we'll always have Kinko's!" it finally looked like the book would be published. I'm glad I was able to tell Newt that.

I just wish Newt could be here to see it finished.

Acknowledgements

This book wouldn't have been possible without a veritable army of friends and family. My parents encouraged and helped me from the start, allowing me to spend the summer of 2008 in Ann Arbor for research, and helping me do a fifth year at Michigan. Peggy Keller, my fantastic agent, looked out for me every step of the way.

My colleagues at *The Michigan Daily*, who may or may not have known I was writing a book at the time, were nonetheless always supportive of my ever-deepening men's gymnastics obsession. Thank you to everyone in *Daily Sports* who helped me follow my passion. Thanks to the staff of *The Minnesota Daily* as well, who allowed me to poke around in their archives during the 2009 NCAA Championships. And huge thanks, of course, to "The Kids," without whom I probably never would have become the men's gymnastics beat writer: Michael Rabinowitz, Katie Stamer, Shubha Rao, Nichole Hansen and Sara Rust.

"My" class of gymnasts at Michigan (2009) were instrumental in this whole process. Joe Catrambone and Jamie Thompson were two of the first to know about the book—their enthusiasm and excitement over the project convinced me once and for all that people really wanted to hear this story. Ralph Rosso, thanks for never failing to ask, "When's the book coming out?" Scott Bregman gave *NEWT* one of its early and excellent edits, something for which I'll forever be grateful. Kent Caldwell provided graphics for the interior layout.

Without the support and friendship of the Michigan men's gymnastics team and coaches, I could never have written *NEWT*. Justin Toman, former U.S. National Team member and the first (and best!) sports information director I worked with; class of 2006 Luke Bottke, Drew DiGiore, Gerry Signorelli, and Derek Croad; class of 2007 Andrew Elkind, Aaron Rakes, and Justin Laury; class of 2008 Dan Rais and Paul Woodward; class of 2009 Joe Catrambone, Jamie Thompson, Kent Caldwell, Scott Bregman, Phillip Goldberg, Ralph Rosso, Ryan McCarthy, and John Sawicki; class of 2010 Torrance Laury, Mel Santander, David Chan, Evan Heiter, and Joe Levine; class of 2011 Ben Baldus-Strauss, Thomas Kelley, Ian Makowske, Chris Cameron, Devan Cote, Adam Hamers, Andrew Vance, and Steve Crabtree; and class of 2012 Syque Caesar and Douglass Johnson. Head coach Kurt Golder has been one of the book's biggest proponents, along with assistant coaches Xiao Yuan and Scott Vetere, and alumni Rich Dopp and Eddie Umphrey. I can't thank Kurt enough for his support and encouragement from the very beginning. Thanks also to the many gymnastics parents who always made me feel like part of a huge extended family.

I loved talking to so many of Newt's gymnasts and colleagues—thank you to everyone who so generously shared your time, recollections and sometimes even photos with me: Phil Bolton, Ed Buchanan, Ray Gura, Jim Hayslett, Dick Kimball, Nino Marion, Chico Miele, Dan Millman, Joe Neuenswander, Ron Rapper, Bill Skinner, George Szypula, Bob Willoughby and Darrell Yee. I was also privileged to meet and speak with more of Newt's "boys" at his Celebration of Life, including

John Corritore, Carey Culbertson, Bob Darden, Dave Eddy, Don Hurst, Sid Jensen, Dave Lake, Bill Mackie, Kevin McKee, Murray Plotkin, Nigel Rothwell and Chuck Stillerman. The Celebration could have lasted a week and everyone would still be happily recounting their favorite Newt stories.

Thank you to Newt's wife, Dorothy, and wonderful children, Chris, Lani, Jon and Newt Jr.

Of course, the biggest thank-you of all goes to Newt. I am so thankful that our paths crossed—after meeting Newt, life was never the same.

Chapter 1

The End of an Era

On March 17, 1983, the University of Michigan Sports Information Department sent out a press release. No one who saw it, or the multitude of subsequent newspaper articles making the same announcement, could quite believe what they were reading.

After thirty-six years as the head coach of the men's gymnastics team and one of the best coaches in the entire collegiate sport, Newt Loken, was retiring. It was the end of an era.

It wasn't just that Newt was one of the most successful men's gymnastics coaches in history, though that was part of it. The two-time national Coach of the Year led his teams to a 250-72-1 all-time record, twelve Big Ten titles (a number matched by no other coach), and two national championships. When Newt won his 200th meet, no other coach had done that, either. Newt guided the Wolverines to two NCAA team championships in 1963 and 1970. Or three team titles, depending on how you look at it. In 1970, as the NCAA phased out Newt's beloved trampoline as a gymnastics event, separate championships were held—one for trampoline and one for all the other gymnastic events. Newt's "bouncers," as he affectionately called them, matched the rest of their championship teammates by taking

1

home the NCAA team trampoline title as well. As individuals, "Newt's boys" won seventy-one Big Ten titles and twenty-one NCAA titles. Newt himself won two Big Ten All-Around titles as a gymnast at Minnesota in the early 1940s, along with an NCAA high bar title and, in 1942, the NCAA All-Around championship.

It wasn't just that he'd been at Michigan so long, though that was part of it, too. Since the team's reinstatement as a varsity sport in 1948, Newt had been there. Even before that, he'd been the volunteer cheerleading coach, back when all cheerleaders were men. He led his troupe all over the Midwest, hoping to boost enthusiasm for the Michigan sports teams on the field. And his cheerleaders were gymnasts, performing tumbling and mini-trampoline tricks during basketball and football games and thrilling the crowds.

The boys, Newt and their sport were popular enough that in late 1947, instead of boxing, men's gymnastics was raised to the varsity level, and Newt was asked to be the head coach. Only a tiny group of people—anyone at the University from 1931-33, when Wilbur West was the coach—could actually remember a time when the school had a team and Newt wasn't the coach. For nearly everyone, Newt Loken and Michigan men's gymnastics were synonymous terms. Could one possibly exist without the other?

Newt did it all with a smile on his face and nothing but encouragement for his athletes. In a time when many coaches, like Michigan football coach Bo Schembechler, affected a gruff drill-sergeant exterior, only yielding their softer selves after much digging, Newt wore his heart on his sleeve.

"I wonder, I really do," Newt said when asked how he kept up such a constant positive attitude. "It wasn't fake. It might be my natural tendency to be happy and smile. It did happen. … I was very enthused about everything. I had a job, I was employed, and they kept me on the payroll thirty-eight years. Jeez, who's going to last that long. I was down after we lost the Big Ten championships, obviously, but I was always smiling because I had malocclusion, too many teeth for my mouth. Even the Big Ten coaches, when I retired, gave me a plaque. It said, 'To the man that's always got a smile.' That was so sweet."

Much of his coaching style was contained in these simple words: Be happy. "What's there to be sad about? Plenty, but fake it out and be happy. Be encouraging. That's the main thing. Encourage them." Sometimes he joked that his main goal was to keep his gymnasts "happy, unmarried and solvent." There was a reason happy came first.

Winning wasn't everything to him—it was just a pleasant side effect of focusing on clean routines and developing each athlete into the best gymnast he could be. Especially toward the beginning of his coaching career, Newt often spent hours working with gymnasts he knew would never make the competition lineup, sometimes focusing on the mastery of a single skill. For Newt, it was all about the human relationships. Even after sixty years, Newt kept in touch with an unbelievable number of his former athletes—at the drop of a hat, he could tell you what the man was doing, where he was living and even the names of his wife and children.

He became like a second father to many of the gymnasts, concerning himself as much with their personal and academic lives as he did with their athletic endeavors. He was always there to support them, whether inside or outside of their sport. To Newt, their lives as gymnasts were secondary to their lives as people—a big reason why the vast majority of his gymnasts went on to successful lives after college.

It turned out that the kind words and unbridled optimism—not to mention Newt's ever-present flair for showmanship—were exactly what the gymnasts needed. More than any antagonizing would have, Newt's obvious love for them inspired them to great heights, year after year. His talent for coaching was obvious, too.

Whereas many great athletes aren't able to articulate the nuts and bolts of their successful technique, Newt was the rare man who could both perform and coach at the highest level. And unlike many sports, gymnastics has changed drastically over the years.

Looking at, for example, baseball a century ago, the game itself is different in small, trivial ways. Over just a half-century or so, gymnastics has morphed almost into a new sport. Skills that were once the pinnacle of achievement, like giants on the high bar, are now basic tasks, stepping-stones on the way to more difficult tricks like complicated release moves. A meet used to consist of tumbling, side horse (now known as the pommel horse), parallel bars, high bar and the flying rings; depending on your location, a rope climb might be thrown in too. Trampoline came and went; "long horse" appeared and evolved into vaulting, which eventually gave way to a tongue-shaped vault rather than a pommel horse without pommels; tumbling was replaced by the floor exercise, the flying rings by the still rings. Newt's long-term success is a testament to his cheerful talent for adaptability in coaching this quicksilver sport.

A fair portion of this success can also be attributed to Newt's excellent communication skills. Each day, he would leave individualized notes for his gymnasts on the bulletin board, always keeping them on track and on the same page regarding the team's common goals. Often, he would post countdowns to the next year's Big Ten or NCAA championships. Each year before the start of the school year, he would send out a long, chatty newsletter to all the team members, updating them on summer developments and their new freshman teammates. Ron Rapper, the captain of the 1970 NCAA champions, adopted Newt's strategy of constant communication during that season, using it to great advantage. And of course, talking has always been effortless for Newt. It's easy to imagine him scampering from one part of the practice gym to another, describing what he wants his boys to do with both words and gestures, grinning as he bounces away to coach another athlete. His most recalled exhortation was, "GREAT! GREAT! GREAT!" Always in capitals, with exclamation points (sometimes lots of those). He was always ready with a wise or funny quotation—he became so known for these that he later compiled a small pamphlet called "Newt's Sayings."

Throughout his career, Newt was also exceptionally innovative. He was one of the first coaches in the country to start using foam-filled pits for safely practicing new or more difficult skills, rather than just heavy horsehair mats. When video cameras became available late in his tenure, Newt immediately began using one to film practices and competitions, in order to better show his athletes where and how they could improve. A coach of Newt's eventual status and longevity could easily have settled into a rut, refusing to change with the times; for Newt, the only thing that would never change was his happy-go-lucky, fatherly treatment of his gymnasts.

The coach made the gymnasts feel like part of his family, and part of that came from keeping his family involved in his gymnastics activities. Newt's four children, in order of age, were Christine, Lani, Jon and Newt Jr., and all of them accompanied their father to the gym on a regular basis. When Chris was just two years old, Newt constructed a tiny trampoline for her to bounce on while he coached. By the time they were three or four, Chris and Lani were performing acrobatics in Newt's signature trampoline act, which he performed in various locations during the off-season. At five, they began bouncing with Dad. Once Jon and Newt Jr., born in 1955 and 1957, reached age four, they became part of the well-loved routine, too. To no one's surprise, all the Loken children graduated from Michigan, fulfilling their Wolverine heritage.

Throughout their childhoods, Newt made sure his kids' lives

were filled with physical activities. They all began tumbling and trampolining as toddlers, but he also had them skiing, figure skating, swimming and playing golf. Newt loved golf and practically lived at the UM Golf Course. He sometimes golfed even after it snowed in Ann Arbor. In an effort to entice the kids to enjoy his favorite game, he tried to think of ways to make it more fun. When they reached Hole No.2—out of sight of the clubhouse—he often had them remove their shoes and socks so that they could feel the beautiful turf beneath their feet.

True to his Nordic roots, skiing and ice skating were big on the Loken family agenda. After starting the kids out at the University of Michigan Arboretum, Newt took the family to Michigan ski resorts. The Lokens were also active members of the Ann Arbor Figure Skating Club. The girls, Chris and Lani, were members of the Hocketts for many years, and Dotty chaired the annual ice carnival, Melody on Ice, for ten years. Newt performed featured comedy skits in the show when his gymnastics schedule made him available.

As much as the Michigan community loved the coach, even Ohio State head coach Mike Wilson had nothing bad to say about Newt. The family spirit of gymnastics and Newt's own warmth easily overcame the ancient rivalry.

"He's always a delight to be around and compete against," Wilson told Paul Resnick of *The Michigan Daily*.* "Great showman, great coach, great gentleman. … I hope he keeps his finger in the sport. It's equivalent to losing Bear Bryant in football, having Newt Loken retire in gymnastics."

What really touched people wasn't Newt's longevity or his sparkling record: it was the man himself. The first in his family to go to college, Newt pulled himself out of the Depression by his bootstraps, always leaving smiles in his wake. Thanks to a set of buck teeth, Newt literally couldn't help smiling, his pug nose

*Henceforward, any reference to the *Daily* refers to the Michigan student paper, unless otherwise noted.

crinkling in a grin under sparkling hazel eyes. Newt exuded an infectious glee for life, his hands flickering in the distinctive sign language of gymnasts throughout his storytelling. Sometimes he'd insert a random "Dammit!" as if to appear a little more gruff, but his smile always gave the lie to any crustiness. Reporters of all ages throughout the years were awed by his seemingly boundless energy. Being exceptionally energetic is a normal trait for most gymnasts, but Newt took it to another level.

"Fun is over at the big 'M,'" lamented Jesse Barkin, a *Daily* sports columnist, after Newt announced his retirement, comparing legendary Michigan football coach Bo Schembechler and former Michigan Athletic Director Don Canham rather unfavorably with the beloved gymnastics coach. "[Newt is] like a super ball let loose in Chuck-E-Cheese's on a Saturday afternoon. Wait, check that; he's more like one of Chuck E's buddies. He's the most animated character in cartoon history. Only he's real." Barkin went on to declare Newt "the most likeable coach in Michigan's history."

Newt was all over campus. As a full professor, he taught physical education and dance classes in the Department of Kinesiology and headed the cheerleading squad, bringing the same verve to those tasks as to coaching his "boys." For twelve years, he directed the Huron Valley Swim Club; for fifty years, he was in charge of the extremely popular trampoline float in the Thanksgiving Day Parade in Detroit, usually roping several good-natured gymnasts into performing. He was a consummate teacher, constantly touching so many lives and changing them for the better. His performances at Homecoming games became the stuff of legend; no matter what his age, Newt was always the most enthusiastic one on the field as he led his cheerleaders through their routines. He was a fixture—no Wolverine could imagine life at Michigan without him.

On January 14, 1984, the Michigan men's and women's

gymnastics teams held a co-ed meet against Illinois in Crisler Arena. Just before the start of the competition, Athletic Director Don Canham presented Newt with an enormous scrapbook. Made by his daughter, Lani, Newt's Wonderful Book of Memories was a work of art. Along with photos of each one of Newt's teams and a multitude of newspaper clippings about the coach and his gymnasts, it (and a large handmade box) was full of letters from people across the country, telling Newt just what he'd meant to them. Newt's four children, Chris, Lani, Jon and Newt, Jr., had sent out a letter to all their father's friends, announcing the retirement, the creation of the book, and Newt's desire to explore his ancestral home, Norway, with his wife, Dotty. They asked for letters to Newt and donations to the trip, both of which poured in.

Some were from former gymnasts, marveling at the impact Newt had made on their lives. Many of those letters came on the stationery of prominent universities' athletic departments—Newt prepared his boys for success in everything, not just gymnastics. Some were from fellow coaches, expressing admiration for one of their own. Charlie Pond, Illinois' legendary coach, was moved to near-incoherence by the retirement of the man who broke his record for Big Ten championships. Pond's great teams had won eleven in a row; Newt's 1975 team snagged the coach's twelfth Big Ten title.

One letter was from Newt's own coach, Minnesota's venerable Ralph Piper, whose chance encounter with the tumbling cheerleader at a 1937 West High School football game in Minneapolis set Newt on his path toward prominence in gymnastics.

Jerome Poynton, a former gymnast, absolutely could not believe what he'd heard.

"Newt retiring? For me it is not possible," Poynton wrote. "Newt is a manufacturer of people, not envelopes. Eighteen-year-old raw material, his work is one of establishing, developing, and maintaining relationships.

"Newt cannot retire from these relationships just as my father cannot retire from being my father. I try to imagine the letter my mother would write:

> Your father has announced his retirement from his parental relationship. He has served our family well for thirty-eight years and although sad to see him go we wish him luck in his future endeavors.
>
> Applications are being accepted for this position. To date we have one resume from a Mr. Smith in Duluth who says he has always wanted ten dark haired children."

Poynton remembered Newt's enthusiastic pronouncements of "Great, Great, Great," and the coach, "dancing up the steps of a hotel in Iowa City after a Big Ten gym meet."

Lawrence Herkimer fondly recalled nights sitting with Newt "in the bunk house at Smith Waldbridge Camp mapping out curriculum for the day for the cheerleaders."

Loyal W. Jodar, a member of Newt's very first team in 1948, wrote of Newt's kindness to an "uncoordinated pre-med student who was really trying to get his body to follow Newt's instructions."

John C. Kauffman, a trampolinist in the '70s, recalled some of Newt's more common exhortations: "Triffis pike, half-in half-out, double back, barani-in-full-out, etc.; GREAT! GREAT! GREAT!" For so many people, Newt was a connection to one of the best times in their lives. His belief in his athletes was so pure and unshakable that they couldn't help but feel it, too.

As Newt often said, "Those who bring sunshine to others can hardly keep it from themselves." No one brought more sunshine to those around him than Newt Loken.

Chapter 2

Minnesota Beginnings

Newton C. Loken was born to Alfred and Clara Loken on February 27, 1919, in Breckenridge, Minnesota. Alfred was a traveling entrepreneur with a fourth-grade education, moving all across the country in search of his fortune. Breckenridge was just a stop on the way to the West Coast. Newt remembered his father always winning awards in whichever job he tried.

Alfred, Newt proudly noted, was known as the Switch-Kicking Champion of Hayfield, the little Norwegian-American farming community in southern Minnesota where the Lokens lived. The Lokens had emigrated from the Hallingdal region of Norway, where the Hallingdans, a men's folk dance, was famous. In the dance, men would take turns kicking a hat off a stick, held by a girl standing on a chair.

Alfred kept the tradition going in his own way. As the elder Loken entered the small town's pool hall, patrons inside would call, "Okay, Al, do your thing!"

"With a smile, he'd back up a few steps and get set," Newt remembered. "Then with a couple branching steps he'd head for the doorway. Then he'd kick one leg up into the air, followed by the other. In midair he'd switch legs and continue up, with the bottom leg eventually hitting the doorsill about six feet above him. Then both feet would drop to the floor, and he'd simply walk casually into the hall with a resounding applause from those inside." Maybe Newt inherited some of his skill from Alfred.

"Dear Dad, he worked hard," Newt said. "He had a fourth-grade education ... [but] he was ambitious and a seeker of excellence. ... Everywhere he worked, he got a plaque for outstanding work. Jeez, a guy like that should be rewarded. But he didn't have the so-called education. ... I think he got somewhat discouraged toward the end of his life. His final job when he was seventy years old was to clean up the church after service. Imagine that."

Newt was the fifth Loken child, and according to his siblings, he was tumbling from the day he was born. In the next few years, traveling westward in search of Alfred's entrepreneurial fortune, the Lokens welcomed three more children, including Newt's younger brothers Herb and Don. It made for some crowded conditions—the three little boys shared one bed, sleeping crosswise. "In the middle of the night we'd receive a poke on our back with the words, 'On the count of five we'll rotate,'" Newt said. "We did and continued our sleep. Such simple and harsh living, but we thought nothing of it." Newt told his stories of hardship with a little smile, proud to have made it through and gone on to make a success of himself as his father, for all his effort, never quite could. His experiences as a child of the Depression gave him considerable empathy later for other people's struggles.

After several years' travel, Alfred and Clara decided there were more opportunities for the family in Minneapolis. On the way back from "out West," Alfred spotted a beet farmer's sign, stating that the man needed two acres to be tended and harvested. So the Lokens temporarily became sharecroppers, the whole family pitching in to cultivate the beets. Throughout Newt's childhood, the Loken children might be sent to relatives for short periods of time to help on their farms. Newt remembered tying rags on his knees and going up and down the rows, pulling any weeds that might interfere with the plants' growth. The farmer was so pleased with the crop that he paid Alfred five hundred dollars. "Man," said Newt, "that was like five thousand in those days!" The Loken patriarch was quick to reward his hardworking children: Each one was allowed to pick one item for themselves out of the Sears & Roebuck catalogue. And for Newt, even a seemingly small reward was an important confirmation that hard work and determination would yield positive results.

Newt didn't waffle. He knew exactly what he wanted: A brand-new pair of tennis shoes. Even as a youngster, Newt always had to be active and doing something, anything. Surely with tennis shoes, he could do whatever he wanted even faster. Two weeks later, a box arrived with the shoes inside. Tremendously excited, Newt laced up his new tennis shoes and begged to go outside. Noting that it had just rained, his mother was reluctant to let him go. But with a child as agile as Newt, she need not have worried that his new shoes would be ruined.

"I assured her that I'd jump over and around the puddles if I could just wear them outside for a while," Newt remembered, still savoring the simple pleasures that marked his childhood. "Hesitantly, she approved and I had the ball of my life, jumping and skipping with my new tennis shoes on."

When the family finally made it back to Minneapolis, Alfred took a job as a milk deliveryman for the Norris Creamery. Sunday mornings in Minneapolis held two treats for Newt and his brothers: a ride in the milk wagon and practicing their tumbling at a sawdust pile outside the nearby brick factory.

One or two lucky Loken kids would accompany their father on his Sunday deliveries, waiting in the milk wagon as Alfred's horse, Nellie, walked placidly down the street, with Alfred switching the empty milk bottles for full ones.

"He'd tell us, 'I'll give you a little surprise if you just don't say anything to Nellie!' " Newt remembered. " 'Don't pull those reins. Nellie knows what she's doing. Just let her be.' So we'd sit there and watch Dad run up those steps and down again. We didn't say boo. And at the end of the day, he'd give us a pint of chocolate milk."

And a pint of chocolate milk was all it took to make little Newt's day. Early on, he learned to find joy in small pleasures.

"It was worth all the silence from us," he said later, as if he could still taste the sweetness.

The sawdust pile, at least at the time, was just a treat for Newt. The exuberant youngster would have to root his brothers out each Sunday morning, as they tried to find excuses why they couldn't accompany him. They'd even volunteer to help his mother with chores—she replied that the chores could wait until the brothers had finished their fun at the sawdust pile.

At the time, bricks were shipped packed in sawdust. So at the brick factory, excess sawdust would collect in piles up to thirty feet high, loosely packed and perfect for practicing tumbling tricks in relative safety. Many hard-up kids might have scratched their gymnastics dreams in the absence of mats or equipment. But when Newt wanted to make something work, he'd find a way, somehow. Determined to tumble—and to tumble better, every day—Newt turned the humble sawdust pile into a makeshift gym for him and his brothers.

"We'd try anything," Newt recalled. "A cartwheel with a side somersault. Nobody had heard of that. ... We'd sprawl all over, and then we tried double twisters [double twisting backflips]. We didn't know what we were doing, but we did it. We weren't coached. Somehow or other we'd make the two twists and we felt pretty proud about that. Then we'd swim in the Mississippi River and get the sawdust off our bodies."

Though they may not have been so enthusiastic at the time,

the sawdust pile made an impact on Herb and Don, too. Like their older brother, they became cheerleaders and gymnasts at the University of Minnesota. And many years later, Don even wrote a poem about the old days with his brothers called, appropriately, "The Ol' Sawdust Pile."

*I don't know how he found it
Out scorching in the sun.*

*To Herb and I 'twas misery
To Newt was lots of fun.*

*With mounds of sawdust everywhere
But some of it was flat*

*And Newt was going to learn some tricks
Quite simply that was that.*

*When he would say, "It's time to go,"
My heart would fill with dread*

*Was this not Sunday morning?
I'd rather stay in bed.*

*Then I would say to Mother
"Have I got chores to do?"*

*But she would smile and pat my head
"They'll wait till you get through."*

*Then Herb would say so all could hear
"I think I'll go to church"*

*And then he'd go and hide somewhere
But Newt would find his perch.*

*So every Sunday morning
While Newt was still in school*

*We'd get our Sabbath lesson
But not the Golden Rule*

Newt became a champion
Of whom we are so proud.

Herb and I—we followed suit
With footsteps not so loud.

And now on Sunday mornings
I often get a smile

To think of all the fun we had
At the ol' sawdust pile.

The brothers were well versed in the childhood art of improvising their own playthings. A favorite pastime was to find an old car seat and an old mattress, and drag them into the backyard for some abuse.

"The mattress would be a crash pad and the single car seat would be a spring board!" Newt remembered with obvious delight. "We'd bounce, turn a somersault. We didn't always land on our feet, but we'd land on our buttocks and think we did a flip. We invented our own things, all the time. When I think about it, I'd like to go back and just walk by my backyard, walk by our apartment, and see Newtie and Donnie and Herbie, my younger brothers, just see them as it was at that time."

This knack for improvisation served Newt well in his coaching career. Car seats even made another appearance, when Newt became one of the first to use a foam-filled pit for trying new skills more safely. The foam? Cut-up car-seat cushions.

Another treat for young Newt was Christmas time, when the Salvation Army sleigh made its annual visit. "We didn't know any better," Newt remembered. "At Christmas time, our family was poor. We really were on poverty row." The Salvation Army notified the Lokens that a horse-drawn sleigh would come by with Christmas presents for the children.

Newt and his siblings waited anxiously by the window of their two-bedroom apartment on Dupont Avenue, eyes searching for that horse-drawn sleigh, ears tuned for the sound of the horse's bells. Finally, the sleigh would pull up in front of the building, and someone "dressed like Santa's helper" would leap out to deliver the gifts.

"I think I got a dump truck," Newt remembered, laughing, of one particularly memorable Christmas. "We were so happy, because Christmas had arrived. And those were the times when we didn't know, we were just happy to have that damn sleigh stop by, you know?" Even after he became a successful coach, Newt never stopped taking delight in all the pleasures, large and small, that life brought him.

The Loken family may not have had much money, but they were extremely tight-knit. Newt's older sisters, Esther and Pearl, became like mothers to the youngster.

"When Mother couldn't take us to the doctor or the dentist or whatever, why, there was Esther," Newt said. "Yet she had a job. I don't know how the hell she did it, but she was always available. So I think some of the mild success that I might have had is because we had a close family." When Newt became the first Loken to graduate from college, it was Esther who attended the graduation ceremonies.

Pearl, too, was instrumental in Newt's early life as a mother figure. As a coach, Newt kept in his office one large photo of his mother—and an equally large photo of Pearl, whom he referred to as the family "matriarch." Newt and Pearl's close relationship endured throughout their whole lives—Pearl died at 96—with the siblings speaking on a near-daily basis.

Were Newt a child today, his family probably wouldn't have had the money for him to enroll in gymnastics. But growing up in Minneapolis, Newt had ample opportunities for "pickup" gymnastics. At the time, Newt likely didn't have long-term gymnastics goals; it was just something he loved to do, more than anything else. When other kids might be meeting each other to play baseball on a sandlot, Newt developed his gymnastics skills on equipment in public parks and on the beach, showing off for the girls. A favorite hangout was Bryant Square Park, where Newt could experiment on a high bar, parallel bars and some other assorted apparatus.

One day, Newt began trying to teach himself a kip on the high bar. A kip is a basic skill, which like much of gymnastics looks effortless but can be extremely difficult to learn. In a kip, the gymnast swings forward below the bar, then uses a combination of timing, swing, muscle and physics to swing himself up into a support position over the bar.

"The way you learn a kip is you wait," Newt said. "You don't do a kip too soon, because you'll run into your belly. You're going nowhere. You wa-a-ait and then you kip, and you're right up on top. I couldn't get the thing."

So Newt improvised, as he had with the sawdust pile. After another unsuccessful day of attempting kips at Bryant Square Park, Newt strayed into a stranger's backyard on his way home.

"In those days, they had their laundry on laundry pipes, on wires that went across, where you'd hang [the clothes]," Newt said. "So on the way home from the park, I couldn't make that kip, I just couldn't make it. And I was rather tired. So I jumped up on this laundry pipe, swung and decided to do a kip. And I was so tired, I waited. And I ended up on top of the bar! Wow! It was the most exciting thing in my life. I made a kip on this funny little pipe!" One of Newt's first "coaching" successes came with himself as the student.

Newt could even develop his skills in school, unlike today, when high school gymnastics is basically extinct. One of the many clubs offered at his grade school was the tumbling club. Two days a week, the boys pulled out all the old horsehair mats in the gym and taught each other tricks. With his compact stature, Newt had an advantage over taller classmates in gymnastics.

The tumbling group became so good, they were invited to put on an exhibition at the school assembly hall. Newt's tumbling continued into his career at West High School, where he was not only the state all-around gymnastics champion but Minneapolis city diving champion as well.

"At one time, the whole city of Minneapolis was just [filled] with interscholastic gymnastics teams," remembered Newt, who would arrive at school an hour early each day to work out in the gym. "They had the high bar raised up against the wall. Somebody had to crank it down, and somebody always had to crank it up. And the fickle finger of fate was always pointed at Newt!" His skills beyond cranking continued to improve, though he avoided the side horse (now known as the pommel horse) as much as he could. Pommel horse, then and now, is widely regarded as the most difficult event in gymnastics on which to succeed—and the easiest one on which to screw up. Missing a hand placement by less than an inch can send the gymnast spinning to the ground. Successful horse workers depend tremendously on upper body strength and precision; Newt's well-developed air sense and other tumbling talents were not much help when it came to the side horse.

In high school, Newt was also bitten by the show-business bug, a flair that would stay with him, and serve him well, for the rest of his life. He wanted to learn any dance steps he could, in addition to gymnastics. So Newt would clean up any gym or dance studio he could find, in exchange for the proprietor teaching him a few dance steps. After that, Newt would run off to teach the steps to his friend Johnny Frankus.

The pair practiced together constantly, and soon began performing at different taverns on "Amateur Night." Of course, Newt just couldn't resist throwing some gymnastics into the act as well.

"Occasionally we would win a second or third!" Newt remembered with undimmed enthusiasm. "That was worth a five dollar bill, or maybe seven dollars! Seven dollars in those times, that's like a five-hundred dollar bill! Mother, she was my chaperone. She didn't smoke or drink or nothing. She'd just sit there and enjoy her little Newtie doing his dance. When we'd do our tap-dancing, then we'd turn around and we'd tumble. We'd throw each other into somersaults and do back handsprings with a half twist. Johnny would do butterflies or something."

Newt also earned a place in a professional clown-and-acrobatics act called "Kent & Quigley." Newt and his partner performed balancing moves, tumbling stunts and risky acrobatic moves, such as "Quigley" (Newt) backflipping up onto "Kent's" shoulders. Although Newt was the straight man of the comedy duo, the act foreshadowed his later trampoline clown act in which he dressed as a bum in multiple layers of clothing.

Newt's schoolboy tumbling attracted the attention of the cheerleading coach, who began recruiting him for the cheer team.

"I can't cheer," Newt informed the coach, who desperately wanted the tumbler to add some pizzazz along the sidelines.

"That's all right," the coach said. "You just tumble up and down the sidelines and leave the people in the stands wanting to do the same thing."

One day, Ralph Piper was officiating a game between Newt's West High School and its arch-rival, Central High School. In his regular job, Piper was the head coach of the University of Minnesota men's gymnastics team, but like many coaches of the day, took extra jobs to supplement his income. One can almost picture the dark-haired Piper sternly making a call with his seemingly ever-present cigar stub migrating from one corner of his mouth to the other. Piper spotted a cheerleader doing back handsprings up and down the sidelines, and during a lull, he patted the youngster on the shoulder.

"Young man?"

"Yes, what is it, sir?" Newt Loken replied, wondering what

he'd done wrong. Later, he remembered, "I thought he was going to tell me to get off the field!"

"What's your name?"

"Newt."

"Do you know what you should do?"

"No, I don't know what I should do, sir."

"You ought to enroll at Minnesota and try out for the gym team."

That was Ralph Piper's entire recruiting spiel to Newt Loken, one of the best high school athletes in Minneapolis. Newt had already made it farther educationally than anyone in his family up to that time. Despite his desire to go into show business, one of his older brothers, Clifford, gave him a serious talk about the importance of staying in school.

At the kitchen table one day, Clifford told his little brother, "You can do your show business as a hobby, a sideline. But get your education. You might have a chance to go to Minnesota. Get that damn degree. I'm telling you, I know." Clifford's words turned out to be right on the money. But when Ralph Piper discovered Newt, the gymnast had already taken his brother's words to heart and earned a partial scholarship to Gustavus Adolphus College. He was reluctant to change his plans—and Minnesota, undoubtedly, was a bit more intimidating than Newt's small initial choice.

Enter Sid Wolfenson, one of Newt's best friends. A year ahead of Newt in school, Wolfenson was a star tumbler at Minnesota and Newt's mentor. Wolfenson took Newt to Richman's Ice Cream Shop, just across the street from West High School, and asked him the same question as Piper had.

"You know what you should do?"

"No, I don't, Sid."

"You should go to Minnesota," Wolfenson said firmly. "Don't go to Gustavus Adolphus." Even telling the story many years later, Newt would imitate Wolfenson's snort of disdain at the mention of Newt's initial college choice. While Gustavus Adolphus was a good small college, evidently in Wolfenson's mind, it couldn't hope to measure up to the great University of Minnesota. "Minnesota has a varsity gymnastics team and you could make a contribution. Make a name for yourself in gymnastics."

All Newt could say was, "Yes, sir, Sid."

About 50 years later, Piper acknowledged, "I suggested that you go to the U., but I guess Sid Wolfenson had more influence on your decision than I did."

Thanks to a few well-timed words from Ralph Piper and Sid Wolfenson, Newt's gymnastics career didn't end at eighteen. His sporting dreams, vague up to now despite his talent, took on a concrete shape. Through his athletic talent, Newt would gain the education that no one in his family had yet had, fulfilling his brother's dream. All his improvisation and skill, his hard-won determination and enthusiasm, had earned him a place at a top university, in a top gymnastics program. And Newt would never forget what effect a few words of advice at the right moment could have on the course of a young man's life.

Chapter 3

Leading the Gophers

In his first year of collegiate gymnastics, like all freshmen of the day, Newt only trained with the varsity team, participating in few competitions. But as a Minnesota freshman, Newt did enter the Northwest meet, along with half his team.

The Gophers hosted the massive meet each year in Cooke Hall, an elegant square brick building on University Avenue. Today, it's just across the street from the Minnesota Sports Pavilion, where the team now competes. According to *The Minnesota Daily*, it was the only meet of its kind in the country. It was actually composed of three competitions, designated A, B and C. The A competition involved the Gopher varsity and usually a few other collegiate squads. The B meet was "intermediate," the C "novice"—and college freshmen could participate as individuals. Newt knew he wouldn't have many other opportunities to impress as a freshman, so in the Northwest meet in 1939, he packed in a season's worth of highlights. He took the all-around title despite competition from all his older teammates in addition to the rest of the opponents.

"I won the damn [Northwest] all-around title, against some of Minnesota's varsity athletes!" Newt remembered gleefully. "Man, that was unheard of. Who's this guy Newt with the buck teeth, always smiling because he can't close his mouth? Got too many teeth in his mouth. I went out there and won the all-around, and it was a pretty big meet." And while Newt never lacked for a positive attitude, the big win in front of so many spectators and gymnasts must have given him an extra boost of confidence. Ralph Piper couldn't help but notice: Later that season, he chose Newt to compete at the Big Ten championships.

"I was lucky as hell," Newt said. "The night before, I was so nervous. I was going through the routines in my head, over and over and over. I mustn't forget them! Then, I got in the damn meet and the adrenaline shot up and away!"

For Newt, excelling in gymnastics wasn't enough—he also had to pay his way through school. Putting his boundless determination and energy to work, he took two jobs, including one ushering at the Rialto Theatre for twenty-five cents an hour. When he bought a 1932 Ford Victoria before his junior year, Newt made that work for him too, providing rides to campus for his fellow students. The car had solid sides and a canvas top, which Newt could slide back on runners so it would look like a convertible.

"Every morning I'd drive around and pick up five guys that wanted a ride to campus at a nickel a ride," Newt remembered. "I'd pick them all up but I wouldn't take them home, because I'd go from the gym to Brown's Drug Store and get a malted milk (that's where my anemic condition came from) and then go to the library for an hour. The engineering library. Those engineers—you drop a pencil and everybody goes, 'Whoa. You're making too much noise.' So at the end of the week, I'd get twenty-five cents from each rider. That's a dollar and a quarter. Wow. And gasoline at twelve cents a gallon! Boy, did I cruise and cruise and cruise." He always found a way to make situations work to his advantage.

Newt was the first of the Loken family to attend college but certainly not the last. Both his younger brothers, Herb and Don, matriculated at the University of Minnesota as well and competed for the gymnastics team. Herb even worked at the Rialto, just like his big brother. Newt's accomplishments had provided a road map to success for his brothers.

Newt and the Gophers practiced, as well as competed, at Cooke Hall, with Piper prowling between events, always chewing on his cigar. The practice area was packed with apparatus from one end to the other. Each gymnast could compete on up to five events in a meet for his team, with each team limited to three men on a given event. The gymnasts were judged out of fifteen points—seven for difficulty, five for form and three for unity and rhythm.

The training was a bit different from today, where varsity teams often have a trainer and one or two student trainers ever-ready to deal with the minor and major injuries that are a trademark of gymnastics. For the Gophers, their only trainer was old "Snapper," whose usual response to a request for ankle-taping was, "Can't you tape your own damn ankles?" Once, after a visit from Newt, Snapper sent him off with the instructions to put marbles on the floor at home, then pick them up with his toes.

"Why?" Newt dared to ask.

"Don't ask why," Snapper snapped. "Just do it."

Maybe it was the marbles. Though his old enemy the side horse continued to give him some trouble, Newt excelled at nearly everything else and loved tumbling above all, as he always had. Informal tumbling tends to be the first skill a gymnast learns, and Newt had taken to it from the first. Though he may have been better at high bar—he won the NCAA title in the event in 1941—tumbling was first in his heart. The event of tumbling should not be confused with the more familiar floor exercise. It involved four or five passes up and down a long, narrow mat, fifty feet long and five feet wide. If any part of a gymnast's body touched the floor, he was disqualified. Newt remembered his friend Sid Wolfenson sobbing for an hour after a competition in which he touched the floor and was disqualified from tumbling.

Every year of college, however, Newt seemed to come in second to fellow tumbler George Szypula, who later became the head coach at Michigan State. But Szypula owed at least a portion of his success to his rival. A bit taller and rangier than Newt, even back then Szypula needed thick glasses to see. But he couldn't wear them while tumbling.

At the national AAU meet, Szypula would approach his rival before the tumbling competition.

"Put me in front of the mat," he'd say to Newt. "I took my glasses off and I can't see very well. Just steer me [to] the mat. Once I know where it is, I can do my routine."

"He was a great tumbler, really very good. Thoughtlessly, I actually steered him to the mat. Maybe I should have steered him in the other direction!" Newt joked. "I beat him in the all-around and in other events, but not tumbling. He was a superb tumbler."

Newt and his teammates especially loved traveling to Wisconsin—the only Big Ten town with a drinking age of eighteen rather than twenty-one. After a meet in the old Armory, the Gophers would head for the student union, where they could enjoy a glass of cold beer (all that their leader "ol' drill sergeant Loken" would allow) and pick up girls, who, in Newt's memory, were invariably "cute."

Piper knew exactly what he had in Newt, and in November of Loken's sophomore year, *The Minnesota Daily* singled him out as one of the hot prospects for the coming season. "The outstanding sophomore is Newt Loken, former state tumbling champion, adept in gym work and considered by [Ralph] Piper to be one of the strongest first-year men he has had," *The Minnesota Daily* reported. And starting with the team's first intrasquad, Newt began a career of serial show-stealing.

No one had seen such versatility in a first-year competitor. In his first Big Ten meet, a dual at the University of Chicago in January of 1940, Newt brought home the tumbling title as he led the Gophers to victory. A month later, in the Northwest meet, Minnesota put on a "blitzkrieg" performance before 1,500 fans, the largest crowd in the history of the event. Newt won his second consecutive A open title, posting the highest individual and collective scores for his team and winning the flying rings event while placing second on the parallel and high bars. Despite his love for tumbling, Newt put just as much effort into his other events, and in his sophomore year it really began to show.

The Gophers went on to claim the Big Ten title by just five tenths over Illinois, 105.50-105.00. Possibly due to impending war and the aftereffects of the Depression, only four schools sent teams to the conference championships in 1940. Third-place Chicago was a full fifty points behind Illinois, with last-place Iowa earning fewer than ten points. Newt came in second to top tumbler Joe Giallombardo at the Big Ten meet, and third in the event at the NCAA Championships. Of the Gophers, only Del Daly was tapped to compete in the all-around at NCAAs.

For the 1941 season, Newt, along with Daly, Bill Anderson and Bob Hanning formed the nucleus of the team. And Newt had some more duties to add on top of his gymnastics regimen: He had been elected "assistant rooter king" of the cheerleading team. Stan Cunningham would serve as rooter king, or head cheerleader, a post Newt earned in his senior year. "Show business had to take a backseat, a little bit," Newt laughed, but clearly the showbiz bug had not released its hold on the young gymnast. His cheer team performed at every home football game for no pay, inventing a different theme for their show each week. Only the rooter king got to make the road trips. The University of Minnesota was one of the first squads to incorporate gymnastics and tumbling into its cheerleading—no doubt the result of many varsity gymnasts joining its ranks.

"We did a lot of tumbling, all the time," Newt said. "We had a rule: We never sat on the sidelines. ... We always made a point of trying to lead the crowd in the cheer that they wanted to do, and not us forcing it." Like Newt, the cheerleaders "were always inventing something."

Like an audio testing device, for instance. Once, the cheerleaders rigged up what appeared to be such a machine, rolling it out on the football field to measure the crowd noise at the start of the game. *The Minnesota Daily* printed the results from the test, that week and for weeks thereafter. It was all a big joke.

"It was all fake—we got it from the music school," Newt said. "It was a cart with a thing here and a speaker, testing the decibels of the crowd when the football team would come out of the locker room and onto the field for the first time. It was fake. We'd turn the little dial in the back of it to show that the volume was going up. Then we'd have it in the paper, the volume was whatever, two hundred ten decibels. Let's see if we can beat that next Saturday! It was so crazy. Yet the crowd kind of chuckled a little bit, and maybe cheered a little louder so the football team felt they were being welcomed in their own home."

In 1941, no "co-eds" were allowed on the team—the University Senate had actually passed a rule banning them, even though cheerleading was already starting to become a female-dominated sport. Rooter king Cunningham told *The Minnesota Daily* he had no problem with female cheerleaders. He thought the team might have an easier time finding a "sugar daddy" if a few girls were incorporated into the squad—then all the cheerleaders could attend away games.

In addition to helping lead Minnesota's cheerleading team, Newt would have to deal with rule changes to gymnastics for the 1941 season. Gymnastics tends to institute modifications to its rules on a regular basis, but these were bigger changes than usual. The long horse (which evolved into modern-day vault) would be a regular event in the conference meet, with just one man from each school competing. Inexplicably, the event wouldn't be included in dual meets, the meat of the regular season. "Free exercise," the forerunner of today's floor exercise, became a required event for all-arounders, but wouldn't count toward the team total. And following the season, the rope climb, which was won by speed alone, would change classifications to a "special event," no longer counting toward the team score.

The change that would affect Newt the most was the addition of free exercise; he'd never been known for rope climbing, and long horse didn't factor into his all-around competitions. Free exercise must have been a delight for him—tumbling without the restrictions of the five-foot-wide mat! The major drawback, though, was the lack of any kind of padding on the free exercise floor. However, because the gymnasts did not attempt skills nearly on the level of those done today, they were far less likely to get hurt on the hardwood floor. Without the padding and springs used today, there was no way for a gymnast of the 1940s to try modern skills like a triple twisting backflip or a Thomas roll-out. Newt and the rest of the Gophers were used to constantly changing rules and requirements, and as usual, handled those of the 1941 season with grace.

As the team headed into its packed and demanding regular-season slate, Newt truly came into his own. *The Minnesota Daily* had predicted that the "sophomore sensation of last year's gym team and the most versatile of Coach Piper's pupils ... [would] carry a heavy load on his shoulders." Newt seemed to pick up the burden without a hiccup. In one meet against Chicago, with two bad cuts on his hands, Newt won three events and placed third on another, earning 146.90 of his team's 476.60 total points. Piper called him "unbeatable." When the Gophers beat the Hawkeyes late in the season, the headline read: "Gymnasts (Loken) Defeat Iowa." He won the Big Ten all-around title and headed into NCAAs rightfully confident in his ability to win the title there, too.

Piper thought the whole team had a chance to bring home the championship. "We're after the championship," he told *The Minnesota Daily*, "even though it does seem that Illinois will win it for the second straight year." Louie Fina was supposed to give Newt his toughest competition in the all-around.

The meet turned out to be full of upsets, except in the team competition, where Illinois won again. Jack Adkins of Illinois beat out Newt—and George Szypula, the usual champion—for the tumbling title. Newt won the high bar crown and Daly the flying rings, as many had predicted, but in the all-around, Newt was edged out by Courtney Shankens. The unexpected success of Courtney and his twin brother at NCAAs was the story of the competition. For Newt, the high bar title was wonderful, but it was made bittersweet by losing the all-around crown. Newt would have just one more shot at his ultimate college goal, the national all-around title.

After Newt won the Big Ten all-around championship and NCAA high bar title in his junior season, Piper named him team captain for 1942. It was the start of a banner year for Newt. In addition to more gymnastics accolades, he earned an award from Alpha Sigma Pi, Minnesota's honorary education fraternity. Coach Piper received word that Newt was going to be honored, but his gymnast couldn't quite believe what he was hearing.

"Newt, you should go to that banquet tonight," Piper said, referring to the fraternity's awards banquet.

"What am I going to a banquet for?" Newt wondered. "I'm not going to win anything."

Piper didn't appreciate having to tell him twice. "Just get over there, period."

So off Newt went. Even after the hint from Piper, he was still shocked when he received the award for physical education.

Even while he was still competing, his talents for teaching and coaching were clearly apparent to his peers.

"I thought my dear rival Frank Grossman would win," Newt said. "He was a pre-med student, he got good grades, and he was a pretty good gymnast. Maybe not quite as many awards as I luckily won. ... That was one of the high spots in my life."

And another high point was coming. Yet after repeating as Big Ten all-around champ, Newt headed into the NCAA championships a little nervous.

Piper, however, couldn't have been more confident. Newt had complained that he'd never gotten a trophy for any of his accomplishments, so for his 1942 NCAA all-around title, Piper had a large trophy engraved with Newt's name, the year, and his achievement. There was a slight catch, though—he gave Newt the trophy two weeks before the competition. Newt made Piper look like a genius, culminating his collegiate career with the highest possible individual honor. In his forty years as Minnesota gymnastics coach, Ralph Piper would coach only one gymnast to two NCAA titles in the same year: Newt Loken. Newt's picture would be the first to go up at the new Sports Pavilion.

Newt was on top of the world: national all-around champ, and with his own spread in the May 18, 1942 issue of LIFE magazine, announcing his prowess—and the importance of gymnastics to the military.

Just before the start of Newt's senior season, on December 7, 1941, the Japanese had bombed the U.S. Navy at Pearl Harbor. The U.S. was now involved in the Second World War, and suddenly people were looking at gymnastics in a new light. Newt, because he was colorblind, could not be on active service, but thanks to his considerable athletic talents, he had been tagged for development as a physical fitness officer.

"Failure of a high percentage of draft-age men to pass Army and Navy physical requirements has stimulated fresh interest

in the need for body-building gymnastics," the article began.
LIFE photographer Gjon Mili took "high-speed and repetitive-
flash pictures of Newt Loken, winner of the Intercollegiate All-
Around Championship this spring." Twenty-three-year-old Newt
performed basic gymnastics skills on the tumbling mats, pommel
horse, rings, parallel bars and high bar, yielding breathtaking
multiple exposure photos showing every aspect of the skill.

"Last month [after graduation], with an ensign's commission,
he entered the Navy's V-5 training course for specialists," LIFE
reported. "When he completes his training, Ensign Loken expects
to condition Navy fliers so they can execute smooth reverse
flyaways over Tokyo and Berlin."

Over sixty years later, the LIFE photo spread remained one
of Newt's favorite clippings. He had reached the pinnacle of
his own athletic career, and the entire country knew about it.
Later, when he was coaching at Michigan, recruits sometimes
recognized him with awe from the photos that appeared just
before Newt went into the Navy.

Chapter 4

A Trampoline at Sea

Like so many young men in the months after Pearl Harbor, Newt had volunteered without hesitation for the U.S. military. Despite the new national appreciation for gymnasts, Newt wouldn't be in the actual fighting. A somewhat circuitous route led him to become an ensign in the V-5 program, a Navy program for pilots, as reported in LIFE.

After volunteering, Newt had gone through a fitness program run by Gene Tunney down in St. Louis. Upon completing the program, the examining doctor told Newt he was disqualified from active service. He was colorblind.

"Well, I knew that," Newt said, unsurprised. He returned to Tunney, who was incensed at the disqualification of one of his most promising men. A *gymnast*, no less!

"He went back to the doctor's office and said, 'What's this? What's going on? We need this guy! Gymnastics—that's the type!'" Newt recalled. The doctor apologized, but refused to reverse his decision.

"Colorblind!" snorted Tunney. "Whose examination do we use?"

"Oh, Ishihara's," the doctor replied.

"We're fighting the Japanese and we're using the Japanese colorblindness test?" Tunney exclaimed. "Dang it!"

"He couldn't do anything about it," Newt said. "All the way up to Minneapolis, I was laughing about this comment."

But Newt's colorblindness turned out to be a blessing. Bernie Bierman, the recruiting officer for the V-5 program and former football coach at the University of Minnesota, was searching out athletes and coaches from around the country to serve as fitness officers for pre-flight school after three weeks of training.

Bierman, of course, recruited the newly available Newt for the program.

"I have to ask you a question," Bierman said. "Is there anything wrong with you?"

"Yeah," Newt replied brightly, informing Bierman that he was colorblind, among other small physical defects.

"Great, great," Bierman said, his dark piercing eyes lighting up. "Because anybody under twenty-seven has to be a pilot, not a fitness officer. With those defects you've got with your body, you qualify. You'll be an ensign." Thus began Newt's military career.

Newt was sent to the Naval Academy in Annapolis for more training. There, he was exposed to some of the most successful coaches in the country, like Bierman; Dr. Hartley Price, who coached the Illinois gymnastics team; Don Faurot, who went on to legendary status coaching the Missouri football team; Lou Bordo, a standout in Penn State gymnastics; Ed Haislet, a well-known boxing coach; and Forest Evashevski, a former University of Michigan quarterback who taught hand-to-hand fighting along with his sport. Each coach focused on his specialty—"We did very little roaming about to witness our fellow coaches and their traits," Newt reminisced. Newt remembers that every coach was supremely organized. Newt himself was already an orderly sort, but seeing the success that meticulous ways had brought the other coaches, he emphasized that trait in himself. It was a big part of his success both in his Navy career and after, when he was coaching at Michigan. Newt's organizational knack kept everything running so smoothly that he was able to write a considerable amount of his instructional cheerleading book while serving at sea.

After Annapolis he was stationed in Iowa City at the naval aviation preflight school, teaching basic gymnastics to the future pilots and getting them into shape. It was there that he met his wife, Dorothy.

The University of Iowa's nursing dormitories were quite near the preflight school, so Newt and the others often got blind dates with nursing students. When dark-haired beauty Dorothy Haight showed up as Newt's blind date one night, he was in disbelief.

"I'll never forget how impressed I was when I first saw her," he said. "She just looked like an absolute doll."

In addition to being a beauty, Dorothy was a very determined young woman. With ancestral roots in pre-Revolutionary War New England, her primary and secondary education took place in a one-room schoolhouse in Missouri Valley in western Iowa. She, like Newt, was the first person in her family to get a college education, earning both a B.S. Degree and her RN degree from the University of Iowa.

After several months, Newt proposed to this remarkable woman. Dorothy accepted, and the two decided on a December 24, 1942 wedding.

"Then we won't ever forget there's something important on that day," said Dorothy—a consideration many forgetful husbands might appreciate. It was a small wedding, attended by Newt's mother, brother Herb, and a few officers from the school. The two remained married for nearly seventy years. They raised four successful children, Christine, Lani, Jon and Newt Jr., in order of age, with Dorothy steadfastly supporting Newt through his entire career. A private, realistic person, Dorothy, who Newt affectionately called "Dotty," provided a needed counterpoint to Newt's bubbly showmanship.

But even after getting married, the young couple couldn't be together all the time.

"They had a rule at the dorms that the nurses had to stay in the dorms, so for six months I would say goodnight to my wife and go back to my apartment with the little roof over my head and my roommate, wishing I was with her," Newt recalled.

After their enforced separation, Newt and Dorothy spent nearly a year in Iowa City, with her finishing her nursing degree and him training the naval aviators. At one point, the captain at the pre-flight school suggested that the coaches go through the training program of each department. And the memory of encountering Forest Evashevski, the head of the hand-to-hand department, has never left Newt.

Evashevski had been a blocking back for legendary Michigan quarterback Tom "Ol' 98" Harmon and would go on to coach Iowa's football team. Spotting Newt in his audience for the day, Evashevski called him to the front of the class. It's easy to imagine him crooking a finger with a bit of evil glee in his eyes—because Evashevski was about to demonstrate to the aviators how to knock someone out.

"He demonstrated on me how to block the blood flow to the head by placing his fingers on my cardiac vein," Newt remembered. "And I promptly fainted. He of course quickly recovered me and I hardly knew that I had been out."

Despite the adventures in other departments, Newt was getting restless in Iowa. He requested other duties, and was assigned to the aircraft carrier, the *USS Prince William*. First, the Navy assigned the bewildered coach to the engineering department—"Can you imagine," he'd say, "me with my P.E. degree in the engineering department?"—but he quickly "engineered" a move to the communications department and served as the fitness officer for the carrier. He climbed aboard on February 1, 1944, and was discharged on June 20, 1945.

Dorothy and Newt said goodbye to their parents in Minneapolis, bought a Buick with their last $900, and set off for San Francisco to meet the *Prince William*. As Newt's partner, Dorothy would continue working as a nurse wherever Newt's career took him. She worked in an Oakland hospital while he was serving in the Pacific, and in a Norfolk, Va., hospital while he served in the Atlantic. She continued her work as a nurse later in Ann Arbor, while raising the four Loken children and taking a leading role in many local volunteer activities. (She even continued working for two years after Newt retired—as she always said, "Once a nurse, always a nurse.")

The road trip with his new bride made a lasting impression on Newt.

"It was the first time I'd ever driven that far," said Newt. "The first time I'd ever seen a motel. ... I never saw so much [snow] as in Donner Pass. And then down into Sacramento, oh jeez, the red clay and earth after the snow was so exciting."

The *Prince William* was a converted tanker with a five-hundred-foot-long flight deck, used for escort duties across the Atlantic, and as the ship's athletic officer, Lieutenant Loken took his duties seriously. Listed among his official duties was: "Make quarterly requests for athletic gear." Thanks to its new fitness officer, the "P. Willy," as it was affectionately known, soon became the only ship in the entire Navy with a trampoline.

Newt had loved the trampoline from its inception—George Nissen and Larry Griswold began manufacturing trampolines commercially in 1942, expecting them to be used in training tumblers like Loken—but the Navy had recognized its uses too, at least in flight schools. Through the concentrated use of a trampoline, future pilots could develop their "air sense" in ways that hadn't been possible outside of an airplane.

Nonetheless, Newt had some difficulty explaining the new acquisition to the executive officer of the *Prince William*.

"What the hell is a tram-bo-line?" asked the perplexed officer, signing the purchase order.

"Tram-*po*-line, P-O," his athletic officer helpfully replied.

"You want it? Okay, you can get it."

Newt kept the trampoline on the flight deck when he could—sometimes the space was inconveniently full of planes. Sometimes the men could find a little corner belowdecks to set it up. In addition to helping hone the pilots' air sense, the trampoline helped in their gymnastics development as well. Not only was it a competitive event, but in the days when "safety equipment" generally consisted of a few heavy, horsehair mats, bouncing on the trampoline was by far the safest way to learn and practice flipping and twisting skills. Newt also managed to rig up a high bar and set up tumbling mats for other gymnastic pursuits.

"It was an uphill battle," Newt remembered, "because the purpose of being on an aircraft carrier was to fight the war, not do this athletic stuff. But we squeezed it in here and there."

By September, Newt had received a delighted letter from Lieutenant William H. Sullivan of the Aviation Training Division.

"I know it will interest you to learn that Tom Bilodeau recently wrote to Commander Wickhorst and stated that he felt that your program was one of the finest that he had seen and was so much superior to that aboard his ship, that he felt quite embarrassed by the comparison," Sullivan wrote. "Keep up the good work, Newt, and rest assured that it will pay off not only in the satisfaction you get from doing a good job, but in future billets in this organization."

Newt kept his men busy with more than just bouncing. He organized baseball games, badminton, weightlifting, high-jumping, broad-jumping, even full-blown "athletic days" and complete divisional basketball and volleyball tournaments. From his old photo albums, it's easy to imagine the space belowdecks on the *P. Willy* as crammed with climbing ropes, mats and other athletic equipment. Despite his ever-present seasickness and the inevitable dangers of war, Newt remembers his days aboard the *P. Willy* mostly with fondness. Already, coaching was an immensely satisfying personal passion, even with soldiers whose first priority, understandably, was not necessarily to become top-flight gymnasts. His fitness program became, according to Lieutenant Commander F. C. Lane, "a standard to judge how well other Athletic Officers [were] performing." Undoubtedly, Newt's sparkling personality was a huge factor in inspiring the sailors aboard the ship to attack their fitness training with the enthusiasm that they did.

It was crucial that Newt keep himself busy, because otherwise his seasickness would gain the upper hand. "A good share of the time, I was seasick, and I mean just that," Newt recalled. "We had over five hundred enlisted men and seventy-five officers, and it seemed that I was always the first one seasick—hanging over the side of the carrier emptying out my stomach." He never forgot the weathered old sailor, with twenty years' experience, who explained confidently to Newt that the seasickness was all in his head.

"But sir," Newt replied, his self-deprecating humor always near the surface, "you have no idea how my stomach is acting." Then he ran off for another session over the side of the ship.

Newt never had a problem with a swelled head, but he maintains that his stint in the Navy taught him "humbleness," and how to use the proper channels in order to accomplish his goals.

When the war finally ended in 1945, Newt was discharged and headed for the University of Michigan, where he'd been awarded a fellowship to pursue his master's degree in physical education. He had written letters to about thirty different schools, but Michigan would allow him to start the day after his discharge. In his spare time, he co-authored *Gymnastics and Tumbling* for the Navy and finished the book on cheerleading that he'd begun aboard the *Prince William*. Always looking for a way to make his passions easily understood by those unfamiliar with them, Newt used abundant photos in order to illustrate the techniques for various cheers and tumbling tricks. Newt's enthusiasm came through even in his writing; in his coaching career, the knack for teaching both verbally and visually that he demonstrated in his books would serve him well. Unsurprisingly, Newt would become one of the first coaches in college gymnastics to utilize the video camera as a training tool.

After spreading the gospel of the trampoline to so many soldiers, Newt was ready as ever for a new adventure. In Ann Arbor, plenty of people knew what a trampoline was and how to use it, especially now that it had become its own event in competitive gymnastics. Newt was in exactly the right place at exactly the right time.

Chapter 5

Newt Finds a Team

Newt didn't arrive at Michigan planning to take over the reins for the cheerleading program, much less revive men's gymnastics as a varsity sport. He was in Ann Arbor to earn his master's, then his Ph.D., in physical education/kinesiology. But he harbored dreams of building a gymnastics club. Basically, he was a coach without a team, on the lookout for one.

The association with the cheerleaders just happened, as one day he passed a field where the cheerleaders were practicing, and everything followed from there. His own days as a "rooter king" at Minnesota and West High School weren't so far away, and after his November discharge, he'd earned his master's degree by June—and Newt sensed an opening.

Approaching the squad, he asked if they had a coach, or advisor of any kind. They didn't, though they wouldn't mind one. Newt jumped at the chance. And in a time when cheerleaders were expected to do far more than just yell and clap their hands, Newt's new gang doubled as neophyte gymnasts.

Thanks to the Navy's V-12 program, a trampoline was already present and accounted for on the Michigan campus in Ann Arbor, in Waterman Gym, when Newt arrived. He quickly worked out a routine with his boys, featuring Newt in a black-and-white striped Gay Nineties bathing suit. As his budding acrobats performed graceful tricks, Newt made the crowd laugh by stumbling and clowning around—then finishing off the performance with forty or fifty straight flips on the trampoline.

Newt's flair for show business, after being forced to hibernate somewhat during World War II, now came into full flower. Of course, his own enthusiasm couldn't help but spread to the gymnasts. If an act with just him and Johnny Frankus was fun, how much *more* fun must it be to perform with a whole group? He took his band of tumblers on tour in 1946, traveling nearly three thousand miles to do twenty-nine exhibitions. To other people, the schedule might have sounded grueling, but to Newt, it sounded like a grand old time. From the first, even unofficially, Newt's calling seemed to be bringing joy and verve to Michigan and its students.

And from the first football game of the 1946 season, Michigan fans knew something had changed with their cheerleaders. The eight men still wore their traditional bright yellow sweaters bearing the blue block M, the tight white pants, the white tennis shoes. They still did their traditional "trumpet yell." But in 1946, they replaced their "jitterbug step" with not another dance move, but a series of gymnastic stunts, including backflips, somersaults and a "sky rocket." All the cheerleaders would stack up on top of one another, and then yell, "Now!" As the crowd whistled, the top man would leap off to land on his feet, somersault forward and spring to his feet again with a flourish.

They counted off the Michigan football team's points by doing flips off the low wall, a tradition that continues in the form of standing backflips in the end zone. As always, the cheerleaders were led by their elected "Rooter King." This year, it was cheerleading veteran Bill MacGowan, who'd already been on the squad three years. But he was now joined by Newt Loken, physical education instructor.

Under Newt's instruction, the cheerleaders quickly became a beloved, exciting institution, not only on the campus but across the Midwest as Newt led them on tours. Twenty-seven-year-old Newt, as ever bouncing off the walls with energy and exuberance, often joined his boys in their stunts. When Tom Tillman was hurt and out for the season, Newt filled in during the halftime show. At Varsity Night, an annual band-sponsored variety show, Newt and cheerleader Glenn Neff performed an impressive hand-balancing act. (Another cheerleader, Chico Kennedy, did a Russian dance called "Crazy Ivan." It must have been a sight to behold.)

And Newt was always looking for new, crazier ways to wow the crowds.

"We even went over to some hockey games and tried to lead cheers on skates," gymnast and cheerleader Bob Willoughby remembered. "Newt was right in there with us. He would do horse-vaulting at the basketball games. He was the clown, really in it. When we'd do a trampoline show, he'd always have the big ladder out there, so he was ready for the climax of the thing." Pictures from that time show Newt in his striped bathing suit, perched high atop a ladder above his trampoline, grinning and ready to leap off.

In December of 1946, the month his first child, Christine, was born, Newt and Howard Leibee organized a gymnastics clinic for high school and college coaches that would become an annual event. Leibee was the director of Waterman Gym where Newt's boys held their practices. The program featured a presentation of teaching techniques, an explanation of new apparatus, and a stunt demo by twelve Michigan students and Newt. Already acquainted with the cheerleaders-cum-gymnasts' talents from football games, interest from Michigan's student population was high enough that Newt finally extended them an invitation.

The event, which he'd been planning for weeks, was a definite success. For the budding coach, the most important thing was to get more people excited about gymnastics, tumbling and cheerleading. Especially in these early days, he often put on his own performances, but they were never for the sake of showing himself off. He wanted everyone there to know that with hard work and good coaching, they could do the same tricks Newt did before their amazed eyes. At the clinic, Newt performed thirty-six continuous front and back flips, featuring twists and turns, wowing the huge crowd that showed up. Two female gymnasts even performed—more of a rarity in those days. And every trick that Ruth Bush and Elaine Kuzlinski executed on the trampoline was the product of months of work under Newt's coaching, something the coach reveled in far more than his own tricks.

Shortly after the clinic, Newt's cheerleaders and a smattering of other gymnastics enthusiasts asked him for his approval to form a Gymnastic Club. Of course Newt gave it readily, perhaps unaware of just what he was about to get into. He had wanted a team to coach—here it was. The club would not be just a club for very long.

As winter set in, Newt and his boys were as busy as ever, performing vaults at the halftime of Michigan basketball games and touring Michigan cities with a larger variety of equipment—trampolines, tumbling mats, a high bar and flying rings. By February 14, 1947, few people anywhere near the University of Michigan could avoid knowing about the well-traveled Michigan gymnasts. On that day, Athletic Director Fritz Crisler made an announcement that set everything in motion.

Over the next eighteen months, he announced, the athletic facilities at the University would be expanded significantly, to the point of being "just about tops in the nation." A large new 20,000-seat arena for hockey and basketball was planned, along with an enlarged Intramural Building, an overhaul to the golf course, and a new women's sports building on Palmer Field. With the expansion of athletic facilities, three clubs, along with the accommodating *Michigan Daily*, began lobbying for recognition as varsity sports. The clubs were the fencers, the boxers—and the gymnasts.

The boxers were the only club advocating a totally new sport, as both fencing and gymnastics had been supported at the University before cutbacks during the Great Depression. But the boxing club had gathered thousands of signatures on a petition for its recognition as varsity. The sport had never failed yet as a drawing card, noted *Daily* Sports Editor Jack Martin, and there existed sufficient interest, practice space and competition for boxing to be viable. The same applied to the fencers, whose team had been cut, like the gymnasts', in 1933.

The Gymnastic Club was the best known of the three, as Newt's boys had spent the school year performing all over the Midwest, and logging a mind-boggling three thousand miles traveling to their twenty-nine gigs. A men's gymnastics conference championship was scheduled for March 15, 1947—the first in four years, since World War II had intervened. Interest was high, Martin remarked, if the response from the basketball crowds was any indication. The only roadblock to the gymnasts was the lack of proper facilities—but the massive expansion project would "undoubtedly provide suitable space."

With his team being considered for varsity status, Newt's excitement reached new levels. There were no guarantees, especially with boxing the seeming front-runner, but suddenly it looked as though Newt might be able to follow in the footsteps of his own mentor, Ralph Piper. Performance gigs remained constant, to show the administration just what a draw the team's feats were, and Newt planned another trip for his team as well.

On March 15—the Big Nine Championships—Newt took

his boys to Champaign, Illinois, at the invitation of the host Illini. His gymnasts wouldn't get a chance to compete, but they would be able to make valuable observations about the atmosphere and requirements of a championship meet. Newt harbored not-so-secret hopes that those observations would come in quite handy in the following year. And as usual, while in Illinois, they gave an exhibition on Newt's beloved trampoline. By now it was old hat—they had six more engagements to perform in the two months following the championships.

The Daily, as if to prod the Athletic Board, doggedly printed regular coverage of all three clubs fighting for recognition. All three participated in the IM Open House in late March, with the boxers stealing the show before a crowd of 5,000 people. Newt's boys were the halftime entertainment during the fraternity basketball championship game. Finally, a month later, the Board in Control of Intercollegiate Athletics met in Detroit to decide the fate of the three teams.

"According to reliable sources," *The Daily* reported, "boxing is the only sport that will merit serious consideration at this time" by virtue of its petition. Newt had been worried about this, and called Athletic Director Fritz Crisler before the meeting.

"Boss," he said, "I can run out and get a petition if you want me to, because I've seen from *The Daily* that boxing has 500 [signatures]."

Boxing may have had the signatures; gymnastics, however, had Newt, and to Crisler, that mattered far more. Crisler reassured the young coach: "No, that's okay, we know what you've been doing. You've done a lot of exhibitions." Newt nonetheless waited anxiously in Ann Arbor for news. Coaching a club was fun, and he probably could have continued to do it happily. But now his hopes had been raised to something grander: varsity status, a chance to compete instead of just put on exhibitions. His own days of competing as a Gopher weren't that far away; Newt must have missed the rush of the meets, and assuredly he wanted his own gymnasts to have the same chances he'd had to compete and succeed against the best.

On Sunday, April 27, 1947, the wait ended. *The Daily* reported that the University's Board in Control of Intercollegiate Athletics had awarded varsity status solely to the gymnastics team. While the boxers and fencers were understandably disappointed with the decision, *The Daily* declared it "no real surprise, for Newt Loken has had a proficient group of athletes under his tutelege (sic) at Waterman Gymnasium for the past year."

Newt was delighted; even with Crisler's assurances, he still hadn't completely believed it was going to happen for his team. "The forming of a gymnastic (sic) team for next year comes as a wonderful surprise to all of us," he told *The Daily*. "The boys are looking forward to competition next year and a chance to show what they can do."

Crisler contacted Newt about the possibility of coaching the team.

"Would you accept the gymnastics coaching job if it was offered to you?" he asked. Newt didn't need to be asked twice; of course, he would be the coach. This was *his team*, and he had big plans for his athletes. Crisler promised a $1,000 yearly salary.

"I thought that was great!" Newt remembered. "I didn't have any scholarships, because at that time you had to be funded. All my kids were walk-ons. Rarely do you get a champion out of the walk-ons, though it's been done before, and we've had the pleasure of coaching some."

On Saturday, May 3, 1947, Newt Loken was officially named the head coach of the men's gymnastics team. His dream for the past year had come true; his lifelong love of gymnastics, showmanship, and teaching people would now have a constant outlet. And over the next thirty-six years, Newt and Michigan men's gymnastics would become nearly the same entity.

Chapter 6

The First Season

Newt led his boys through the doors of the imposing brick Intramural Building on Hoover Street. One of the structures built during Athletic Director Fielding Yost's tenure, it was much like the others: beautiful and built to last, with majestic arches across the side of the building facing Hoover. Turning left at the main lobby, the gymnasts entered the auxiliary gym, soon to be affectionately known as "the little gym." This was to be their new, varsity home: a big step up from owning one end of big Waterman Gym and using the old equipment that Wilbur West's Depression-era teams had left behind. A removable wall separated the gymnastics area from the varsity pool next door, where Matt Mann (known to Newt as "The Great Matt Mann") trained his champion swimmers. Down the hall was the big gym, where IM basketball tournaments were held—and where the varsity gymnasts would hold their meets, sometimes in front of a few thousand spectators.

"I had six guys, all neophytes," Newt remembered. He gathered them together in their new gym, six gymnasts who had performed only in exhibitions. A far cry from the intense pressure of competitions, to be sure, they were about to take a huge step into the land of varsity sports. "Here goes," Newt said—possibly wondering just what he'd gotten himself into. In all the tension and excitement of the team's road to becoming varsity, no one had talked much about the new responsibilities Newt would have to shoulder. Preparing gymnasts to compete against other schools was far different than preparing them to do exhibitions.

"What did I know about coaching?" Newt said later. "I was just a gymnast. When Fritz Crisler said they had a little gym for me in the IM Building, and okay, you're head coach, I went in there and I had six cheerleading gymnasts. And all we did was frolic around. What did we know about routines and months and months of practice? Now it's thirteen months a year. Back in those days, in the summer I'd go off to various camps so I gave the kids time off. I thought that was not a bad program but it meant they weren't learning skills. In my early days, I was kind of naïve about how much intensive work you really have to do."

In the late 1940s, gymnastics wasn't yet the "thirteen months a year" sport it has now become, but coaching a varsity team was still a far bigger commitment than leading a traveling group on exhibitions. He'd be not just teaching and refining, but handling the team through competitions and somehow finding time to watch amateur meets, pick out up-and-coming talent and recruit new gymnasts.

In November of 1947, Newt held the first of a series of intrasquads to add gymnasts to his team. By December, he needed to choose the squad that would compete against a number of other first year programs—Ohio State, Michigan State and Central Michigan—in six events that may be unfamiliar to today's gymnastics fans. Along with the familiar side horse (now called pommel horse), high bar and parallel bars, gymnasts competed in tumbling, down a long, thin mat; the dangerous flying rings, which instead of hanging straight down like today's still rings, swung in huge, dramatic arcs as the gymnast performed; and a new crowd-pleaser of an event that had caught on in the Midwest—trampoline.

"We were bad," remembered Bob Willoughby, a member of that first team. "I had to work all-around, and I'm far from an all-arounder. ... I think it was pretty much true of the other guys, too. We had one or two events where we did enough of a good routine, and the others we filled in. When I think of the stuff we did ..." Willoughby, still living in Ann Arbor, can't quite believe the changes that have occurred in his sport. "[Now] they can try an awful lot more, and not worry about getting hurt. ... For tumbling, we put down big horsehair mats. ... They were just as heavy as can be."

Newt was one of the first coaches to start using a pit filled with foam to help his gymnasts safely practice new skills. Loose-foam pits are now a staple at most gyms, immeasurably useful for experimenting on every event but pommel horse. At any moment an athlete can suddenly disappear, mid-routine, into one of them. At Whitmore Lake was a company that made seat cushions for cars produced in nearby Detroit, and Newt would visit periodically to collect the scraps for his pit. "I remember when they started using that for the horse vaulting so you had something to land on," Willoughby said.

November 12, 1948 saw the first varsity event for men's gymnastics at Michigan since 1933. Thirty spectators, *The Daily* reported, attended the Maize and Blue intrasquad in the gym, their cheers echoing in the big space usually used for intramural basketball games. Tom Tillman, who was later named a team captain, earned the most points of the night. A second Maize and Blue intrasquad was held on December 7, this time in front of 250 people. Because several Blue gymnasts missed the competition for a psychology exam, the ever-resourceful Newt filled their spots with gymnasts from Detroit clubs. It was a good show for the fans, but Newt deemed more hard work necessary before the team could be chosen. He wouldn't choose his final squad until he had satisfied himself that he knew which athletes were the right ones.

Gymnastics in those days followed a far different set of rules than those of today. Performers could earn up to one hundred points for a routine. Sixty points were based on the gymnast's gracefulness and form, forty on the difficulty of his routine. However, gymnasts' rankings in comparison to their opponents was the real key. Rather than combining the gymnasts' individual scores into a team total, teams received a certain number of points for each gymnast who finished in the top five. A first place finish in an event, regardless of the gymnast's actual score, earned the most points for his team. Ten men at most comprised a competing varsity team, with three men performing on each apparatus. The last man up was usually the team's top performer.

Difficult "tricks" in 1948 were not exactly on par with the skills of sixty years later. The "crowning point" of a high bar routine was said to be a perfectly executed giant swing, now a very basic skill that every college gymnast can perform almost without thinking. Circles on pommel horse, now a basic move and often used as a repetitive drill, were also considered spectacular.

Through the years, the scoring code, equipment and safety measures have changed so much that gymnasts must perform skills of far greater difficulty in order to get good scores. Each time gymnasts push the limits of what is possible on a given event, the Code of Points will change to reflect that. Attempting a triple-twisting backflip in tumbling in 1948, for example, would have been unthinkable, not to mention impossible and dangerous given the lack of springs and padding. Now, there are many gymnasts who can successfully complete such a skill on the floor exercise, and one, former Michigan gymnast Kent Caldwell, who even executed a quadruple-twisting backflip.

The trampoline, though 1948 was its first year as a regular

NCAA gymnastics event, would probably be the most impressive to the contemporary gymnastics fan, just as it was then. Along with the growing number of private gymnastics clubs springing up all over the country, the trampoline was a huge reason for the sport's rise after World War II. Crowds gaped at the small muscular men shooting high into the air, performing a double backflip or a fliffis—a double somersault with a half twist— among his ten or twelve tricks. A few years later, Newt conducted an informal poll of fans to find out which event they liked most. By a huge margin, trampoline was the winner. And from the start, Newt's teams specialized in the event—he loved trampoline above anything else, and the fact that the crowds did too only increased its appeal to the show-business part of his nature. Trampoline's prominence at Michigan came from a happy confluence of Newt's preference for it; the excellent talent he recruited over the years; and the fact that it was the flashiest, most crowd-pleasing event. (Ironically, Illinois coach Charlie Pond, later to become one of Newt's biggest rivals, was the man who originally introduced trampoline to gymnastics as a special event at the 1946 NCAA Championships in Dallas.)

Finally, on December 13, Newt named his team. Glenn Neff and Tom Tillman, both varsity cheerleaders, would co-captain the squad, which featured several more of their cheerleading teammates: Dave Lake, Bob Willoughby, Bob Schoendube and Chico Kennedy, as well as gymnast Dick Fashbaugh.

High-bar and flying-rings specialist Willoughby, along with Lake, became a lifelong Ann Arborite; he still attends every home meet. His former coach not only provided unfailing support through Willoughby's gymnastics career, but helped him earn a bachelor's degree and then offered him a teaching assistant job leading trampoline classes at Waterman Gym. Willoughby, rather than becoming a doctor as he'd originally planned, became a coach like Newt.

When a gymnastics coaching job opened up at Alpena High School, Willoughby's experiences under Newt helped him get it. When the former gymnast returned from serving in Germany during the Korean War, Newt invited him back to Michigan for a teaching fellowship so he could earn his doctorate. Willoughby ended up at Eastern Michigan University, just a few minutes' drive from the University of Michigan, started a gymnastics team and taught there for thirty-five years.

And when the department head at Eastern went on a long leave of absence, Willoughby was able to bring in another Wolverine gymnast to help shoulder the load: Marv Johnson, the 1954 Michigan team captain.

"We were able to keep Marv on after that," Willoughby remembered. "He was there forever; [he's] still hanging around over there. ... Marv was another gymnast at Michigan, so Newt had an influence there, all the way through on that, as far as my career was concerned, and a number of others, too."

Preparing for their season opener in January of 1948, Newt and all but two of his gymnasts spent their 1947 Christmas break performing as cheerleaders for the Rose Bowl game and visiting Santa Monica's Muscle Beach, practicing on the gymnastic equipment down in the sand. By now, Newt was also developing his "Loken Trampoline Act," which would become so well-known that he would be featured on the TV show *Super Circus*. Sometimes Newt's gymnasts participated; later on, Newt's daughters, then his sons, would supplement his own performance. "I could talk on and on about how much fun we had as a 'circus family,' " Newt's second-oldest daughter, Lani, said.

Newt had been tossing around the idea of his own trampoline act for a long time. The show his gymnasts put on was quite popular, but due to classes and schoolwork, they couldn't always appear everywhere they were wanted. Newt's schedule was far more flexible. And as always, Newt gave his act everything he had, earning himself the title of Comedy King of the Trampoline.

Newt's costume was an act in itself. At the start of his performance, he'd be dressed in multiple jackets and vests atop two or three bathing suits, with various caps hidden about his person. First stepping on the stage, Newt, upon approaching and exploring this strange contraption, would immediately step through a spring of his trampoline and fall on his face. Pulling off his current cap, Newt made it clear through body language that this was the headgear's fault. On would go a new cap. Newt then headed for the enormous stepladder inserted into one end of the springs of the trampoline—and put a foot through the rungs. His face slammed into the ladder. Again, it had to be the hat's fault.

"Jeez, that ladder would shake!" Newt remembered. "It was a ten-foot ladder. Then I'd get up to the top and miss a step, and I'd fall on my face! I'd laugh and the crowd would giggle. Then when I finally got up on the top, I would do a swing time. I'd jump off and do a back somersault, Barani, back and bounce backward. Then somehow or other, I always landed on the ladder."

Well, almost all the time. Not the time Newt got a chance to perform outdoors.

"I'm outside in the open sky and I felt so fresh I bounced back, and went up and over the top!" Newt said. "I'd never done that. Usually I'd hit a step or three or four, and then my back would run into the steps of the ladder. Wow. I looked down and there was the ground. If I'd fallen on my neck, I'd have been broken. But the crowd loved it!"

As Newt's tricks with the ladder and trampoline progressed, he began to shed pieces of clothing—so many amazing stunts, the implication went, made the exuberant performer a tad warm. More hats, a jacket, and four vests eventually littered the stage.

"Then I'd come down and do a back somersault and kick my pants off," Newt said. "Wham, they'd fly off, and I'd have this striped, old-fashioned bathing suit. Yellow and black. It had a hole in the back, and under that I had [another] striped bathing suit. Stripes all over the place. ... It finally got to the point where I'd get all the way down, and I had a nice white rayon ... elasticized bathing suit, and I was in pretty good shape. And I would look out at the audience and say, 'You think this is the last suit I've got on?' And I would hold the suit off my waist, look, and say, 'It is!' They would laugh and say, 'Don't take any more off!' "

Newt then grabbed an old metal bicycle hoop tied to the trampoline frame, and declared that he was going to do a backflip into the hoop.

"Do you think I can do it?" he yelled to the crowd, before gleefully performing the trick. Then he asked the crowd if they thought he could do a front flip into the hoop. He did the flip, but finished with only one leg through the hoop. Once more, he turned to the crowd and announced, "It must be the hat!"

Newt reached into his trunks and out came another hat. Finally, the big announcement came: "Now, I'm going to do a back flip into the hoop and a front flip out of the hoop—and I 'hoop' I make it!"

As the audience roared with laughter, Newt completed those flips, then threw the hoop off the trampoline and continued with several flips in a row. As Newt dismounted the trampoline, the crowd applauded and yelled, "More, more!"

This was a perfect time to introduce a little "crowd participation"—actually Newt's daughters, Chris and Lani. Known in the show as "the Apple Sisters, Seedie and Corey," they would come out of the crowd and onto the stage. Wearing special bouncing outfits, they demonstrated a series of trampoline skills, finishing with an eye-catching jump rope routine.

During summers and at Christmas time, the girls participated in nearly all the shows. Later, Newt's sons Jon and Newt Jr. also became part of the act. For twenty-five years, the trampoline act was Newt Loken's calling card—other than Michigan men's gymnastics and cheerleading, of course.

The Daily trumpeted Michigan's first meet, to be held January 9, 1948, against fellow varsity newcomer Central Michigan. Seven of the gymnasts were slated to perform: Neff, Tillman, Fashbaugh, Willoughby, Lake, Coplin and Schoendube.

Then, the day before the meet, disaster hit. The dark, intense Tillman, already standing out as the team's top all-arounder, was forced to stay behind in Ann Arbor for a psychology exam. Hack Coplin fractured his wrist practicing on the high bar and was out indefinitely. Schoendube contracted the chicken pox. Newt added Butt to the roster and planned to send up three men on each event (today, coaches typically use six men in each rotation). The team was holding together with spit, good wishes and Newt's unfailing optimism.

And that turned out to be enough. No matter what the situation, Newt's belief in his athletes never wavered. He had been through everything they were going through as competitors, and if he thought they could succeed despite the setbacks, who were the gymnasts to think otherwise? In Michigan's first gymnastics competition in fifteen years, the Wolverines rolled over Central Michigan in Mt. Pleasant, 59-30. They wore white step-in uniforms, MICHIGAN embroidered across the chest in blue, loose white pants and soft white shoes as they earned four of the six first-place spots, sweeping the top three spots on the flying rings. Head cheerleader Dave Lake bested all comers in tumbling and Bob Willoughby won high bar in front of a huge crowd.

The fans weren't just there for the gymnastics competition, however. Staying true to their roots, the Wolverines and Chippewas were the opening act for an upcoming basketball game—and between halves, Newt, Tillman, Loyal Jodar and Fred Thompson put on a trampoline exhibition. Michigan was off to a great start, but a big test loomed ahead of them: the powerful

Minnesota Gophers, led by Newt's old coach Ralph Piper, and his star tumbler—Herb Loken.

Herb, like Newt, had served in World War II and was one of many former GIs who took advantage of the opportunity to get a college education. The twenty-three-year-old sophomore had been a high school champ on the parallel bars. In Europe, he was a paratrooper.

"There was a $50 a month increase in your salary [for being a paratrooper]," Newt remembered. "Fifty was like five hundred back in those days, so he jumped at the chance. Jumped is right! He said, 'Every time I jumped out of that damn airplane, I thought, "I don't want that $50! I just want to go back to the ground!" ' It was pretty hairy—they'd jump out of the plane and hope that the parachute would open."

Herb jumped into the Battle of the Bulge and ended up landing right in the middle of a German troop. The Germans shot everyone from the platoon but Herb and one of his friends, who then had to fight their way back to their fellow Americans from behind German lines. But "he made it through the rain," as Newt likes to say. Now, in 1948, he and Don, the youngest Loken brother and a Gopher freshman, were following in their big brother's footsteps on the Minnesota gymnastics team. *The Daily* ran a prominent story on the head coach's kid brother and his juggernaut team, which featured three 1947 Big Nine champions. Ralph Piper called his boys the best team of his career.

Newt was already molding himself in the image of his old coach. "The thing [Piper] was involved with, was everything in the world, along with coaching," said Newt, who, as the years progressed, became involved with ever more activities around Ann Arbor. "[Piper] was chairman of the [athletic] department, was a folk dance expert, he received many awards. He was a folk dance [and] square dance authority. [Piper] got two Fulbright Awards and went overseas to teach ... So maybe his diversity was one thing that allowed him to win very successfully six Big Ten titles." With Newt's energy and zest for life in general, it's not surprising that he followed in Piper's footsteps, learning to call square dances and teaching social dance forms at Michigan. "Diversity" certainly worked for Newt as well, as he won twelve Big Ten titles. Over the years, he became an Ann Arbor fixture as well as a men's gymnastics stalwart. He taught physical education classes, dance classes, coached the cheerleaders, did his trampoline act and served as the manager of the Huron Valley Swim Club from 1961-1972, all while coaching and recruiting for the men's (and for a year, the women's) gymnastics team. Working at the swim club actually aided Newt's coaching regimen—instead of being away from Ann Arbor at various tumbling and cheerleading camps, he could be in town to coach his gymnasts.

Predictably, when the lordly Gophers arrived in Ann Arbor they handed Newt's boys their first loss. But Newt's face still lights up when he remembers the joy of his team competing against his brothers and old coach. And despite falling to Minnesota, the Wolverines had some surprises in store.

A month later, after another thumping of Central Michigan, the Wolverines held tough final workouts in preparation for the meet against Illinois, the defending national champion. Newt placed the most emphasis on the high bar and flying rings, which were the undefeated Fighting Illini's major strengths. Illinois captain Vito Zinzi was the defending side horse champion, Johnny O'Heron the defending long horse (vault) champ. The team had also regained the services of 1942 letter-winner Joe Calvetti. It would be a combo meet, with the first three events in the little gym, then finishing at impressive Yost Fieldhouse after the evening's basketball game.

The Illini edged Michigan out for the win with a sweep of the top three places in the final event, trampoline—before that, the defending champs had actually been trailing. Michigan lost by just five points, a huge accomplishment for such a new and inexperienced team. *The Daily* called Michigan's season thus far a "meteoric rise to a prominent place in the nation's gymnastic constellation." Even for someone as positive as Newt, Michigan's ability to compete at the same level as a team like Illinois so quickly must have been a very pleasant surprise. And given that his team was basically a troop of unrecruited volunteers, the majority of their success had to be credited to Newt, with his ability to both teach them and inspire them to heights they might not have dreamed possible. In just Newt's first year coaching, Michigan's future trademarks of optimism and success were already making themselves apparent.

Even when co-captain Glenn Neff, one of the tallest of Newt's boys and a parallel bars and rings specialist, was hospitalized with the flu after the Illinois meet, Michigan wasn't daunted. Despite his sickness, Neff joined his teammates for a trip to East Lansing where the Wolverines soundly trounced the Spartans, 62.5-32.5. The Wolverines took first in five events, tying for the lead in the sixth, in front of 10,000 enthusiastic fans. And Neff? He got the top spot on flying rings.

Eleven days later the Wolverines notched another significant victory, beating both the University of Chicago and the University of Wisconsin at Chicago. They only managed to squeak out a "photo finish" win with a tremendous performance on the trampoline. Newt called it "one of the most interesting meets of the season. It was well-received by a nice crowd and the officiating was excellent." He must have been impressed by his admitted novices' ability to grit their way through a meet to a win, and especially gratified to see them using trampoline performances to secure the victory.

And now came the Big Nine Championships, this year to be held on Chicago's Navy Pier. *The Daily* billed it as the "biggest and most appealing event in Big Nine history," with

Minnesota, Illinois, Michigan, Wisconsin, Ohio State, Purdue, Iowa, Chicago, Michigan State, Nebraska and a team of Navy Pier gymnasts all invited to compete. Three judges would evaluate each performance, awarding points for performance (out of five points), continuity (three), and difficulty (seven). Teams would receive ten points for a first-place event finish, nine for a second-place finish, and so on. The Gophers and Illini were the teams to beat, though Newt believed the addition of trampoline as an event could do nothing but help his boys.

For the first time in history, the conference meet was televised, even if it was only to the Metro Chicago area. And if *The Daily* of the time is any indication, hopes were high for the Wolverines. A team that preseason predictors had placed in the cellar, Michigan was entering the championships with a 6-2 record and fresh off beating two of the hottest teams in Chicago. Despite their "spectacular rise," however, the Wolverines were still considered underdogs.

And in front of an overflow crowd on Navy Pier on March 14, 1948, the Wolverines finished third behind powerhouses Minnesota, the new champion, and Illinois. Bob Schoendube, who won the Big Nine trampoline title, was the only Wolverine to place in the top three on any event. Newt was thrilled with his boys' inaugural season, singing their praises to a *Daily* reporter while acknowledging that the Gophers superior experience had allowed them to snag the championship. To him, Schoendube's championship performance was "flawless"—he did "every maneuver with perfect ease." Though they hadn't won, Newt couldn't be anything but hopeful about what the future held for him and his teams. With a team of all walk-ons, Michigan had still managed to make a strong impression on the gymnastics world. Newt's coaching philosophy was not as finished as it would become in later years, but his tendency to encourage rather than berate, to treat his gymnasts as part of his family, to try anything to make them successful, was clearly working with great effectiveness. In the coming years, Newt would get the chance to refine his technique, as well as apply it to ever more gifted athletes—a potent combination.

Not even Newt could imagine just how successful his team would eventually be, which became clear when the team returned home. Newt found himself staring up at the blank white wall of the IM Building. Suddenly, he had an idea: Why not paint the name of every Michigan event champion on the wall? Bob Schoendube would be the first.

"Earl Riskey, who was intramural director at that time, was very handy with printing," Newt said later in an interview with the U.S. Gymnastics Federation. "I asked him if he would mind putting up the wall of champions sign, and we centered it right in the middle. We thought a champion a year would be pretty good for us. So here we were in the center and we thought it would take twenty years to fill up this one panel."

Thirty-six years later, running out of room for all the names that had joined Schoendube, Newt wished he had told Riskey to start painting on the end instead of the center. He joked that he might "put their names on the ceiling! So that the incoming freshmen would truly look up to the champions of the years of yore that are no more."

Chapter 7

Gathering Stars

Thanks to a cross-country trip to the 1948 Rose Bowl, the gymnastics team of 1949 gained its first star. Dave Lake convinced the local Kaiser-Frazer dealer to give the cheerleading team the use of a beautiful car all season. It was a bright yellow sedan with rounded lines and blue block M's along the sides. According to Bob Willoughby, he and his mates had grand plans to get the car autographed by all the movie stars roaming the streets of Pasadena. Though they only got two autographs, from actors Olga San Juan and Donald O'Connor, the trip was a tremendous success. A drive from Ann Arbor to Pasadena, even today, is a big undertaking, and in 1948 the trip took days longer. Newt's carload, consisting of Dorothy, Bill MacGowan and Bob Willoughby, stopped to sightsee at every opportunity. The rest of the team, driving the Kaiser, drove straight through to Pasadena.

Like many gymnasts, Newt possessed a nearly unshakeable inner confidence—something that tends to lead them into performing handstands on all manner of objects in widely varied places. Add that to Newt's flair for flash and showiness, and you had a recipe for some amazing handstand photos. Newt's handstands on the trip started small, posing upside down on signs marking the caravan's crossing from state to state. When they reached the Grand Canyon, the coach was ready for his star turn. The photo, even sixty years later, is enough to send a viewer's heart into their throat. Newt grasped the railing and pushed himself into a handstand, grinning upside-down at the camera with only his athletic talent between him and a mile-long fall to the bottom of the canyon.

The most important moment of the trip, however, wasn't the daredevilry at the Grand Canyon or the football team's 49-0 drubbing of USC. Along the way, Newt made a strategic stop in Amarillo, Texas, to check out a young trampolinist of whom Newt had heard great things. The local Texas Maverick Boys Club was having an exhibition, and the moment Newt saw young Henry Edsel Buchanan perform on the trampoline, he knew he wanted him for his team. As the coach would prove over the coming seasons, his eye for fresh talent was unerring. Over some barbecue, Newt convinced the slender wavy-haired trampolinist that Michigan was the place for him. "Tex," as young Ed became known, spent the next four years proving Newt right.

Buchanan had been the club's most experienced tumbler when Nard Cazzell, according to Buchanan a "great booster of the Maverick Club," bought a trampoline for the boys to try. Young Ed took to trampoline like he was born to bounce, using his tumbling experiences and overall gymnastic ability to adapt skills to the new event.

"The club director [Ralphy Dykeman] gave me Newt Loken's name at Michigan and I wrote Newt telling him of the skills we were achieving on the trampoline," Buchanan remembered. With an academic scholarship and some financial aid from Cazzell, he was able to go to the University of Michigan.

Through the fall of 1948, more than twenty gymnasts worked out in the IM Building with hopes of making Newt's team. The cheerleaders continued to be an extension of the team, as they would for many years to come. This year, they introduced a new method of counting the football team's score, performing as many flips off the wall as the team had earned points. The popular halftime trampoline-and-tumbling exhibitions at basketball games continued—Newt's boys were not yet a team that could stand completely on its own.

Christine Loken, Newt's two-year-old daughter, had no such problems standing on her own. Newt, never one to spend more time with his team than with his family, had introduced the trampoline to Chris when she was just six months old. Before Chris even learned to stand on the ground, she was standing on her father's strong, capable hands.

And she was certainly her father's daughter. Following her dad to work, she immediately made a beeline for the IM Building's big trampoline. Newt quickly realized that this might not be the best place for a six-month-old to play, and promptly constructed a tiny version of canvas, cut up inner tubes, and leftover pipes so Chris could bounce away to her heart's content. By the ripe old age of two, the curly-haired cherub was now pirouetting, executing seat drops and flying through the air with ease. When Newt's back was turned, she'd often clamber up onto her tramp by herself.

"I never expected our play sessions would lead to this," Newt said modestly. "Friends who've seen her practice are asking for stunts to do with their own children."

Newt never pushed his oldest daughter to become a gymnast, despite her early aptitude. Instead, she followed Newt's interest in dance and the tales of his coach Ralph Piper and earned a Ph.D. in anthropology.

By now, Newt had the basics of what would become his distinctive coaching style down pat. These aspects of his program became his trademark: unflagging enthusiasm for everything in his sport, a sense of genuine optimism and a willingness to work individually with any athlete, regardless of his skill, on improving his gymnastics. There were countless walk-ons with no shot of making the team that Newt nevertheless made time for as if they were his stars.

"I had this one guy, never made the team, trying to learn a full twisting flyaway on the rings," Newt remembered. "He spent endless hours on the trampoline with me spotting him trying to learn the full twist. Just a somersault with a full twist. I don't know if he learned it or not. But now he comes to all the gym meets, comes up with his two boys, again and again."

Newt's boys were visibly improved thanks to his recruiting, which would only get better. Michigan added Buchanan, the trampoline ace, and Pete Barthell, who would earn the nickname "Daily Double." In nearly every meet of the 1949 season, the protégé of national tumbling champion Joe Giallombardo earned two first-place finishes, usually in the parallel bars and tumbling. And Buchanan began one of the most impressive careers in Michigan gymnastics history.

"He was our first real champion," Newt said of Buchanan, who was one of the only competitors capable of a backflip with a triple twist on trampoline. In those days, competitors used a "solid bed" trampoline, unlike the "web beds" currently used, which make higher-flying, more difficult tricks easier to perform.

No one could best Buchanan on trampoline—not in the regular season duals, not at the conference championships, not in AAU championships, and not even at the NCAA championships. Additionally, Dick "Old Reliable" Fashbaugh was back, along with Bob Willoughby, Bob Schoendube, Dave Lake and Tom Tillman.

"Newt had great talent in analyzing both individual skills and combinations of skills," Buchanan said of his coach's early years. "Newt was very insightful in analyzing skills of gymnasts … [His] background was exceptional across gymnastic events and skills." This meant Newt could help his gymnasts build the best possible routines, composed of elements they could perform with a high level of success and perfection and which would get them the highest possible scores. Newt could also suggest new tricks which an individual gymnast's aptitude indicated would be easy for him to learn and add to his repertoire. While Newt recruited the best he could, he never stopped trying to make them even better.

Beyond his obvious technical expertise, Newt's trademark was his willingness to tailor his program to his gymnasts' individual needs. Regardless of the athlete's skill level, Newt would make it work. If one of his boys needed some one-on-one instruction around noon, Newt made peanut butter sandwiches and ate them while coaching in the little IM gym. If a Wolverine couldn't make it to practice until late in the evening, Newt would find a way to be there. For those who would never make the competition team, these sessions were individually affirming; for Newt's stars, they were a way to improve already solid performances. Instead of instilling respect in the manner of most coaches—through behavior reminiscent of a drill sergeant—Newt earned their trust, respect and love through his own tireless work ethic. His boys' success, in and out of the gym, meant the world to him, and Newt wasn't shy about telling them so.

"I think [my coaching philosophy was] to be continuously optimistic about what they can do and realistic, of course, overall," Newt said. "I think I was a friend of the athletes. I've seen some of their comments. If they had any problems, I wanted to hear about it. I wasn't sure I could solve them, but I was interested in their welfare and I was always encouraging the elevation of their skills. I haven't won as many dual meets as some other people have, so I'm not all alone in the win and loss column. But we were fortunate in recruiting. I always showed a keen fatherly interest in any athlete who came to Michigan, and

I think the parents detected this. 'Go to Michigan—Coach will watch over you.' I'd do everything but go to class for them. So it felt like we had a family. Many of the kids thought they were members of my family, and I wonder if my two boys and two girls wondered who was really part of the family. Just human being to human being with the athletes, more than anything, and help them wherever possible."

The Wolverines lost just one regular season meet, to the ever-powerful Illini. Illinois lost the conference crown to Minnesota, but Michigan joined those two teams in proving to be the class of the Big Nine. Of 154 possible points in the championship, only sixteen went to other teams. Held in Ann Arbor for the first time, the conference championships drew more competitors than ever before, with 50 entries from seven different schools. With ten gymnasts competing, Michigan boasted the largest contingent. "Daily Double" Barthell claimed the conference titles on the parallel bars and tumbling, while Buchanan took the trampoline title with ease. Impressed, Fritz Crisler gave the go-ahead for the pair to travel to NCAAs at Berkeley. Barthell, recently elected as team captain for the upcoming season, was slightly off form, but Buchanan came home with the trampoline title. Only two years into its existence, Newt's team had established its calling card: mastery of the trampoline.

Back in Ann Arbor after NCAAs, Newt's home team was growing also. In April, Dorothy delivered the Lokens' second daughter, Alanna (known as Lani).

Through the 1950 season, it seemed that Michigan's rise to prominence was unstoppable. The Wolverines, led by Barthell and Buchanan, added upcoming sophomore Connie Ettl to the mix and posted win after win, often coming from behind to snatch victory from their opponents. The final two events at that time—tumbling and trampoline. Michigan could always count on tumbling as half of Barthell's Daily Double, and Buchanan seemed impossible to best as a "bouncer." But two weeks before Michigan risked its perfect record against Kent State and its two Olympians, all-arounder Joe Kotys and Ed Bijack, one of Newt's best bouncers, Gordie Levenson, injured himself on the trampoline. He would certainly miss the upcoming Michigan State meet (which the Wolverines won after being down two points heading into trampoline, the final event), and maybe the finale against Kent State.

Kent State had lost just once in 1950, and had beaten the powerhouse Illinois team. Head coach Vic Moore, fully aware of Michigan's tendency to rally in the final two events, stacked the lineups for the preceding four events with his very best men. It almost worked.

The meet seesawed constantly, putting the largest crowd of the season at the IM Building into a state of high tension. The teams were tied after the first two events, side horse and rings. With Barthell having notched his usual double win, Michigan was ahead by just two points heading into trampoline, and Newt held back Levenson in favor of Sam Dudley, who had filled his slot against the Spartans. Buchanan, Tillman and Dudley swept the top three spots on trampoline, finishing up an unbeaten season for Tex and the Wolverines. Newt's never-give-up attitude had clearly caught on with his gymnasts, and thanks to the talent he was now able to attract, the team was now able to pull out victories in the clutch.

When the final score was posted, Newt's boys—now nicknamed the "Lokenmen"—picked him up, carried him down the hall, and dumped him in the varsity pool. Newt bobbed to the surface with a huge smile. It tasted like victory, and with a team like this, no one could blame him if he thought, just maybe, this might be the year Michigan finally got its first gymnastics conference championship.

The consensus among experts, however, was that Michigan

could at best hope to improve to second place. No one was going to unseat the Illini this year. But Newt, his boys, and Marv Epstein, the *Daily* beat writer who had become emotionally invested in the team, held out hope. Newt's enthusiasm had spread even to the press.

On the night of March 25, 1950, Marv Epstein kept a vigil over the phone at 420 Maynard, the Student Publications Building, waiting for news of his team at the conference meet. When it finally rang, he lunged for it, grabbing the receiver before anyone else could move. It was the track coach calling in results. Epstein handed off the phone, and settled back into his wait. After a while, the phone rang again. Epstein snatched it, his face brightening as he heard Newt Loken's voice on the other end. Just seconds later, his expression turned to one of disappointment. The Wolverines had come in second to the Illinois juggernaut.

The 1950 conference championship had seen the largest field in the meet's history, with nine teams participating. Illinois coasted easily to yet another championship, with the Wolverines coming in second, just as the experts had predicted. Buchanan suffered a stunning upset at the hands of Iowa's Bill Harris, losing the trampoline competition for the first time in nearly two years. Newt, though disappointed, had to admit that red-hot Illinois was the superior team. There was nothing more the Wolverines could have done—Newt couldn't, and wouldn't, fault his boys for coming up short when they did their best. And there were NCAA Championships still ahead.

At nationals in West Point, N. Y., Buchanan got his revenge on Bill Harris, beating him out for the national trampoline title. Kent State's Joe Kotys barely held off Barthell for the parallel bars title. And no one was surprised when the Illini won the team title, beating out defending champion Temple.

Newt had every reason to believe his was a team on the rise. His boys, for the most part, were young and promising. He would only lose Levenson, Tillman and Dudley to graduation. And Fritz Crisler had just announced that Ann Arbor would host the 1951 NCAA gymnastics championships.

"You've just been in the business two years!" Newt remembers Crisler saying incredulously when Newt posed the idea of hosting NCAAs. But Crisler quickly relented, perhaps thinking of Michigan's unbelievably fast rise to prominence within the gymnastics world. Maybe they hadn't beaten Illinois, but with the returning talent, and Newt's already obvious knack for bringing in strong young freshmen, the Wolverines were sure to keep challenging for the Big Ten title. Acquiescing, Crisler likely favored Newt with a rueful grin as he said, "Well, we can do a good job [of] it."

Newt's show-business flair immediately took over. "We created excitement, got posters all over," Newt remembered gleefully. "Big banner outside the intramural lobby, and drew a reasonable crowd, especially when this Springfield lad ... was doing a cut and catch on the flying rings, and he missed the catch part." Like many NASCAR fans, people showed up in droves afterwards hoping to see a crash.

Little did Newt know, one of the most challenging periods of his career lay ahead.

Chapter 8

A Rivalry Begins

For Newt, the two highlights heading into the 1950s were the 1951 NCAA championships and Ed Buchanan. The trampolinist, sometimes known as that "darn rebel" or "jumping jackrabbit," piled up dual meet titles, Big Ten crowns and NCAA championships. Clearly, Newt had chosen well on his trip to Amarillo. One of only three collegiate gymnasts who could successfully perform a back triple twist, the confident Buchanan refused to use a safety belt when learning new tricks, saying he'd feel like someone was jumping along with him. "Besides," he laughed, "we didn't have safety belts when I learned."

Obviously, he wasn't shy about speaking his mind. When asked about his hopes for the 1951 football season, during which he would serve as "Lord High Yeller" of the Michigan cheerleaders, he said, "I hope we'll be able to do something to all those cadavers who roll around campus, and get them to do a little cheering next year."

Outside of Buchanan, though, no one else seemed to be more than a flash in the pan. Michigan opened its 1951 season—in which it was to host the best-attended NCAA championship meet to date—missing five of its key gymnasts, mostly to ineligibility from "scholarship difficulties." One of those was Pete Barthell, who'd been featured on the cover of *Athletic Journal's* January issue; the Daily Double never returned. The team didn't win its first dual until March, ending up seventh at Big Tens.

But Newt had a surprise up his sleeve. Actually, the surprise fairly landed in his lap when a virtual unknown named Harry Luchs enrolled at Michigan, but many coaches might not have taken a chance on him. With Tex graduating after the 1951 fall semester, though, Newt had to do something.

Luchs had arrived in Ann Arbor after escaping the Russians in Latvia, Poland and Germany. Finally caught in East Germany in 1944 and told that his high school diploma would be withheld unless he joined the Communist Party, Luchs refused and was sent to a Communist "convincer" course—a concentration camp. The camp didn't work, and Luchs was left lying in a gutter, temporarily paralyzed from the rough treatment.

Luckily for Luchs, he was discovered by friends and smuggled to West Germany, where a doctor at the University of Marburg told him he would never walk again, much less return to practicing his beloved gymnastics.

"I simply said no," Luchs told *The Michigan Daily*. "This can't be true."

After months of physical therapy and corrective tumbling, Luchs could thumb his nose at the doctors and crow, "I told you so!" though he never did. He was even selected for the German Gymnastics Association in 1950, which went on a six-month trip to the United States. Luchs liked it so much that he decided to stay. Attracted by the university's pre-med program, Luchs enrolled at the University of Michigan. Newt's gymnastics team didn't hurt Michigan in Luchs' eyes, either.

In gymnastic competition, nothing could faze him—this was what he'd been working toward for years, even through the torture of the Communist camp. After an experience like that, taking on the Illini was nothing. Newt must have believed he'd found the core man for his team for the next few years, and at the start, it looked like he was correct.

By midseason in 1952, he was a "stalwart" of the gymnastics team, always contributing a few first place finishes to the cause, nearly always finishing third or better in any event he entered. But only he and fellow sophomore Duncan Erley, a tumbler, were predicted to do anything noteworthy at Big Tens. Despite Luchs' eventual parallel bars title, and Erley's second-place finish in tumbling, Illinois once again coasted to a conference victory as Michigan straggled into fourth.

Instead of becoming a three-year star, though, after his initial success Luchs continually fought eligibility problems that prevented his ever becoming a factor again. With no scholarships available for gymnasts, Luchs not only had to balance schoolwork and the practice schedule, but also had to work enough to pay his way as well. He lived out at the university president's retirement home in Dexter, struggling to make ends meet by doing chores there.

Newt felt terrible, but there wasn't anything he could do. In those early days, he had no scholarships to offer anyone, and certainly did not earn enough money himself to help his gymnasts financially. Newt always did as much as he could to help his gymnasts through their athletic, academic and general life issues, and for such a promising career as Luchs not to end in success hurt as much or more than any loss to the Illini at Big Ten Championships.

"He was a really good gymnast, possibly better at the all-around than just one event, like parallel bars," Newt remembered of Luchs. "He still excelled despite all the problems he had."

Newt himself knew well the trials of balancing gymnastics and school, and must have been looking forward to taking one thing off his very full plate. By the end of 1955, Newt finally finished his doctorate in physical education at Michigan, earning the rare dual title of full-time faculty member and full-time coach. By 1959, he would publish *The Complete Book of Gymnastics*. For years, Newt had been using all his breaks from gymnastics to score one hundred Michigan high schools' physical education programs as part of his doctorate research.

"There were one hundred questions that I'd go through," Newt said. "Then I'd run them through a machine and we would find out what area of the state had the best programs [for physical education]. ... One of our master's degree students in the department of phys ed said, 'How many schools did you really visit, Newt?' Wow, it never entered my mind [not to visit every school]. I should have done that, but oh no, I did every damn school, even during spring vacation when we went up north to the Upper Peninsula."

Dorothy and his growing daughters, Chris and Lani, accompanied him on these trips to the Upper Peninsula, and the girls became part of Newt's ever-evolving trampoline act. The show business bug still had not let go of Newt, and never really would. A coach in those days had to supplement his coaching income, and with his regular forays into showbiz, Newt had found a most enjoyable way to do so.

The fact that Newt had finished his doctorate before the 1956 season meant that he could devote even more energy and focus to the gymnastics team. It was a good thing, too, because by then Michigan despaired of ever even finishing second to the Illini, much less winning the Big Ten crown. But finally, the first of Newt's outstanding Canadian gymnasts had arrived: Ed Gagnier. Gagnier's arrival signaled the start of a veritable pipeline of gymnasts from Canada, a pipeline that proved key to Newt's success. (It also helped that Newt seemed to know absolutely everyone in the gymnastics world—and of course, Newt being Newt, everyone adored him.)

Gagnier was Canada's "outstanding athlete of 1954," and after his freshman year, Newt felt that he could give an outstanding performance on any event. The diminutive gymnast loved football and basketball, but quickly realized he was too small to go far in either. Beginning in high school, he threw himself into gymnastics, competing for the Windsor Gymnastics Club under Newt's old friend Bernie Newman in both Canadian and U.S. open meets. Many of Newt's stars would be Windsor Gymnastics Club alumni. In 1956, he would join seven returning regulars, including fellow all-arounder Nick Wiese and Chico San Antonio.

Chico was hardly your average Wolverine. A few years later, he would follow his brothers' lead in changing his last name to Miele, a switch that would prompt Newt, upon meeting his charge after graduation, to inquire, "Chico, who did you marry?"* In fact, Chico was married before he ever joined the team. A standout at the Providence Turners, he was discovered by Walt Tyszkowski, a visiting gymnast. Tyszkowski, naturally, was a friend of Newt's and immediately dashed off a letter to him telling him he needed to see this kid.

Chico wasn't much of a kid, though—after serving in the Navy during World War II, he was twenty-four and about to get married. He'd already been offered a two-year scholarship by the Normal School, an American Gymnastics Union school in Indiana from which he'd be able to transfer to the University of Indiana. Newt couldn't promise anything in the way of financial assistance; but Tyszkowski passed along two critical pieces of information.

"You won't find anyone better than Coach Loken, as a coach and a friend," he told Chico. Told of the young man's Indiana plans, he brushed them aside: "There's no comparison. There's no school like Michigan."

So in August of 1952, with his new bride Maria in tow, Chico added Ann Arbor to the list of stops on their honeymoon.

"The first time I saw him walking towards us, I recognized him right off because I knew him from pictures in LIFE magazine," Chico remembered, referring to the 1942 spread that appeared after Newt's senior year at the University of Minnesota. "'Wow, this is Newt!' It was like looking at a movie star."

---

* To avoid any confusion, therefore, he will be referred to as Chico.

Newt hustled the newlywed off to the administration building, where a bewildered Chico took tests for five hours. Newt assured him that both he and his wife would be able to find part-time jobs in Ann Arbor; Newt would shepherd Chico's application through the admissions process personally; and perhaps some financial aid could even be worked out. A few weeks later, Chico and Maria packed up their belongings in Providence and headed back to Michigan—by living in Ann Arbor while skipping the fall term, Chico would be able to establish residency and thus cut his tuition costs considerably. That winter—with a new baby on the way—the twenty-four-year-old freshman embarked on an exhausting schedule of classes, wiring planes built at the Willow Run manufacturing plant, sneaking in workouts in the gym whenever he could, competing for the team, and adjusting to his new duties as a husband and a father. The areas of his life often overlapped. Working at Willow Run, he would tape his reading assignments to the belly of the plane he was wiring, in order to do homework at the same time. Once, with an anatomy exam approaching, he carried a box of human bones to a dual meet, studying them between routines until his fellow gymnasts told him to "Put those bones away!"

Just before the 1956 season, Newt and Dorothy's third child, a boy named Jon Newton, was born. That season, Chico San Antonio was more than ever the beloved "old man" of the team, and his teammates had elected him captain for his senior year. And thanks to the quality of those teammates, Newt's smile and optimism were more irrepressible than ever.

"I guess I should be worried this early in the season," he told a *Daily* reporter, "but I've got some really sensational boys."

Sensational was the perfect word for Newt's Wolverines that year. Chico provided excellent leadership on and off the competition floor for his younger teammates. Gagnier had impressed Newt with his skills throughout his freshman year and now would finally have a chance to compete. And in Nick

Wiese Newt had found a man to bring home first more often than not on the flying rings.

In his first varsity meet, sophomore Gagnier made Michigan history by winning five of his six events. But several roadblocks still stood in the way of Michigan's goal of a perfect regular season record, and none bigger than the Illini. That was the one mark against the undefeated 1950 Wolverines—they'd never put their record to the test against the Orange and Blue. Now, Newt's boys would put their record on the line in one of the first meets of the season.

On January 13, 1956, the Wolverines strode into Illinois' Huff Hall, hoping for the impossible. Never in Newt's years of coaching had Michigan beaten the Illini head to head.

But they'd never had anyone like Gagnier either.

With the little Canadian leading the way, Michigan finally beat its archrival, clinching the historic 57-55 victory with a sweep of the top three places on parallel bars. Gagnier led the parallel bars squad as well as winning the floor title, while his partner in crime Nick Wiese took the crown on his specialty, the flying rings. And the following week, the team didn't let up, despite competing against bottom-dweller Indiana—a far cry from lordly Illinois. Michigan romped over the Hoosiers, with Gagnier taking home a whopping five first-place finishes.

But even as the wins piled up, the fans didn't multiply as they should have. Only about three hundred fans showed up on a regular basis to see the sublime feats of Gagnier and his teammates.

"One of Michigan's 'winningest' teams this winter has been going virtually unwatched as it piles up triumph after triumph," griped a *Daily* columnist. Newt, of course, had a plan.

The way he saw it, the lack of interest must stem from a lack of knowledge—a reasonable assumption, given the confusing nature of gymnastics even in the 1950s. Like today, gymnastics was not a sport that the majority of kids grew up watching and understanding by osmosis, like baseball or football. Newt gathered his freshmen and set them to work—now, though they still wouldn't compete with the varsity, they would demonstrate each stunt for the home crowd before the routines, with Newt providing explanations over the P. A. system. It was a perfect marriage between Newt's three loves: gymnastics, teaching, and showmanship.

In the final meet of the season, Newt's plan and team were both unmitigated successes. The Badgers entered the large gym with just a 4-4 record—but all four wins had come in their last five meets. This was not a team to take lightly. The Wolverines' seriousness paid huge dividends, as they routed Wisconsin 73-39 before an "unprecedented" crowd of 2,000 fans, the largest gymnastics crowd in Michigan history. According to *The Daily*, Gagnier drew "gasps of amazement" from the packed throng, winning four event titles; Wiese nabbed two. Grinning ear-to-ear, Newt was lifted to the shoulders of his ecstatic and undefeated gymnasts, who, after giving the coach a brief ride of triumph, threw him gleefully into the pool.

If there was any year to challenge Illinois' supremacy at Big Tens, it was this one. And Michigan's captain, Chico, almost got left behind.

The day of the drive to the big meet, Newt and his carload of boys pulled up at Chico's house. As usual, Newt sent one of the gymnasts to knock on the door and fetch the captain. But the boy came back empty-handed.

"They're fighting!" he reported.

Maria, understandably, had just about had it with Chico being away from her every weekend. Every few minutes, Newt would send another gymnast to the door; each time, he'd come back and report that the argument was getting louder. Finally, Maria posed the unanswerable question to Chico, her husband and his team's captain: "What's more important—the Big Tens, or me?"

Everyone looked up as the door slammed and Chico threw

his bags into the car. "He said, 'Damn it all, Coach, I might lose my wife but I'm not going to lose my team!'" Newt recalled with evident relish, finishing off one of his all-time favorite stories. (Chico, it should be noted, did *not* lose his wife; he refused his later invitation to compete individually at NCAAs, and they remained happily married for 59 years.)

Chico actually might have been better off staying home; by the time the Wolverines got to the biggest meet of their season, Chico's cold had become a full-blown illness. But for his teammates, he would be there, even with his wife at home, and for Newt, he would participate in the all-around.

Drill-sergeant coaches might order athletes to run through the proverbial brick wall and be obeyed; for Newt, the gymnasts would just volunteer. His heroic effort, unfortunately, didn't pay off, and other Wolverines ran into trouble as well.

Running a 103-degree fever, Chico didn't have near the energy he needed to succeed in the all-around, spending what little he had on parallel bars. For the first time in a year and a half, Gagnier fell from the high bar—his bicep had torn. The trampoline squad failed to come through as it had all year. Perhaps the pressure of the meet got to them; perhaps it was the injury to Gagnier. And as usual, the Illini dominated and squashed Michigan's dreams of glory, occupying twenty-two qualifying spots in the finals and effectively turning the second day of competition into a battle for second place between Michigan, Iowa and the surprisingly tough Spartans—a battle Michigan won.

Gagnier and Chico provided the highlight of the weekend, going one-two on the parallel bars. As always, the champion's name was painted onto the gym wall, along with his year and event. Just as the artist finished painting Ed Gagnier's statistics, Newt made an impulsive decision. His captain may not have won a first-place title, but his actions on behalf of the team went beyond mere competition results.

"Up to that time the names on the wall were all champions, only champions," Newt said. "I looked at Chico and said to the little artist, 'Put Chico San Antonio's name up there—runner-up, parallel bar Big Ten title. He deserves his name on the wall.' That name on the wall was so precious. The kids would come up to me after they'd won a title. 'Coach! Do I get my name on the wall?' Not the medal in the hand, but the name on the wall. It was the most important thing in the world."

To Newt, Chico had clearly proven himself a champion. He wasn't the sort of coach who would declare competitions a tie to save his athletes' feelings, but Newt knew exactly how to make the important gesture to make a gymnast feel like a million bucks—even if he hadn't won a title.

Even so, for Newt it was still disappointing. Even his naturally sunny nature took a big hit. He'd never show it with his team, but at home, it was obvious just how much he wanted to win a Big Ten title and how much it hurt him to keep coming in second. Just because Newt's trademark was happiness didn't preclude the fact that he was just as competitive as any elite athlete or coach. That Newt could be credited with bringing Michigan to an elite level so fast also meant he could be blamed for the Wolverines continually falling just short. And while Newt often brushed off credit for winning in his modest way, he was quick to take it all when the team lost. No good coach would ever blame his athletes; Newt certainly wouldn't. Maybe Big Ten results weren't completely within his control, but Newt couldn't shake the feeling that he was somehow responsible for all the second-place finishes.

"My wife said she could hardly live with me after a Big Ten meet," said Newt later, recalling all those years when Illinois seemed unbeatable. "I kept blaming myself. ... I was quite a depressed person, and in some respects I probably didn't need to be, but that was just my nature about competition."

There was always next year, though—and in 1957, Michigan pushed Illinois to the brink.

Chapter 9

The Rivalry Heats Up

Thanks to Gagnier's skill and Newt's exuberance, crowds were starting to fill the IM gym on a regular basis. "If you watch this team in action," one *Daily* columnist noted, "you'll notice that they probably have as good a time as any varsity sport here. Loken's enthusiasm carries over to his team members."

Newt and his boys had a lot to be excited about, as the 1957 squad had gained several fine sophomores. Ed Cole and Dick Kimball were both varsity divers who also excelled at trampoline. Cole had been a state diving champion in Illinois, and only started practicing the trampoline when he arrived at Michigan. Like many of Newt's early gymnasts, the dark-haired boy with a sweet smile was plucked from one of Newt's gymnastics classes when he gravitated toward the trampoline and looked promising.

Another sophomore, Jim Hayslett, had been expected for some time. Nurturing dreams of becoming an acrobat, Hayslett spent much of his childhood hanging from trees by his knees. He and gymnastics were fated to be together—the first day he went to his local YMCA, the usual instructor was sick and his place filled by a former gymnast. The gymnast spent the whole day teaching the boys to tumble, and Hayslett was hooked. Most families went on picnics—the Haysletts went to the Turners, a "German family society which makes gymnastics a family outing."

83

Two seniors, Wayne Warren, another product of the Windsor Gymnastics Club, and Nick Wiese, who'd won the Dutch AAU national championship at fifteen, would serve as captains for the squad. And of course, there was Gagnier.

Before the start of the regular season, the Wolverines made their now-customary trip to Sarasota, Florida, for the National Gymnastics Clinic. Six years old in 1956, the clinic had become a huge success, with more and more gymnasts attending each year in the week between Christmas and New Year's Day.

The clinic was started in order "to promote interest in a sport long neglected in this country," according to the 1956-57 official program. It was also part of a country-wide attempt to address the "alarming evidence, gathered by scientific research, of the poor physical condition of [America's] youth."

People had originally become "alarmed" during World War II. Before that time, gymnastics barely hung on in the United States thanks to the efforts of Czech Sokol clubs and the better-known German Turnvereins, commonly referred to as the Turners. Once war broke out, the clinic's program noted, "Gymnastic instruction became an important part of the physical education program conducted by [the] armed forces." And like Newt, many of the instructors and participants returned to coach the rapidly multiplying college teams.

Newt certainly wasn't alarmed, but he could never get enough of gymnastics. Additionally, college coaches of the time weren't expected to subsist entirely on their coaching salaries; they always had to have at least one, sometimes multiple, extra jobs. What better side job than another gymnastics coaching gig?

"Basically it appealed to us with the idea of Christmas break in sunny Florida, and a month of getting in some good workouts, whether in the gym or on the beach before the throngs," Newt said. "Quite an incentive."

"The National Gymnastic Clinic," wrote clinic president

Edward J. Scrobe, "since its inception, has labored toward [improving America's fitness] armed with the knowledge and experience of the hundreds of physical educators, gymnastic coaches and gymnasts who constitute its membership and support." Over a decade after the end of World War II, the sport and clinic were both booming. Nearly every major university had a team, and many of those teams traveled to Sarasota each year for some early competition. And Newt, naturally, was a big part of the clinic's program. While his old rival George Szypula taught clinics on tumbling, Newt instructed clinic youngsters in the nuances of his beloved trampoline. The whole Loken family joined in on the yearly pilgrimage to Florida, with all four children, according to Newt, having "a glorious time romping in the Lido Beach sand."

Sarasota also provided opportunities for a little recruiting— many circus families used Sarasota as their headquarters for training—and scouting the competition.

One night during the clinic, all the gymnasts would gather at Sarasota High School to put on "A Night of Stars," performing in acts they had made up themselves. And, going out with a bang, the clinic always ended with the North-South meet, featuring all the collegiate gymnasts divided up into two competing squads. In 1956, Newt, in addition to his other coaching duties, was the director of the North-South meet.

"I coached for only a couple of periods, and then the clinic director decided they needed someone to handle the mic for the North-South gymnastics meet at the end of the clinic," Newt remembered. "[They thought] that I had some mild technique as an announcer"—an understatement if ever there was one—"and that I knew many of the gymnasts, many from the Big Ten schools. They decided to point their finger at me and thus the position became a reality. And I must say, it was fun."

One year, the clinic even added a "senior" gymnastics meet to the bill, so the coaches could get in on the action. Newt managed to best all comers, including Szypula, in a competition held out in the Florida sunshine on Lido Beach.

"I'll never forget when the clinic held a senior Gymnastics meet," Newt recalled fondly. "I managed to get through parts of my old routine. I asked Ed Scrobe, a well-known gymnast from the East, to spot me on my high-flying reverse flyaway. He stood on the beach ready to grasp me on my dismount. I recall how he reached up and literally grabbed my waist as I was sailing toward the sand and gently placed me on my feet, resulting in my taking first place in the senior meet."

When the Wolverines' 1957 regular season commenced a few weeks later, Newt's boys lost just once. The loss came, of course, at the hands of the Illini, who were undefeated since their tight loss to Michigan in 1956. Even with his team peaking in its last dual meet, a romp over Ohio State before a capacity crowd in the large gym, and even with the Big Tens to be held in Ann Arbor, Newt still held out little hope of beating the Illini.

He was as surprised as anyone else when the Wolverines finished up the first day of competition in a dead heat with their archrivals.

Gagnier and Illinois' Olympian and star, Abie Grossfeld, were locked in a battle as tight and tense as their teams'. Both gunning for the all-around crown, they were separated by six points after five events. Grossfeld had claimed the still rings title, Gagnier the long horse championship. Neither event counted toward a team total, but they were an integral part of the all-around. Parallel bars, one of Gagnier's strengths, was the final event. He beat Grossfeld's score by six points, pulling himself—and Michigan—into a tie.

But the judges' initial tabulations were mistaken, showing Grossfeld beating Gagnier by two (and thus giving Illinois the lead, with eleven points from finishing first in the all-around). Medals were even awarded, with Gagnier standing to Grossfeld's left, eyes gleaming as if he knew something no one else did. Finally, someone caught the calculating error. Michigan had never been in a better position to take home the Big Ten title.

But Illinois was not to be stopped. Despite its best performances of the season, Michigan's scores were only good enough for second. The huge gulf between Michigan and the rest of the finishers was not much consolation; neither were Gagnier's parallel-bars title or Cole's trampoline championship. He wanted that Big Ten crown, and once again, it had eluded him. Even a trip to NCAAs with Gagnier, Cole and Hayslett wasn't much of a lift. Three gymnasts were all Michigan could financially afford to send; and for Newt, it was "quite depressing to enter a meet with three men when three of the schools had ten or eleven-man teams present." Newt and his boys could have all the optimism in the world, but no one could win a national title with such a small squad. To enter a meet with absolutely no chance of winning was strange, and clearly unpleasant, for Newt. The Big Ten title was the only one within reach, and once again it had slipped out of Michigan's grasp.

"We thought we might win—this was after how many years of trying to beat Illinois, and just such a juggernaut," Newt said. "It was very, very tough. And when we tied the all-around, it saved the sadness of the results somewhat. Big Ten all-around is a top prize in any competition. ... So we salvaged something there."

As the 1957-58 school year began, Newt couldn't keep the grin off his face. This wasn't an entirely unusual state of affairs, but now he had more of a reason than ever to smile. In addition to welcoming his fourth child, Newt Jr., in October of 1957, Newt got the good news that the Big Ten had finally decreed that athletes with need could be given scholarships.

"Gymnasts were poverty-stricken," Newt joked. "Not really, but they needed the help ... Suddenly, we were able to get two or three scholarships!" Now if he had promising gymnasts like Harry Luchs on his team, facing challenges they couldn't surmount without aid, Newt would be able to help them stay in school and on the team.

The scholarships also gave Newt an equal footing with Illinois for recruiting in the Chicago area, a hotbed of high school gymnastics. For many years, the top Chicago gymnasts had gravitated naturally to Champaign, with its excellent team and in-state tuition. Now, Newt had something extra to entice them away to Ann Arbor. The days of his gymnasts running themselves ragged keeping up with school, a full- or part-time job, and practice seemed to be over.

Newt's first scholarship acquisition was another Canadian, Richard Montpetit, who had been the Canadian junior champion. The coach's practiced eye for talent picked Montpetit out immediately, seeing in him a breathtaking all-around talent.

"He appears to be another Gagnier at this stage of his progress," Newt told *The Daily* when Montpetit was just an untried freshman.

Montpetit's first love, like many Canadians, was hockey. But when he was fifteen, a former German Olympian named Fritz Besslich introduced him to gymnastics. Montpetit caught on quickly, excelling on his high school team. In his numerous competitions, he struck up a friendship with Ed Gagnier and Nino Marion, both Canadian Wolverines. Add in the scholarship, and there was nothing to keep Montpetit away from Michigan. He was so good, everyone could overlook one odd little habit.

"Johnny Martin [a younger Wolverine] was given the responsibility of going into the practice gym and telling Richard, or Mr. Montpetit, whatever, that you're next up on high bar," Newt remembered. "So then he'd go in and he was so proud of his duties, because he was talking to the champ. 'Montpetit, you're next up on high bar.' He'd get on his handgrips and in the meantime he'd just been sitting there reading his schoolbooks, not watching the meet! 'Coach, I've seen enough of these gymnasts all my life. I don't have to see them again to get nervous, seeing their routines and saying, "Oh my god, that's pretty good stuff. I don't know whether I'll do well against them or not." I don't need that. I just need to walk out there just like in practice.' That's what we used to tell the kids, just do your routines like in the practice gym in the meet."

Marion and Montpetit, combined with the tremendous tumbling duo of Bill Skinner and Jimmy Brown, convinced Newt that his team was the strongest it had been in years. Skinner and Brown couldn't have taken more different roads to tumbling dominance.

Skinner, who'd moved to Canada as an infant, got only spotty exposure to gymnastics in high school, where he played hockey, football and basketball and ran track. He taught himself to do a back handspring with spotting from a few friends, but that was it. Then, in July of 1956 he arrived at Lowry Air Force Base in Denver to begin his schooling at the Air Force Academy.

"I had no idea what was available in sports but one of the fitness training tasks for incoming 'plebes' was to try out for every athletic team," Skinner said. "At the end of about six weeks they had me pegged to be a springboard diver or a gymnast."

He came under the tutelage of Bob Sullivan, a former NCAA tumbling champ, and spent the next two months learning the fundamentals of his new sport. But a wrench was thrown into his plans at the Academy when in late October, he suddenly passed out while kneeling for prayer in church. At the hospital, he was told that he had a heart problem that hadn't shown up on his physicals. He would never be able to fly, and probably wouldn't even be able to receive a commission. The Academy, however, still wanted him to stay.

"My decision was made in about thirty seconds and I chose to resign," Skinner said. He went to Sullivan, who'd visited him frequently in the hospital, for advice on where to go next in order to pursue an engineering degree as well as a career in collegiate gymnastics.

"Sully did not hesitate—Illinois at Champaign, Penn State or Michigan," remembered Skinner. "He was a graduate of Illinois." But he told Skinner to go to Michigan. He didn't say why, but it's fair to assume the recommendation had a little something to do with Newt Loken.

The afternoon after his discussion with Sullivan, Skinner arrived in Ann Arbor. He quickly found the gym and the enthusiastic coach, bouncing off the walls as usual. Newt handed the prospective gymnast a pair of shorts and a towel and said, "Let's see what Sully has taught you." Evidently, he'd taught Skinner enough, because after the brief tryout Newt got the boy a room at the Union and an appointment with the admissions office.

"The rest is history," says Skinner, whose mysterious heart problem never resurfaced. "I started school in January of 1957. I never went to Illinois or Penn State."

Jimmy Brown, on the other hand, had had a bit more experience. After beginning his athletic career as a diver, he switched to gymnastics as a high school sophomore. The good-humored Georgian had won the State Gymnastics Championships twice before entering college. He and Skinner became close friends, their fierce competition in the gym driving both to new heights. The two even spent a summer teaching gymnastics together in a Traverse City summer camp.

"[Bill Skinner] and Jimmy Brown, they were competitors and friends," Newt remembered. "One would win in one meet and the other would win in another meet. Back and forth."

In trampoline as well, Newt had a crack unit: Dick Kimball and Ed Cole, boosted by the arrival of a standout freshman named Ronnie Munn. He announced his presence with a surprise win over both Dick Kimball and Ed Cole in an intrasquad in November. Though his career at Michigan would be short, it was memorable for his outstanding skill.

Like Newt, Charlie Pond of Illinois was convinced that *his* team was one of the best he'd had yet. Not only were the Illini their usual powerful selves, riding a winning streak now stretched to fourteen duals, they now possessed two former Olympians, Abie Grossfeld and Don Tonry, who later scored ninety four and a half of Illinois' 143 points in the Big Ten championships. With an unblemished record, the Wolverines prepared to take on the Illini in the cozy confines of their own IM gym.

With tumbling as the final event in the meet, Newt knew that Skinner and Brown would be keys to victory. For the past four meets, the two had alternated winning first and second in their specialty event.

All the stops were pulled out for the Illinois meet. In a time when it was perfectly acceptable for the press—especially a college paper—to root openly for the home team, *The Daily* urged students to get out and see their undefeated team take on its archrival. One reporter called it "one of the biggest meets in Michigan history."

On Friday night—February 27, 1959, Newt's fortieth birthday—a standing room only crowd wedged itself into the large gym. Going into the final event, Michigan was behind 49-47. The only way to pull off a win would be to take three of the top four places. Anything else would result in either a loss or a tie. The crowd was hushed with tension, quiet "to the point of explosion" during the routines.

Dick Kimball's set was good enough for fourth, and was followed by a top-notch performance from Jimmy Brown. *The Daily* called it a "stunning performance that topped anything he had ever done before, perhaps symbolic of the entire team's effort." Skinner finished six points behind Brown, and to everyone's amazement, Grossfeld faltered and was out of the running. But Allan Harvey, Illinois' best tumbler, was up last. If he beat Brown's mark of 277, Illinois would force a tie.

Harvey bounced gracefully through his routine, as everyone in the crowd felt their stomachs knot with the suspense. Once he was finished the Wolverine gymnasts huddled around Newt, near the scorer's table. It was readily apparent that they weren't feeling much calmer than their fans. After a few moments' deliberation, the judges began putting up their scores. Five would go up, with the highest and lowest being eliminated; the middle three scores would be added together for Harvey's final total.

Ninety-six. Ninety-two. Ninety-two. Ninety. Ninety.

Dick Kimball did the math quickly in his head. The crowd was still puzzling out the formula when the cheerleading captain yelped loudly with glee. About three seconds later, the crowd finally realized why: Harvey had scored a 274. Michigan had beaten Illinois, 58-54!

The Wolverines exploded, celebrating with Newt on their shoulders. Newt later got soaked, of course—tossing him into the pool was becoming a regular tradition. Sure, it wasn't Big Tens, but beating Illinois was always something Newt savored. To do it before a rocking sellout crowd in Ann Arbor made it even better. Even Charlie Pond, an intense competitor who sometimes spoke before thinking, couldn't help but be thrilled with such an intense meet. This was, he said firmly, "the best dual meet we've had in eight years."

Immediately after this pronouncement, he informed the *Daily* reporter that he expected to win Big Tens by twenty points. He gave the young writer a friendly punch in the shoulder. "That should fire up your boys, shouldn't it?"

It would have been nice. Instead of breaking Illinois' other streak—the eight-year Big Ten streak—Michigan, despite being a legitimate challenger, faltered again in the Big Ten championships. Illinois won easily for the ninth straight year. Ed Cole provided Michigan's only title on the trampoline. Skinner grabbed a third place in the tumbling, and convinced Newt to allow him to make the trip to Berkeley, Calif., for NCAAs. Michigan would only pay for its first- and second-place finishers to go, so Skinner had to scrape up the money himself. Ed Cole finally captured an NCAA trampoline title, and Skinner snagged a bronze, beating out the two other Big Ten tumblers (including his teammate Jimmy Brown).

But for the team as a whole, it was another collective opportunity blown. And Newt, not to mention Dorothy, was in for another off-season of what-ifs.

A bright spot of the late 1950s Michigan squads was the team daredevil, Al Stall. Teammate Nino Marion thought he should have been in a circus.

"I watched him do some high bar stunts and fly off the bar to the point where we thought he might kill himself," said Bill Skinner. "But he would get back up and try it again—usually with bloodied hands, because he did not like to wear the leathers."

"He'd try something he'd dreamed up, and maybe he was far ahead of the crowd," Newt remembered. "All these releases and stuff."

Marion remembered his teammate's unique way of filling the down time during the 1958 Big Ten Championships at Iowa. The team's motel had a pool out back, but no one was swimming—March in the Midwest is just not the best time for outdoor aquatics. Stall found another use for the pool, however. He announced to his disbelieving teammates that he would jump across it.

"Normally we would be betting on stuff," Marion said. " 'Oh yeah? Well, here's fifty cents, let's see it.' " Knowing Al's personality though, the gymnasts didn't even think of taking bets; they just tried their best to discourage him from attempting the stunt. Undeterred, Stall floated boards across the pool to measure the jump, as he lacked a tape measure. He laid the boards out across the grass and practiced jumping the distance.

Marion, well aware of the vast difference between jumping boards on a lawn and leaping across a pool, feared Stall would be just short and might break his legs against the cement lip of the opposite side of the pool. With his teammates looking on nervously, Stall took his place at the side of the pool. Marion raised his camera to his eye.

"I'll be damned—he took a run at it and he jumped it, and I got a great picture!" Marion said later. "He jumped that darn pool. We were astounded at that. Nobody—we were all athletic guys, eh? —but nobody, none of us, would do that."

In the photo, it seems as though Stall is on his way to an icy dip in the pool. But at that point in the jump, he was still on his way up into the air.

"The bugger cleared it," Marion marveled fifty years later. "That's the kind of guy he was."

But Stall's tenure at Michigan came to a heartbreaking end. With a day to go before graduation in June 1959, Stall, now a senior, hopped into his car with his teammates Ken Sakamoto and Bob Harris. After helping put on a clinic for Florida State University cheerleaders (and visiting a girlfriend in Groveland), the boys were headed back to their house at 509 S. Division Street.

Marion was supposed to be with his teammates, but had cancelled at the last minute because he didn't have enough money to pay for the trip. The boys were near Valdosta, Ga., on U.S. 41 when their car crashed head-on into a truck.

Stall, the driver, and Sakamoto, in the passenger seat, were both killed, with Harris in the backseat escaping alive with cuts and bruises.

"Harris told police he believed the driver of the car dozed at the wheel," reported Harris' hometown *Windsor Star*. That was the normal way the gymnasts traveled then, just driving straight through with few stops to wherever they were going. Yet this was the first time anything tragic had come of it.

"We were very, very sad," Newt recalled. "It happened in the spring of the year, so you had the whole summer to … recover, if there is such a way to recover from the death of a teammate. But it didn't hold them back. The team continued to learn those tricks, we called them, and skills. Whether they ever dedicated a certain meet to Al Stall, I'm not really sure. After four or five months, sometimes these terrible things leave the mind, you go about your way."

Gymnastics continued, of course, but the deaths remained stark in the gymnasts' memories. Whatever recovery may have happened, they never forgot the teammates taken from them too soon. And it was not the last time Newt would have to deal with a tragedy.

Chapter 10

The Birth of a Dynasty

Between the two championship meets in 1959, Newt had taken his boys to State College, Pa., for a meet with Penn State—the only other team in the country with an unblemished dual-meet record. Led by Gene Wettstone, the already-legendary coach, Penn State was a perennial powerhouse.

At the competition, Newt's boys experienced an atmosphere even more electric than at their own clash with Illinois.

A standing-room-only crowd packed old Recreation Hall, a tradition that still continues. Bill Skinner remembered the team arriving on campus late, and spotting a mass of people going into a large building. They assumed it was the basketball crowd and asked one of the fans if he knew where the gymnastics meet was being held.

"Oh, right here!" the fan replied. "We are all going to it."

"I was flabbergasted," Skinner said.

According to Jim Hayslett, Newt couldn't believe they were in the right place. After being directed to Rec Hall, he led his carload of gymnasts up a tunnel and into the gym, where 12,000 overwrought fans were waiting for the meet to start.

The Nittany Lions, led by Armando Vega, one of the best gymnasts in the country, handed Michigan its first dual-meet loss of the season, but the meet wouldn't soon lose its luster in the Wolverines' minds. Skinner vividly remembers doing his best tumbling routine up to that point, and getting "one of those heart-pounding ovations that only happen once in a while." Even the Michigan-Illinois meet couldn't match up to competitions at Penn State's Rec Hall. Not yet, anyway.

Seeing such a talented team perform in front of such a massive, enthusiastic crowd must have been a source of inspiration for Newt to take his own showbiz flair to the next level. Already, people in Ann Arbor were more excited about gymnastics than they'd ever been, but still they had not reached the level of Penn State's manic fans. And Wettstone, who like Newt, would one day have an award for best performance of the meet named after him, was an inspiration too.

"I felt that Gene Wettstone was a master coach," Newt said. Newt felt that one reason why Wettstone was so successful was because he could devote so much time just to coaching in the gym. It was a quality Newt tried to emulate with his own team, even with his busy schedule of activities all over campus along with his growing family. He now had four children, Chris, Lani, Jon and little Newt Jr.

For the 1960 season, Newt brought in his biggest recruiting class ever, thanks in part to the scholarships now at his disposal. The nine-man group included such future standouts as Gil Larose, Jim Hynds and Barry Spicer. They didn't enter regular-season varsity competitions, but early season workouts showed that Larose, especially, was going to be a mainstay. In the team's second public pre-season intrasquad, Newt pitted the freshmen and seniors against the sophomores and juniors. In front of a "surprisingly sizable" crowd—finally, Ann Arborites were waking up to the talent under their noses—the "tiny yearling" Larose was a key factor in the frosh-senior win.

Other youngsters made a splash in 1960—the "tramp twins"

Tom Osterland and Tom Francis. Francis, conveniently, answered to the nickname of "Tee," thus avoiding confusion.

Osterland had only learned to bounce in his freshman year, never having touched a trampoline previously. Bouncing was in his blood, though—at fourteen months, *The Daily* reported, the toddler "executed a flying somersault out of his crib and landed on his feet for his first successful routine."

His first love was diving, but upon his arrival at Michigan, he was told by swimming and diving coach Bruce Harlan that he was too far behind the others to make the team. So Osterland turned to the trampoline, previously only a warmup to diving. He watched the technique of Dick Kimball, Michigan's star diver and trampolinist, as well as Ed Cole; the older bouncers noticed him and began to help him.

As Osterland got serious, Newt gleefully snapped him up for the gymnastics team, and within two years he was ranked among the best in the country at "rebound tumbling," as trampoline was sometimes called. As a sophomore, he claimed the Big Ten trampoline title. (That done, he decided to add tumbling to his repertoire, and one year later, was second only to the great Hal Holmes.)

Tom and Tee were responsible for making up for the points lost in the departures of Ed Cole, Dick Kimball, Frank Newman and Chuck Clarkson, one of Michigan's best-ever trampoline squads. Newt had perfected his recruiting to an art, always with fresh new talent ready to step in as soon as the senior stars had graduated.

Throughout the year, the sophomore sensations consistently placed in the top three for Michigan. Brown and now-captain Skinner in tumbling continued to be each other's toughest opponent, regardless of the opposing team's men. As gymnastic skill level across the board increased, new stunts on all the events began proliferating, exciting Newt even further than usual. Though most of these skills are now considered basic or a bit above basic, they were important enough in 1960 for Newt to grab a microphone at meets and announce each one by name just before the gymnast performed it.

Newt understood the need to explain the complicated sport to the inexperienced fans, telling them what was going on before their eyes with enthusiasm and clarity. Like any good teacher, Newt made learning fun, with his bubbliness and extensive knowledge. And unlike other coaches, Newt didn't assume that winning alone would draw the crowds. He knew it would take a little more effort—and of course, Newt went above and beyond even that, in drawing people in to gymnastics. Once people became familiar with his beloved sport, they loved it as much as he did. The crowd and a good team went hand-in-hand. If potential Wolverines knew that each meet would take place in front of a packed, rollicking house, they were that much more likely to commit to Michigan.

In the opening issue of *The Daily* for the 1960-61 school year, writers urged new students to "see a gymnastics meet this winter. You won't be sorry. This virtually unheard-of sport has been made interesting by a great showman, Newt Loken." But despite Newt's enthusiasm and showmanship, Illinois had up to now thwarted his every effort to lead his boys to the Big Ten championship. The ease with which the Illini—now without Grossfeld and Tonry—disposed of their opponents added insult to injury. They'd now won the conference crown eleven years running. Even with scholarships and Olympians of his own, it seemed to Newt as if he would never be able to best them when it really counted. Even for such a sunny man, keeping a positive attitude was becoming harder.

But things were about to change. More than ever, Newt threw himself into coaching and recruiting for Michigan, gathering all the talent he could for the upcoming season. If he could inspire even middle-of-the-road gymnasts to achievement, like Bob

Schoendube in 1948, surely with a team completely packed with talent, he would be able to best Illinois at Big Ten Championships.

"We're shooting the works this year!" Newt proclaimed to a *Daily* writer in September of 1960. Nineteen-sixty-one would finally be the year—he was convinced—that his boys would wrest the Big Ten title away from Charlie Pond's Illini. Promising sophomores Gil Larose and Jim Hynds were ready to join the varsity, now led by 1960 MVP and new team captain, Richard Montpetit. And the Big Ten championships would be held in Ann Arbor, where Newt had been energetically priming the crowds for years now.

Montpetit, a 5'5" senior from Montreal, was raised in a community where gymnastics was, at the very least, one of the top two most popular sports. He always had a flair for it, but he got even better once he began setting goals for himself, the biggest being to compete for Canada at the 1960 Olympics in Rome. His Olympic dream came true when he became Canada's lone representative in men's gymnastics. With that kind of experience, there was no one better qualified to lead the Wolverines into battle. But with only juniors Tom Osterland and Jimmy Brown remaining of the veterans, a tremendous amount would depend on the success of Newt's upcoming sophomores. In contrast, Illinois had six returning lettermen, including Ray Hadley, the NCAA pommel horse champion, along with its largest sophomore class ever of eight gymnasts.

Jim Hynds, whose career was often overshadowed by his classmate Larose, was Newt's kind of gymnast. Like Newt, he'd grown up practicing on public equipment—in his case, a high bar in a vacant Windsor lot, erected by Bernie Newman, the local gymnastics "promoter." By the age of fifteen, Hynds was working two hours a day on certified tricks and routines, not just whatever he could make up on his own. He became, like so many future Wolverines, a member of the Windsor Gymnastics Club, for which he competed internationally. In 1958, he won the Junior National All Around title at the Canadian National Gymnastics Tournament in Vancouver. Larose was just behind him in second—an occurrence that would happen rarely in college.

So it wasn't surprising when young Hynds began to be recruited. Originally, he leaned toward Michigan State and George Szypula. Then he talked to two former members of the Windsor Gymnastics Club, who also happened to be Wolverines: Nino Marion and the great Ed Gagnier. Whatever they said, it was enough to convince him that Ann Arbor was the place to go—and it's safe to assume that much of it had to do with Newt. Now Newt had Hynds focusing on rings, horse and floor exercise instead of the all-around. Montpetit couldn't get enough of the calm and focused youngster.

Larose seemed to be (and eventually proved himself to be) Montpetit's heir. Like Montpetit, he was a little French-Canadian with big skills. Late into high school, however, his main sport was still hockey, Canada's national pastime. He played right wing on his high school team. But he began to see other boys working out on the gymnastics equipment at the Immaculate Conception Center where he went to school. At 5'4", Larose was extremely small for a hockey player—but he was just the right size for a gymnast.

"From then on, I became a dedicated gymnast," Larose said. "I liked to bounce around on the trampoline when I first started to take the sport seriously, but later the still rings and especially the high bar became my favorites. Like most gymnasts, the only apparatus I didn't care for was the side horse."

He cared even less for the all-or-nothing life of being a specialist, though, so Larose molded himself into an all-arounder, where there was more room for redemption—a botched routine on one event could be made up for with a sparkling performance on another. After a year of training and watching all the meets he could manage, he was ready to compete himself, and entered competitions all across Canada. He earned first place in the novice division in the Canadian National Gymnastics Championships, his first major meet, at fifteen years old. Then, for three years as he moved from the novice division to the junior to the senior, Larose swept the regional honors in his native Quebec.

Larose had encountered Newt at age fifteen, as he competed in his first Canadian National Championships. As always, Newt had made a positive and lasting impression.

"Athletic scholarships aren't given in Canada," Larose said, "so in the choice between Michigan and Michigan State, I followed Newt." Obviously, the coach's personality had made an impression on young Larose, and Newt's eye for talent was only getting sharper.

The one catch was that Larose spoke only French; Jim Hynds had to help him through a tough first semester. His teammates kidded him, putting him at ease. Phil Bolton remembered the team pulling a prank on him once, telling him that "filet mignon" was pronounced in America as if one had no knowledge of how to read French. When Larose ordered his meal that way—"Fill-ett mig-non"—his teammates burst into laughter. Now with his first year past, Larose was just another Wolverine—and possibly the biggest talent on the team.

Newt got his first inkling of what the year might bring when Michigan and Illinois clashed in early February. The Wolverines walked away from the IM Building with a 62 ½-49 ½ victory, snapping Illinois' seven-meet win streak. And it was Larose and Hynds who made the difference, Larose opening the meet with a huge upset of Hadley on the floor exercise. Hynds notched a surprise victory too, on side horse, where he not only beat out Hadley but his own captain. Hadley beat Montpetit in the all-around by half a point, but the Wolverines' confidence shot up nonetheless.

It got another boost when, in a contest predicted to be a nailbiter, Michigan romped over powerful Southern Illinois in the same weekend. Wolverines took six of the seven first places. SIU's coach, Bill Meade, stated emphatically that Michigan was "definitely better than the Illini." Newt's early promises of a team different from all the others that came before seemed to be coming true. He was giddy with the anticipation of finally avenging all those years of coming in behind Illinois. His talents as a coach and recruiter, and the talents of his gymnasts, were all coming together. If Newt felt any sense of unreality or anxiety at the prospect of becoming the top team in the Big Ten, he never showed it.

"We're moving like one of the best teams in the country," he said. "We've been in Illinois's shadow for the past thirteen years and now it's our turn to grab the victory laurels. This is the team which will do it."

Newt's boys rolled to the end of the season undefeated, capping the dual meet schedule with a victory over Michigan State. Charlie Pond, however, remained completely unruffled. He'd seen his Illini lose in the regular season before, and always, the Orange and Blue turned it on for the championship meet. No one could ever catch the Illini in the one meet that really mattered.

"Two years ago," Pond said to a *Daily* writer, "one of your guys got all excited after you beat us in a dual meet, and I said we'd still win the Big Ten meet. Well, I'll say it again."

George Szypula of Michigan State retorted, "[Pond] always says that." But then he added, "And you know, he's probably right."

Newt kept quiet. He had said his piece, and was not one to cross the line from enthusiasm into boasting or arrogance. He knew this team was special—no matter what anyone might say. A team that was doubted for its lack of depth early in the season had shown itself to be plenty deep once the sophomores got their feet wet. And the veterans had come through as well, with

Osterland, Montpetit and Brown accounting for over half the team's points that season.

Finally on March 3, 1961, Big Ten action began in Ann Arbor, with qualifiers held in the familiar IM Building. Richard Montpetit, as always, rose magnificently to the occasion, leading his team to an early 22-17 lead over Illinois and beating Ray Hadley for the all-around title in the process. After the first day of competition, the leader in every event belonged either to Michigan or Illinois.

On Saturday, 1,200 fans crammed themselves into the gym to watch the two heavyweights conclude their long battle. Even before the meet, Newt had to have been well pleased with the turnout. His sport had been called "unheard-of" to start the year; now everyone knew about his team, and the tight little Michigan community was deeply emotionally invested in the outcome of Big Tens. Maybe they hadn't been watching closely over the past eleven years, but they certainly knew by now of the great rivalry between their team and Illinois, and Michigan's burning desire to come out on top for once.

With captain Montpetit leading the way, winning three event titles and tying for a fourth to notch fifty eight of his team's points, Michigan breezed to a 147 ½-122 win—and its long-awaited first Big Ten championship. Tom Tillman, Newt's first captain, was in the stands, along with Ed Gagnier, Ed Cole, Nino Marion, Bill Skinner and a host of other former Michigan gymnasts. They, perhaps more than anyone besides Newt, knew exactly how long the road to this point had been.

And Newt knew what was coming. So did Montpetit, who bear-hugged the coach. "Coach, we did it!" exclaimed the usually subdued captain. "We did it! We won the Big Ten title!"

"He embraced me, and jeez, I'm not used to being embraced by anybody especially another man," Newt remembered with a smile, reliving the euphoria of the moment. "He was so happy."

None of Montpetit's individual awards meant much; it was the team championship that lit up the captain's dark, handsome face.

After the final results were announced, Newt's gymnasts approached and lifted him onto their shoulders. Triumphantly they carried the man who had finally led them to a conference title down the hall of the IM Building—straight to Matt Mann Pool, where, of course, they tossed Newt into the water.

"That was when I really got my dunking in the pool," Newt said. "I was so joyful, I didn't care whether I was soaking wet. Damn it all, I'd be grabbing that trophy." Newt had waited what seemed like eons for this moment, and he wasn't going to let a millisecond of it go by without enjoying it to the fullest. He had finally reached the top of the mountain, and his ever-present smile was so wide it seemed to take over his entire face.

To sports writer Tom Witecki of *The Daily*, no scene could have been more perfect. He recalled his very first visit to the gym in 1957, meeting Newt and Ed Gagnier, and noticing a huge sign on one of the bulletin boards.

"It read—'Only 107 days until the Big Ten meet,'" Witecki wrote after the meet. "The 107 was written on a sheet of paper that was attached to the sign. Under the scrap of paper were 106 similar sheets of paper, each with a number on it. And one sheet was removed every day until the day of the Big Ten meet. ... Who could think of a nicer epilogue to yesterday's success story than an NCAA title—another something Michigan and Loken have never won."

Charlie Pond, loquacious and confident as ever, told anyone within hearing range that things would be different at NCAA championships, to be held this year in Champaign, Ill.

"We'll lick you in the NCAA meet," he promised. "Hadley will never have two bad days like yesterday and today again."

Even assistant coach Pat Bird got in on the action, instructing the Wolverines, "You guys better polish up the trophy real good, 'cause you're only gonna have it for a year."

But on that glorious day, it didn't seem to matter.

"We feel like kids who have been waiting expectantly for Christmas to come, but after it's passed, don't quite realize how they feel about the whole thing," Newt said a few days later, still waiting for the achievement to fully sink in. After waiting so long for this to happen, it's understandable that it took a little while for Newt and his boys to grasp completely that they'd won the Big Ten title. It was to be the first of twelve for Newt, and perhaps the sweetest, simply because of the long hard road to the top.

And Charlie Pond was wrong—between Illinois and Michigan at NCAAs, it was Michigan who did the beating.

In April, Michigan sent seven of the best gymnasts in its history to the NCAA Championships in Champaign. Rich Montpetit, Jim Hynds and Gil Larose would vie for the national all-around title, with Tom Osterland and Mark Erenburg competing in trampoline, Jim Brown in tumbling and Lew Fenner in the side horse. It was the most competitive team Michigan had sent to date—yet they finished fourth, behind champion Penn State, Southern Illinois and USC. Illinois tied with Michigan State for fifth, and Newt was named the Midwest Coach of the Year.

After winning the Big Ten title, Newt wanted to keep up the pressure on his team. After years of various summer activities that had him teaching tumbling, cheerleading and gymnastics at camps in Indiana, Michigan, and Ontario, he decided to take the job as summer manager of the Huron Valley Swim Club on the outskirts of Ann Arbor. Staying in Ann Arbor throughout the summers meant that he would be available to schedule workouts throughout the summer.

It was the start of the most successful period of Newt's career, to be packed full of Big Ten titles and two national championships as he and Michigan ascended to the elite of the sport. Attracting new talent, with every Big Ten championship, only got easier— Newt could have his pick of some of the best young gymnasts in the United States and Canada. Pat Bird, who had expected to regain the Big Ten trophy in 1962, was about as wrong as a person could possibly be.

Newt loved slogans, and for the 1962 season, his team not only came up with one, they had it made into a stamp for Newt to use on all his outgoing mail: "Two in '62!" Other coaches might have chuckled at the beginning, but as the slogans and stamps began to pile up over the next several years, they stopped laughing. Few probably expected it, but a juggernaut was about to start rolling.

The departure of Richard Montpetit might have proved a severe blow to many teams, but as always, Newt had prepared his team well. Gil Larose was ready to step in and assume Montpetit's role. A promising group of sophomores moved up from the freshman team to join the powerful junior class, including Arno Lascari. Lascari and Larose would become arguably the best gymnastics duo in Michigan history.

Lascari had been participating in gymnastics since the age of three, thanks to his father, a Turner instructor in Buffalo. His college decision came down to Illinois and Michigan: "Even though, at the time, Illinois had Olympic competitor Abie Grossfeld, Michigan had Newt." And Lascari, who dreamed of being a coach one day, hoped to learn from one of the very best.

For his part, Newt was overjoyed to have him, though he tried to remain realistic. A few months into Lascari's sophomore campaign, Newt asserted, "Arno has already equaled Montpetit's performance as a sophomore." Then, he cautiously added, "But sophomore performance does not always indicate how a gymnast will do as a senior."

Newt's family continued to support him and the team.

Dorothy brought the children to all the meets. As they got older, the girls worked as "flashers," sitting beside the judges and arranging the scores on flashcards that they held up for the score table to see. Dorothy also supported Newt by being an active member of the UM Coaches' Wives Association.

Newt almost missed the beginning of the season. On December 20, 1961, he was headed up north with his three older children, Chris, Lani and Jon, to go skiing. Dorothy was home with Newt Jr., who was too young to go.

"We were on Main Street in Ann Arbor, near the end of the city," Newt remembered. "Suddenly this lady who all her life has turned into this particular gas station with an order of eggs from her farm, she came into this gas station and she turned in. So what do you do when you see a car turning in? You turn right. Right at the very edge of the damn curb was a telephone pole. A telephone pole! I ran into it. I ran right straight into it."

In the crash, Newt sustained a broken collarbone and a severely broken nose. The girls' faces were cut up, and both of them broke their ankles and wrists. Doctors also found that Lani had broken her left thumb and her nose and needed ten stitches. Jon's head had hit the roof, leaving him with a bloody scalp. Luckily, once the Lokens arrived at the hospital, the doctor informed them that Jon's wound had caused no brain damage, though he would need over thirty stitches. He would go on to recover from the injury and participate in all the favorite Loken family activities, trampoline in particular.

Many years later, Newt could joke about it. "I broke my nose, jeez. That's why I've got the pug nose. The insurance coverage said, 'We'll give you an operation on your nose,' cause I was a good-looking nose guy. 'Or we'll give you $6,000.' Six thousand dollars? That seemed like $600,000 at the time! I said, 'Well, I think I can live with my nose. Give me my six thousand.' I guess we put it on the mortgage on the house."

At the time, though, the accident hit the family hard. "We were very cautious around the outskirts of Ann Arbor," Newt said. "We weren't going very fast [before the crash] because we weren't out of town yet. Most unusual, freakish accident. Every time I go by a telephone pole, I think of that incident. And why are the telephone poles right on the curb by the road? Right there. Why aren't they ten feet back? It gives nobody leeway of escaping something coming at you. So that was very sad, very bad."

"This was a turning point [for] the Loken family," Lani said. The accident shook some of the seemingly unshakeable confidence they'd all had about life in general.

A sense of depression over the accident hung over Dorothy for some time before fading away. Newt, for his part, tried harder than ever to remain unfailingly positive, but for probably the first time, not all of his optimism seemed to fit the situation for his family anymore. It had to have been tough for the Loken children to see the emotions of their parents at such opposite ends of the spectrum.

The family needed time to pick themselves back up; to Newt, picking himself back up meant diving back into his coaching, recruiting and teaching as soon as possible. Nothing would keep the coach away from his team and beloved sport for long, especially not when the very first dual of the year involved the Illini.

Illinois had yet another top-notch team, retaining the services of all-arounder Ray Hadley, who'd come in second to Montpetit in the 1961 Big Ten all-around competition, as well as noted tumbler Hal Holmes. With one event left, the two teams expected to vie for the '62 title were locked in a 48-48 tie. Michigan had made up an early 32-16 deficit; senior Lew Fenner missed his horse dismount after a solid routine, and Lew Hyman had trouble on the trampoline. Even Lascari had a bad moment, with a flukey high bar set. The last event was tumbling, and Holmes effectively "iced" the meet for Illinois and ended Michigan's comeback.

Lascari "came into his own" in Michigan's home opener against Central Michigan, winning three events and coming in second in two more. That victory sent Michigan on a five-meet winning streak entering its final home competition of the season against the Spartans. Michigan State, unlike most of Michigan's other opponents, had several seniors who matched up well with the Wolverine stars on every event, and had only graduated two regulars from the previous year. Their star was the great Dale Cooper, expected to win the Big Ten rings title without much of a fight. After a close victory in 1961, the Wolverines expected another highly charged meet. Extra stands had to be constructed to accommodate a larger crowd in the IM Building.

Michigan ran into several problems in the competition. Larose, the "Little Giant," injured his finger dismounting from parallel bars. He'd already won the floor exercise and high bar titles, but with the swollen knuckle, he couldn't even compete on still rings later. Lew Hyman hit the springs on the trampoline after only eight bounces—a full routine was required to include at least ten. But captain Tom Osterland stepped up to win the event, with Fenner winning the side horse crown. Lascari won another parallel bars title, finishing the regular season unbeaten in the event. Altogether, the good outweighed the bad for the Wolverines, and after the loss to Illinois they finished the season on a 6-0 run.

Heading into Big Tens as the defending champions for the first time ever, the Wolverines' main worry was Larose's grossly swollen finger. Points at the championship meet were awarded based on individual finishes, not accumulated team scores, and Michigan was depending on the Little Giant for multiple high finishes. Newt believed the pair of Larose and Lascari was "more than enough to compensate for the loss of last year's captain, Richard Montpetit." But Lascari probably couldn't carry the team by himself. Luckily, the finger wasn't too much of a problem for Larose on one of his main strengths, floor exercise.

Newt, as always, was optimistic just before heading to Big Tens in Columbus. His team's attitude, despite Larose's injury, was "tremendous," and the group seemed to be the best Newt had ever coached. The gymnasts undoubtedly picked up on and internalized Newt's unwavering confidence in them despite their obstacles, making them a formidable squad even with their captain hurt. All season, if one gymnast faltered, his teammates stepped up to put Michigan right where it needed to be, on top. Newt knew they could do it again on the biggest stage.

And in general, no one could decide whether Michigan or Illinois should be the favorite to win the title. "The dope sheet has Michigan winning by anywhere from one to ten points," a wry *Daily* reporter noted. "It also has Illinois winning by the same margin on the same sheet."

On the first day, Michigan placed twenty men into the finals; points earned on Friday by the top ten qualifiers in each event would contribute half the points for the final total, with the other half coming on the basis of Saturday's routines. Illinois' Ray Hadley, however, took the all-around title, with Lascari and Larose pulling in second and third. Larose's performance was one of the grittiest anyone had ever seen, as he competed the all-around on his painful finger. Tears trickled down his face after his high bar set from the sheer pain of trying to grip the bar.

Sunday, March 4, 1962, saw a huge banner headline splashed across *The Daily* sports page, proclaiming the team's second consecutive Big Ten championship. Rather than drama, the final competition featured the Wolverines coasting to the title, with Michigan State coming in well back in second and Illinois in a distant third. Michigan's only event champion was the still-undefeated Lascari on parallel bars—the Wolverines' balance and depth did them proud.

Out of a possible twenty-four qualifying places, Michigan filled twenty-three, with Larose qualifying into six. He would have qualified for seven, but on side horse three of his teammates had already placed in above him. Lascari earned 38½ points, more than Iowa's entire team. Lew Hyman and Ralph Bromund earned runner-up spots in tumbling and rings, a real shocker, especially for Bromund, who had pulled off two spectacular performances. The only man in the competition to perform the Olympic cross, he admitted to "going for broke" and set two career highs with a 91 on Friday and a 93 on Saturday.

By Saturday, Larose couldn't even grasp the high bar properly, he was in so much pain; but he refused to scratch. Instead, he managed to hang onto the bar using his thumb and wrist and came in third on the event. With Hadley graduating, he and sidekick Lascari now seemed to be the heirs apparent to the all-around crown.

Newt said Saturday's victory without question replaced the 1961 win as his favorite coaching moment. In 1961, Montpetit carried the team on his back; in 1962, Michigan had placed its maximum of three men in every event, with the third- and fourth-place men making all the difference. He'd won Big Ten titles himself as a Gopher; won an NCAA all-around crown; had a write-up in LIFE magazine; and three years earlier, had won the senior all-around competition in the Sarasota clinic. This moment topped them all.

"Seeing everyone coming through last weekend made me feel that I was accomplishing the ultimate in coaching," Newt wrote in a special article for *The Daily*. He added: "I never thought I would be as happy as when the boys threw me into the pool after last year's meet, but when they carried me on their shoulders through the crowd and into the pool Saturday I guess I changed my mind."

The NCAA championships still loomed, and now the Wolverines, with the highest average dual meet score in the nation, were one of the favorite teams. With weeks to recover,

Larose would be back at 100%; but with all the Eastern teams competing, rope climbing would be one of the events counted toward the final score. (While teams in the Midwest and West favored trampoline as the "extra" event, Eastern teams instead did rope climbing. Regardless of method, the first man to the top of his rope won.) Only speed mattered in this odd event, and fans worried that it might be just the fluke to derail the Wolverines.

As the championships got underway, Michigan kept pace with the leaders by placing two men in the top ten of every event but high bar. Lascari, the lone qualifier for high bar, and Larose were in good position in the all-around, and the team looked forward to seeing how the final results would come out when the averages were calculated after the second day of competition.

But for the second time in just a few years, tragedy struck Michigan.

Lew Hyman was expected to be one of Michigan's major players on trampoline. For safety, four spotters were always stationed around the apparatus; on Saturday, they were Tom Osterland, Gil Larose, Jim Hynds and a USC gymnast. Osterland's view was all too good as Hyman bounced toward the ceiling for the last skill of his routine.

"Hyman, going up for his final trick, lost his balance and soared upward, unusually high moving directly over the edge of the frame," Osterland told *The Daily* afterward. "From where I was, it looked like Lew would hit the frame, but he seemed to come straight down and veer off because of his twisting. ... Lew was twisting and moving so fast that it was hard to realize what was happening. Nobody present could predict that Lew would miss the apparatus. We all thought he would hit the edge. One moment he was coming down and in the next he was veering off. Before I knew what was happening, he had hit his back on the floor and in the next instant his head slammed against the wood."

That the third-place finish was Michigan's best in history was lost in the worry over Hyman. When he came out of his sedation (or a coma—he was so sedated doctors couldn't tell which), he was unable to speak and had a weakened right side. A few weeks after the competition, he was able to feed himself and respond to requests to move certain parts of his body. In mid-May, he was finally released from the hospital and flew home to Waslagh, N. Y., with his parents, who still had not left his side. By then, he had regained 90% of the use of his right side, and doctors expected him to make a complete recovery. But unsurprisingly, Hyman never participated in gymnastics again.

The events of the past few years had to have shaken Newt, even with the team's success on the floor. First there was the death of Al Stall and Ken Sakamoto; then his family's own near-tragic car accident; and now Lew Hyman would never compete again after his freak fall off the trampoline. But even as they made him less of a complete optimist, they gave him more depth. He knew the risks associated with gymnastics, just as his athletes did, and they wouldn't stop him from doing what he loved. Newt had bounced back from terrible events, and would continue to do so; his example would prove inspirational to his upcoming generations of gymnasts.

Despite the sad end to the season, Newt was satisfied with his team's finish, especially Lascari and Osterland's recognition as All-Americans. Gil Larose was elected the team's new captain, and embarked on several international meets over the summer as a member of the Canadian National Team. It was a bittersweet end, but Michigan was on the verge of hitting the collegiate gymnastics jackpot.

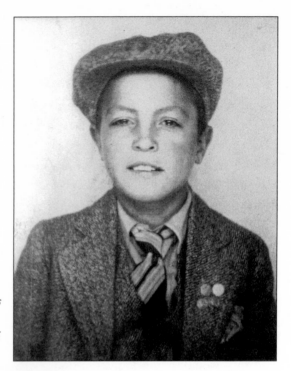

Newt at ten years old, wearing medals for selling magazines.

Newt's father, Alfred Loken, who regularly won accolades at every occupation he tried.

Newt with his mother, Clara, who always encouraged him in his athletic and show-business endeavors.

From bottom: Newt, Herb and Don Loken balance atop each other in Minnesota.

Newt was hired while in high school to perform in the clown and acrobatics act Kent & Quigley—a forerunner of his long-running trampoline act.

Below: Newt with his younger brothers, Herb and Don, in 1939 near the sawdust pile where the boys honed their gymnastics skills.

MINNESOTA 'U'
HAS 'MOST
ACROBATIC'
ROOTER KING

Newt's athletic and entertainment talents made him into an exceptional "rooter king" at the University of Minnesota.

Ralph Piper coached Newt on the University of Minnesota gymnastics team. Piper was a jack-of-all-trades, and Newt followed in his footsteps.

As a Gopher gymnast, Newt won the two Big Ten all-around titles, the 1941 NCAA high bar title, and the 1942 NCAA all-around title.

The Loken brothers: from left, Clifford, Newt, Herb and Don. This is the only photo of all four brothers.

Newt, with characteristic flair, perches on top of a building as a Minnesota cheerleader.

Newt demonstrates the use of a trampoline to cadets at the Iowa Pre-Flight School during World War II.

Newt and Dorothy's wedding photo. The two were married on Christmas Eve, 1942, and had 69 happy years together.

Newt and Dorothy perform a balancing act beside a pool in Iowa.

Newt, Herb and Don in 1943. The three brothers all eventually competed for the University of Minnesota men's gymnastics team.

Newt entered the Navy after graduating from Minnesota in 1942. He served as the Athletic Welfare Officer on the USS Prince William.

Athletic activities aboard the USS Prince William in May 1944, organized by Athletic Welfare Officer Newt Loken—including, of course, a trampoline.

Dotty and Newt with two-month-old Christine, their first child, born in December of 1946.

Newt's first varsity gymnastics team in 1947-48
Back row, from left: John Allred, Dave Lake, Coach Newt Loken and Dick Fashbaugh. Front row, from left: Bob Schoendube, Glen Neff, Tom Tillman and Bob Willoughby.

Glenn Neff and Tom Tillman, co-captains of Newt's first team in 1947-48, pose on the parallel bars.

The urge to do a handstand can strike a gymnast at any moment. Here, Newt performs a handstand on a railing at the Grand Canyon. He was on his way to the 1948 Rose Bowl.

Newt and his cheerleading squad took a road trip to Southern California for the 1948 Rose Bowl. In addition to a couple celebrities, they also met Michigan football great Tom "Ol' 98" Harmon, pictured here with the cheerleaders and their borrowed Kaiser-Frazer car.

Two-year-old Chris bounces on a miniature trampoline Newt made for her.

Newt, shown here in the early 1950s, balances atop his ladder in his trademark trampoline act.

courtesy of Nino Marion

Team daredevil Al Stall, who was later killed in a car accident, leaps over a pool during Big Ten Championships in Iowa, 1958.

Newt added daughters Chris and Lani to his famous trampoline act when they were very young. Here, Lani holds Jon, the newest addition to the show, on her lap for a promotional photo.

Ed Cole, Newt's 1958-59 co-captain, brought home an NCAA trampoline title in 1959.

Below: Ed Gagnier captained the 1958-59 team along with Ed Cole. The star all-around competitor later coached Iowa State to an NCAA title in 1971—the year Michigan hosted the national championship meet.

Newt and Dorothy at Boyne Mountain in the late 1950s, engaging in one of Newt's favorite pastimes, skiing.

All-arounder Richard Montpetit, one of the many talented gymnasts who came through Newt's Canadian pipeline, captained Michigan to its first Big Ten championship in 1961. He also won the Big Ten all around title that year.

Chris, Jon, Newt Jr. and Lani pose at the gym for the family Christmas card: "Hanging Around Waiting for Christmas."

Newt's four children, Chris, Lani, Jon and Newt Jr., sitting on the diving board at the Huron Valley Swim Club in 1963. Newt's summers at the HVSC created many happy memories for his family, and allowed him to continue scheduling workouts for his gymnasts.

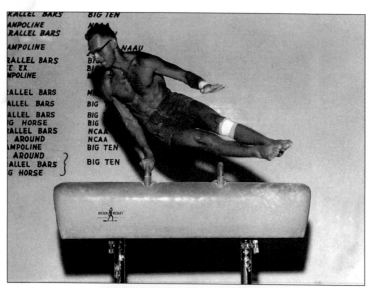

Above: Arno Lascari captained Michigan's team in 1964. Along with teammate Gil Larose, he helped lead Michigan to its first NCAA title in 1963.

Right: Dave Jacobs, one of Newt's three world-class trampolinists. Wayne Miller, Jacobs and George Huntzicker held a lock on the World Trampoline Title in the late 1960s.

1970 Michigan captain Ron Rapper, a parallel bars specialist, helped lead the Wolverines to their second NCAA title. He saw the victory as a tribute to Newt.

Newt and his 1970 NCAA Championship team in front of the Wall of Champions.

Newt pulled out all the promotional stops when Michigan hosted the 1971 NCAA Championships, posing in a variety of ways with the countdown marquee.

Newt dances with his wife, Dorothy, in 1974. In addition to coaching gymnastics, Newt loved to dance and teach dancing classes.

Newt headed the trampoline float in Detroit's Thanksgiving Day Parade for many years. The 1974 entry featured bouncers Newt Jr., Lani, Michigan diving coach Dick Kimball, Newt's grandson Gary Loken-Dahle and Newt himself as bugs.

Performing with the alumni cheerleaders at Homecoming was always a highlight for Newt. This cheer is called the Michigan Locomotive.

Courtesy of Michigan Men's Gymnastics

Newt leads cheers from the field at Michigan Stadium, fondly known as the Big House.

Newt gets passed up to the top of the crowd at Michigan Stadium—an occupational hazard of coaching the cheerleaders.

Lani and Newt demonstrate a balancing skill at one of Newt's cheerleading clinics. This photo also served as the cover of one of Newt's cheerleading books.

*A portrait
of Newt
taken in
1983,
the year
he retired
from
coaching
Michigan
gymnastics.*

courtesy of Michigan Men's Gymnastics

*Dorothy and Newt with the cake celebrating Newt's years at Michigan at his
retirement in 1983.*

Following his retirement, Newt traveled to his ancestral homeland of Norway with Dotty. Uff da!

Newt, with Dotty at his side and Michigan head coach Kurt Golder looking on, cuts the ribbon at the opening of the Newt Loken Gymnastics Training Center in 2003. At each end are Michigan gymnasts Scott Vetere (left) and team captain Chris Gatti.

courtesy of Colt Rosensweig

Newt poses with the 2009 Big Ten champions after telling one of his favorite stories, about a shirt that was "long on quality but short on quantity!"

Newt with some of the original U of M cheerleaders.

Chapter 11

Newt's First National Title

Expectations could not have been higher for Michigan as the 1963 season approached, and three top-notch bouncers were about to join the core of Newt's strong 1962 squad. Trampoline had always been Michigan's trademark, and now, three youngsters had arrived to carry on the tradition: sophomores Gary Erwin, John Hamilton and Fred Sanders. All had been national champions in the event as juniors, Erwin and Sanders in the U. S., Hamilton in Canada. In the Midwest Open, held in late 1962, Erwin took first for the second straight year, with Sanders just behind him. Newt concluded, "you would have to give Erwin the nod as the best of the three because of his win in the Midwest meet."

Erwin, a gymnast from Arlington Heights, Illinois, had picked up the sport late in high school. After being forced to give up tumbling due to injuries, he switched his focus to the trampoline. At Michigan, he practiced ten to fifteen hours per week, with special emphasis on his toughest trick, a triple backflip. Sander was a former pole-vaulter who'd begun working on the trampoline three years previously. Hamilton had begun "rebound tumbling" in 1953 in Amarillo, Texas; due to the lack of good teams, he migrated northward to Canada. He proudly told *The Daily* that he'd never needed a safety belt to learn a new trick. The presence of the three young trampolinists provided a huge lift to a team reeling from the loss of fellow bouncer Lewis Hyman due to a terrible accident the previous year.

"The competition between the three should keep them going all out," Newt said at the time. "The three help each other with their routines, and in addition, Ed Cole sometimes lends a hand in the coaching chores." But Newt was still cautious, reserving his final judgment on the athletes until the close of the season. He knew he had a talented team, but he was soon to find out that he was at the helm of a juggernaut.

Already he was worried about the possible drop in performance from Gil Larose, the team's senior captain. Larose had proved an invaluable asset to the team—until, his coach thought, the summer of 1962.

One of Newt's basic philosophies as a coach was to keep his boys "happy, unmarried and solvent." And just before his senior year, Larose got married.

"That's the end of your career, Gil," Newt sadly told his captain when he heard the news. "You're just not going to make out. You just can't handle the duties at home and the duties at the gym."

His pronouncement only made the talented Canadian work harder to prove his coach wrong.

"He worked so hard," Newt remembered. "He had this trick—he'd stand at the side of the floor before his routine, then put his hand on the floor, lift his body up, and do a one-armed planche!" In a planche, a gymnast holds his body parallel to the floor, supporting his entire weight on his arms. Or in Larose's case, arm. "He'd slowly bring his body into a handstand. Nobody in the world could do that. And he told me after [the season] that he did that every night of his life before he went to bed. He was so determined to show Coach Loken."

Michigan began its season with a second-place overall finish at the Midwest Open in Chicago on December 1, 1962 (a forerunner of today's regular season opener, the Windy City Invitational). Bested only by Southern Illinois, something of a juggernaut in its own right, Michigan received a top-notch performance from Larose that would become a regular occurrence throughout the magical season. Larose snagged the all-around title, also finishing first on rings, second on parallel bars, and third on side horse. With up to 80 gymnasts competing in each event, the presence of at least one Wolverine in the top ten on all of the apparatus was a feat to be proud of. Newt was "optimistic about the season, to say the least," reported *The Daily*.

"Michigan is ready for an all-out effort to win the national title," Newt said emphatically. Just two years after finally winning his first Big Ten title, Newt had already set his sights higher—he could never stand still, either literally or figuratively. Newt was always shooting for bigger things, innovating in the gym and with his coaching style, trying to improve himself and his gymnasts. Beating Illinois wasn't enough anymore, after just two years of besting them in the conference. Now it was time to beat all the best teams in the country.

First, however, the Wolverines had to deal with a layoff that lasted from December 1 to January 12. A *Michigan Daily* reporter visited the gym to see how the boys were keeping up, and came away with the same image of Newt that had impressed so many others.

"Loken, a man who seldom stands still for any length of time, is continually shouting words of encouragement or advice to his charges," the writer noticed. He also noted that Newt seemed to be higher on this team than he'd ever been before. The ebullient coach planned several exhibitions for the layoff, both to keep his gymnasts sharp and to further increase interest in the sport. With only two home meets scheduled for the 1963 season, Newt was even more determined to give the Ann Arbor faithful a good look at their potential champions.

Finally, on January 12 the team kicked off its conference season against Iowa and Indiana in a double dual. In 1963, a double dual meant that each team would be scored against both others—for example, a first place finish in one event was counted as two victories. Indiana's team consisted of only six gymnasts, but Newt expected some trouble from Iowa. The Hawkeyes, he told *The Daily*, hadn't had an outstanding squad since 1960, but like Michigan, boasted a talented crop of sophomores, especially all-arounder Glenn Gailis.

In fact, neither team gave Michigan much trouble. Though Erwin and Sanders were bested on the trampoline, Larose recorded a first place finish on floor. And Arno Lascari took on the hero's role, as he and Larose would so many times that season. Lascari earned top scores on the pommel horse, parallel bars and high bar, while the Wolverines swept the top spots in tumbling.

Newt, predictably, was delighted. Though the competition wasn't too stiff, his boys' morale was high as a kite, exactly where he wanted it. The team planned to take it easy until its next test, February 9 against Ohio State.

For this next test, nearly the entire team planned double somersault dismounts off of every event. "It shows that they're strong enough in their routines to have a little something extra coming off the apparatus," Newt said proudly. Having a little extra early in the season is important, especially considering that often gymnasts don't hit the peak of their endurance until close to championship time, even in today's hyperactive "thirteen months a year" training style. Phil Bolton and Mike Henderson had added double backflips to their tumbling sets, and the Buckeyes seemed to be having a down year. They'd lost captain Stu Greenberg, a Michigan nemesis, as well as their first two meets against Wisconsin and Michigan State.

Michigan rolled over the Buckeyes easily, taking first place in every event before a crowd of 2,000 fans. Larose won the floor exercise, still rings and parallel bars, taking second on high bar. Gary Erwin took first on trampoline, Arno Lascari on the horse, Hynds on high bar, and Bolton in tumbling; the Wolverines also snagged five of the seven seconds and thirds.

"The team as a whole performed very well," Newt told *The Daily*. "Larose was the big wheel, turning in his usual fine show." Already, Newt had seen the signs that Larose, despite following in the footsteps of Gagnier and Montpetit, and despite getting married, would be better than nearly anyone who had gone before. Now the team looked forward to revenge against the Illini, who'd beaten the Wolverines the previous year.

Like Ohio State, Illinois was in a rebuilding year. Though the Illini could boast senior Hal Holmes among their ranks, he was just about the only bright spot on a team that had lost eight lettermen to graduation. Newt called him "the greatest tumbler in the universe" and with good reason: He'd won the Big Ten title in that event the past two years, and was the defending national titleholder. But Bolton and Henderson were ready to challenge him—only they and Holmes, of all the Big Ten gymnasts, included double twists and double backflips in their tumbling routines.

It was Michigan's first home meet of the season, but if the gymnasts felt any pressure they didn't show it. Before a crowd of over 2,000 fans, Larose and Lascari earned two first-place finishes each, with Sanders winning trampoline and Hynds winning horse. Holmes put on an amazing tumbling show, with Bolton and Henderson tying for second just behind him. But Holmes' performance wasn't enough as the Illini fell before the rolling Wolverines, 53-26.

A week later, the Wolverines were set to face some "classy competition"—Michigan State and Minnesota, both previously unbeaten, in the final duals before the Big Ten Championships. Two meets in three days against the best of the Big Ten would be a revealing test for Michigan.

On Wednesday, the Wolverines easily beat the Spartans, taking five of the seven first-place finishes and handing MSU its first loss. For captain Gil Larose, determined to show that his new marital status wouldn't hurt his gymnastics, it was his best performance of the year. He finished first on floor exercise and high bar, and notched three second-place finishes, missing first on pommel horse and parallel bars by just half a point.

By Friday, before the final regular season meet, Newt was convinced that this was the best team he'd had in his fifteen years as the Michigan coach. Nearly every member was carefully recruited, painstakingly chosen for what he could add to the team. Everyone had bought into Newt's confident, enthusiastic mindset, and the team chemistry and sense of collective purpose showed clearly.

"Experienced observers," *The Daily* reported, "said that the Michigan State showing was one of the best team performances they'd ever seen." After a night like that, no one could be entirely surprised when the Wolverines toppled the Gophers on Friday in the IM Building. The team had become prominent enough that now other teams wanted to put on exhibitions at *their* meets! That night, again in front of a crowd of over 2,000, the female gymnasts of Flint Community College performed—as if the fans needed any more entertainment. Friendly Wolverine rivalries— Larose vs. Lascari, Sanders vs. Erwin, Bolton vs. Henderson—all paid dividends. Larose and Lascari led the team with sparkling performances, while Sanders and Erwin tied for first on the trampoline, and Bolton and Henderson tied for first in tumbling.

Minnesota coach Pat Bird was impressed. "There's no doubt in my mind that Michigan will take the Big Ten Championship," he said, "and I'd even give them an edge over Southern Illinois in the NCAA's (sic)."

Before the postseason, though, Newt decided to stage one more exhibition for the Michigan fans. Promoting his team and the sport was never far from his mind—winning was fun, but it wasn't everything, and it was extremely important to Newt that men's gymnastics have a good following in Ann Arbor. And with such a talented team, having an exhibition—where Michigan *couldn't* lose—was a surefire way to get fans even more fired up about the championship meets. Newt had recruited so successfully among Canadian gymnasts that he could split his team into Americans and Canadians for the intrasquad competition. The Canadians came up a little short in numbers, however.

Not a problem for Newt. Other coaches might have just switched one gymnast to the other team; Newt called in Wilhelm Weiler, Canada's top male gymnast from the Pan-American Games, along with former Wolverine Rich Montpetit, who would eventually compete for Canada in the Olympics. Today, even some of the biggest gymnastics competitions of the year aren't televised; sometimes they're on three weeks after they happen. But an exhibition by Newt's 1963 Wolverines rated live coverage on regional TV, with the exhibition to take place (naturally) between halves of the Wisconsin-Michigan basketball game.

Fans were in a fever over their highly favored team. On March 1, *The Daily* ran a plethora of photos, proclaiming, "If ever a Michigan athletic team had a chance for a national championship, it's the gymnasts of 1963." But first, there was a Big Ten crown to claim.

The two-day competition was held at Michigan State's Jenison Field House. Ten gymnasts would qualify to the finals on each event, with teams earning points based on the final standings of their individuals. Newt had stamped "Three in '63!" on every piece of outgoing mail—now it was time to make good on the bold words.

On Friday, Michigan established a commanding lead, sweeping the top three spots in the all-around (Larose, Lascari and Hynds) and qualifying twenty-three of twenty-four individual routines to the finals. It was the first all-around sweep in Big Ten history. In five of the eight preliminary competitions, a Wolverine won or tied for the top spot. And on Saturday, the team rolled to its third consecutive Big Ten title, with Larose and Lascari, as usual, leading the way.

Michigan posted the highest score ever in a Big Ten meet with 210½ points—more than double the total of second-place Iowa (83½). Between them, Larose and Lascari took six first-place finishes. Sanders became the Big Ten champ on the trampoline, and Henderson tied Larose for the floor title.

Afterward, Newt was glowing with happiness.

"Wonderful, wasn't it?" It was all the normally chatty coach could say, and it was enough. Winning Big Tens was a highlight (and one that would become nearly an annual rite)—but now only a stepping-stone to something even greater.

As the NCAA championships, to be held in Pittsburgh, Pa., neared, Michigan was the slight favorite in a gigantic field of forty-two schools. Perennially dominant Southern Illinois was still very much in the running, but had lost two of its best gymnasts to mid-year graduation. As in the Big Ten Championships, NCAAs would span two days, with only the all-around being decided on the first day. Each school was limited to ten competitors—Newt would take Larose, Lascari, Sanders, Erwin, Hamilton, Hynds, Bolton, Henderson, Paul Levy, and Barry Spicer. With gleeful anticipation, *The Daily* reminded readers that this would be the gymnastics program's first national title ever, and a fitting climax to the team's most successful season to date.

The outcome was never in doubt as the juggernaut neared the finish. After the completion of the all-around competition, Larose stood alone as the champion, with his partner in crime, Lascari, finishing third. Michigan led all other schools with twenty-one points, Southern Illinois a distant second with fifteen. Sixteen Wolverine routines qualified to the finals, more than any other school—Southern Illinois qualified thirteen, and no other school more than six.

On Saturday, March 30, 1963, for the first time the Wolverines became national champions. With a grand total of 129 points, Michigan trounced runner-up Southern Illinois (73). Larose, in addition to his all-around crown, took first on vault and high bar, with Lascari winning parallel bars, Erwin trampoline and Henderson floor exercise. Newt, who'd predicted a down year for Larose, couldn't have been happier to find himself wrong, proudly declaring that "Larose was clearly the star of the meet."

"First NCAA championship," Newt remembered with a pleasurable sigh. "We'd been in a bunch of NCAAs, runner-up, bridesmaid. Crying in the mirror for a week afterward, thinking, 'What did I do wrong,' like all coaches do, blaming themselves. I stood in the bleachers there and waited for them to announce that we won, but you never know with the scoring table. And they finally announced, 'And the team title, won by Michigan!' And they played the school song, and the crowd started singing, cause they'd heard it so often! It was so cute. ... Afterward, I kept looking at the scoreboard, thinking the scorekeeper made a mistake. But it stayed."

That was pure Newt—never wanting to celebrate too early, in case things turned out not to go his way, then pulling out all the stops with expressing his joy once the results were final. If Newt ever doubted himself or his coaching after winning those first two Big Ten titles (he certainly must have doubted himself beforehand, during the long off seasons), he never again had a reason to do so after the 1963 NCAA title.

"The win was a great feeling of accomplishment," Phil Bolton remembered. "It left a warm glow in my heart for some time."

A few days later, Newt was still "somewhere between the lower stratosphere and upper ionosphere, still feeling the aftereffects of the Wolverines' first NCAA championship, won Saturday at Pittsburgh," *The Daily* enthused. Ever-smiling Newt was named the outstanding coach of 1963, and Larose was named the best collegiate gymnast in the United States. He'd not only attended to his duties at home and in the gym—he'd won the all-around in every single meet he entered in 1963. And he believed it was largely due to his jack-of-all-trades mentor. Newt hadn't just coached his team to a championship; he had completely befriended his boys, tailoring workouts to each individual while still managing to be one of the best promoters in collegiate men's gymnastics. He wasn't just responsible for the team on the floor—thanks to his tireless efforts, he was responsible for putting ever larger and more enthusiastic crowds in the Michigan stands.

"I owe at least three-quarters of my success to [Newt]," Larose said. "He's everything to the team—organizer, coach, and always one of the guys. He'll do anything for you."

In 1964, without Larose and with every other team in the country gunning for Michigan, Newt remarked, "The higher up you go, the more your rear end is exposed." Nonetheless, the boys presented him with the now customary new stamp, this one reading "Four in '64!" and readied themselves to defend their Big Ten and NCAA titles. In the space of just a few years, Newt had developed a team that decisively replaced Illinois as the class of the Big Ten.

Arno Lascari, now a senior, was named captain—he was out of Larose's shadow. The maturing trampoline squad promised to be better than ever. One *Daily* writer noted that on trampoline, "Michigan is about as safe as Sonny Liston at a sewing circle."

His fellow senior, Phil Bolton, remained in the shadow of his "rival" on the team, Mike Henderson. Like Lascari, he didn't mind much. At 5'9", Bolton was on the big side for a gymnast, but now in his final year, he was the only tumbler in the Big Ten who could perform both a one-and-a-half twisting backflip along with a full-twisting backflip. Born in Jackson, Michigan, he'd grown up in Florida. When Newt offered him a partial scholarship to return to the distinct seasons of Michigan, Bolton jumped at the chance. (Except for a four-year hiatus in San Francisco, Bolton has remained in the Midwest ever since.)

"There isn't another tumbler in the conference that can beat him," Newt said of Bolton, "except Mike."

As 1963 came to a close, Lascari fell off the parallel bars and apparently broke his wrist. The injury actually turned out to be a dislocated elbow, which so scared Newt that until he saw Lascari back on the apparatus, he feared his star wouldn't come back at all.

He made his return in the most dramatic fashion possible at the start of the 1964 season, as his team took on their archrivals, the Michigan State Spartans. Most of the time, a tie is one of the most unsatisfying feelings in all of sport; but that night, the 56-56 tie with Michigan State felt just as good as an outright win to the Wolverines. Their captain earned top honors on parallel bars, and third place on rings, while the tumblers and bouncers together delivered the crucial blow. Both squads—Erwin, Hamilton and Sanders on trampoline, and Henderson, Hamilton and Bolton in tumbling—swept the top three places to clinch the tie at the last moment. Like Lascari, Hamilton was making a comeback; due to an injured knee, he hadn't tumbled competitively all season. It seemed that Michigan's big guns were getting healthy just in time for the most important meets of the season. The team had a middling 3-2-1 Big Ten record, but that wouldn't matter if everything came together in Madison, Wisconsin.

Instead of Illinois, it was Michigan State that seemed to be the biggest roadblock to Michigan's streak. The Spartans boasted, unquestionably, the best ring man in the country in Dale Cooper, and unlike the Wolverines, they hadn't been battling injuries all season. (*The Daily* now lumped Illinois in with the "also-rans," Minnesota and Indiana.)

On the first day of competition, a trio of teams emerged as the leaders. These three would dominate the Big Ten for the rest of the decade—Michigan, Michigan State and Iowa. But in 1964, the other two still hadn't quite caught up to Newt's Wolverines. Lascari finished fourth in the all-around competition, and on the second day, with the pain in his injured elbow so intense that he was forced to ice it after every event, he gutted his way to another parallel bars title. Following in the footsteps of their gallant leader, the tumbling trio of Henderson, Hamilton and Bolton swept the top three spots in the final event to clinch the title for Michigan. Until then, Michigan had been fighting off challenges to its narrow lead all day; but thanks to what *The Daily* called the "splendid threesome," Michigan won its fourth straight conference title by eighteen-and-a-half points over second place Iowa.

Newt, of course, was "ebullient" after the win. In 1961, Michigan rode to its first Big Ten title on the back of the brilliant Richard Montpetit. This year, they'd won it on depth. Though Lascari, Henderson and bouncers Hamilton and Erwin had claimed first place finishes, it was the multitude of seconds, thirds and fourths that proved the difference. Despite their regularity, Big Ten titles remained a thrill for Newt. Nothing fun ever became old, or everyday, for Newt.

The gleeful gymnasts hung a somewhat cryptic sign on the door to their little gym in the IM Building: M Inverted to the Fourth—M inverted is a W, for a win; and the four indicated the number of Big Ten titles. (Newt continued the tradition of mysterious signs for years afterward. In 2009, he secretly posted maize-and-blue numeral threes all over the practice gym right before Big Tens, signifying that the gymnasts were aiming for current coach Kurt Golder's third Big Ten title.)

Once again, Michigan had earned a trip to the NCAA championships as a team. Newt expected another six-team fight, with most of the competition coming from the other Big Ten teams, along with Southern Illinois and USC. Eight men would represent Michigan at Los Angeles State College, including Gary Erwin, who would just have returned from the World Trampoline Championships in London. Lascari, despite his injury, was Newt's main hope in the all-around.

Michigan could also count on a big advantage in the tumbling and trampoline events. Except for one Southern Illinois gymnast, none of Michigan's chief rivals planned for any of their athletes to compete in either event. The Wolverines knew two sweeps were theirs for the taking.

But unlike 1963, this time it was not to be. Southern Illinois won decisively despite Michigan's unprecedented sweep of trampoline. Once again, Erwin, Hamilton and Sanders finished in a pack at the top of the standings. USC, with only two gymnasts competing, managed to collect enough points for second place, nudging Michigan to third. Lascari fought through the pain again, coming in third on parallel bars and eighth on high bar. Erwin, at least, got a measure of revenge. At the World Trampoline Championships, he'd come in a close second to a freshman from the University of California at Berkeley, Danny Millman. Now, he was back on top of the heap. His teammates soon elected him captain for the 1965 season.

The fight for the Big Ten and NCAA titles was on once again.

Chapter 12

Two More Titles—
and Mounting Complications

The push for "Five in '65" marked the first year of tinkering with the Big Ten championship determination process. Only one team would be allowed to represent the conference at the NCAA championships, and the champion would be the team with the best dual-meet conference record. This reduced the big meet at the end of the season to nothing more than an individual competition, where gymnasts vied for event titles. In addition, tumbling was dropped as an event, with floor exercise taking its place.

Floor exercise wasn't just a term in those days. It actually happened on a wooden floor. Even by the 1980s, only a select few schools had added the padding and springs characteristic of floors today. When carpets on the wooden floors appeared, it was an innovation—and in 1965, it was an innovation for which the gymnasts still waited. Newt remembers, with a wince, fastening small Styrofoam pads all along a gymnast's spine, trying to lessen the beating he was about to take on a dive roll to the floor. The rules of tumbling had been unyielding, with disqualification the penalty for putting one finger off the narrow mat; the floor, physically, was just as unyielding.

155

But Newt couldn't have been unhappy with the general development. The horsehair tumbling mat didn't provide a ton of padding, either. Now gymnasts had much more freedom in the composition of their routines thanks to the larger, square area about the size of a wrestling mat. They had much more room to move and experiment, a far bigger margin for error without having to worry about coming off the mats. Of course, going out of bounds on floor was a deduction, but it was easier to avoid.

Newt and his boys were as optimistic as ever. The wall in the gym was now three-quarters filled with names, and Newt merrily admitted regret for starting the list in the middle, instead of on the left side, of the wall. He'd lost three seniors—Lascari, Bolton and Paul Levy. But the identical Fuller twins, Chip and Philip (whose name was promptly shortened to the harmonious "Phip"), were sophomores now, and primed to help out on the floor and vault. Gary Vander Voort, a former Illinois state all-around champion, and John Cashman were expected to contribute on high bar, Art Baessler on the pommel horse, Rich Blanton on the rings.

Newt sometimes complained—good naturedly, of course— that the young Fullers were a little too alike.

"I wish they weren't such identical twins," he quipped. "It's rather difficult to separate them."

Though Chip and Phip didn't engage in the time-honored pastime of identical twins—posing as each other—their friends often did the trick for them. If a friend mysteriously accused one twin of failing to respond to a greeting on the street, he could safely assume that his confused brother had been spotted. They delighted in giving synchronized answers to questions, or, failing that, finishing each other's sentences. When one was asked if he'd gotten his hair cut short, he'd turn to look at his brother rather than in a mirror to check just what his new 'do looked like.

Everything hadn't always been so lighthearted for the twins. When they were freshmen in high school, their father, a naval officer at Pensacola, Fla., passed away. But to keep their minds occupied, their mother sent them to a trampoline course at the base. There, the boys met two ex-Wolverines, Lew Fenner and Phil Noggle; Noggle recommended the twins to Newt. They pronounced themselves thrilled to be "working under a great coach like Loken," with a proven track record not only for turning out great gymnasts, but successful Michigan men. Tragedy had turned into triumph for the Fuller twins. It's likely that Newt provided the father figure they'd been missing—Newt played the surrogate dad for all his athletes, but for the Fuller twins, it probably meant a little more.

Their styles provided one of the few distinct differences between the twins. Chip was exciting and daring on the floor, while Phip was more graceful and fluid. Chip was the first gymnast in the United States to perform a front one-and-three-quarters flip—a rollout skill that may look easy today but was an entirely different creature when done on an actual wooden floor. Phip, for his part, made his trademark skill a full twisting backflip that he landed in a full split position—again on the carpetless, spring-less wooden floor.

Newt's crop of sophomores quickly proved themselves, winning one of the preseason intrasquads and tying the other one against the rest of the team. Newt penned eight of them into his season-opening lineup for the meet against Eastern Michigan, coached by 1954 captain Marv Johnson. Eastern was only expected to provide "token opposition," but Newt still couldn't contain himself when it came to talking about his team's all-around talent. His exceptional coaching was helpful to anyone, but now that Newt was drawing the best of the best to Michigan, he could take his athletes even farther. His style never caused Wolverines to put too much pressure on themselves—they knew their coach only wanted them to hit their routines. However they could make that happen, worked for him. Newt knew that the wins would come on their own.

And this team thrived, like so many others had, under that philosophy.

"I can count on at least one man in the 90s on every event," Newt proudly told *The Daily* "like a man showing off his muscle."*

Eight hundred fans braved "brutal cold" to watch the Wolverines steamroll Eastern Michigan, which never posted an individual finish higher than third. And all Michigan's winners were youngsters; with Newt's teams, there was nearly always a youth movement going on. Phip Fuller took top honors on floor; freshman Wayne Miller on trampoline; sophomore Gary Vander Voort on high bar (he also tied fellow sophomore Kenny Williams for first on the parallel bars); sophomore Rich Blanton on still rings; and freshman Larry Quinn on side horse.

The Wolverines then opened their conference slate with a profound drubbing of Ohio State, 68-43, despite Newt's attempts to keep the score down and minimize the Buckeyes' embarrassment. Ohio State didn't manage even a single first-place finish. With Mike Henderson out with tendonitis, the Fuller twins made their conference debut. "A few suspicious souls," *The Daily* reported, "were mumbling that Loken was trying to enter the same person twice." Phip snagged the floor title, with Chip winning vault. Their pattern of splitting titles would continue for the next three years, to the delight of Wolverine fans.

The next week against Illinois, Michigan proved that it had completely taken on the old foe's role in the conference. Ten years earlier, it was Newt who had schemed frantically in hopes of finding the magic formula to beat the Illini. In 1965, his Wolverines rolled over Illinois by a thirty-point margin—and it was just one more part of the journey leading to the real showdown, with Iowa. While Michigan took every first place except on the still rings, Gary Erwin was in London, winning the World Trampoline Championship. Newt had so much talent now

---

*The 90s are equivalent to the 9.00 range on gymnastics' traditional perfect-ten scale.

under his careful eye that he could even afford to send some of it halfway around the world. He had fashioned not only a supremely talented squad but one that was finely balanced and unfazed by anything, even the temporary loss of their top bouncer.

Erwin added to his hardware collection by teaming up with Southern Illinois' Frank Schmidt to win the World Synchronized Trampoline Championship as well. Erwin topped his biggest rival, a young gymnast named Danny Millman.

Erwin had followed in the footsteps of his particular idol— former Michigan gymnast Ed Cole. Cole was a longtime friend of Erwin's family, and a large part of Erwin's reason for coming to Michigan. He was also a big part of Erwin's success.

"Ed was an inspiration and an idol for me," Erwin told the *Daily*. "He still comes around to most of our home meets to watch and make suggestions."

His teammates John Hamilton and Fred Sanders—the rest of the Big Three—deserved some credit too.

"I know I wouldn't be as good as I am if I didn't have to work so hard just to keep up with Fred and John," Erwin said.

Michigan pulled off a close win against Wisconsin, despite the Badgers grabbing five firsts, then beat Michigan State in front of 2,000 fans for a perfect Big Ten record. The second-to-last meet of the season would be powerhouse Iowa; and though the Wolverines would face Indiana after that, everyone knew that to win against Iowa would be to win the Big Ten team title, now that the conference meet barely mattered.

The *Daily* declared, "It's Armageddon in stretch pants," noting both teams' undefeated records. To add to the drama, three years earlier in 1964, Iowa had snapped Michigan's three-year dual-meet winning streak.

Newt wasn't cocky, but he wasn't intimidated either by Iowa, whose star, Glenn Gailis, could do fingertip handstands among other impressive feats.

"They have the headliners," he allowed, "but we have a fifteen-man team." *The team, the team, the team* may have become the football team's slogan officially, but Newt made it apply to men's gymnastics as well. It may have been the only similarity between the ebullient Newt and the gruff Bo Schembechler (other than winning, naturally).

It was that balance that spelled victory for Michigan, with an overflow crowd of 3,000 on hand in the IM Building. People were literally hanging from the venerable building's rafters. While Gailis won four firsts including the all-around title, Michigan beat the Hawkeyes 64 ½-53 ½. Art Baessler, in the best performance of his career to date, beat out Gailis for first place on the side horse, while Michigan's floor and trampoline squads both swept the top three. On floor, the Fullers, occasionally referred to now as "Chip and Flip," added to their exact likeness by tying for first place. Now, Michigan would have to lose to Indiana—a near impossibility—to end up in a tie with Iowa for the title. To make Newt's achievement even more improbable, he did it all with specialists. Each competition for a first place spot meant points for the team: three for first, two for second, one for third. Without a single all-arounder, that meant Michigan spotted every opponent six points before the meet even began—the other team could put up its most inept three all-arounders, and they would still finish first, second and third.

The meet with Indiana ended up snowed out by the worst storm of the winter, giving Michigan the title outright. Amazingly, every winter team at the University had gone undefeated; but the gymnastics team was the first to sew up its conference title.

There were still more challenges left before the NCAA championships, however. First, Michigan's individual stars competed against the best of their conference for Big Ten event titles. Gary Erwin brought home Michigan's only title, on trampoline. Interestingly, had the Big Ten meet determined the champion rather than the regular season record, Iowa would have broken Michigan's dynastic streak.

And now, the NCAA was experimenting with a system of regionals. Like the basketball tournament, the objective was to reduce the NCAA championship to only two teams. Michigan first had to take on the Salukis of Southern Illinois, the defending NCAA champs. After that they would probably face Penn State in the second regional before NCAAs …

But at the first regional, in Iowa City, Southern Illinois pulled off a narrow victory, beating Michigan by just one and a half points. Newt had warned beforehand that vault might be a key to the meet, and it was—Southern Illinois swept the event to erase its deficit and eliminate the Wolverines as a team. Thirteen Michigan gymnasts would go through to the inter-regional in State College; the top six competitors on each event from that meet would earn the right to compete for individual titles at NCAAs. But the team, which as an entity had been so important to Michigan's success, was broken up. As any team-sport athlete can tell you, there is an excitement and a rush in competing for something larger than yourself that you just can't get when competing as an individual. Newt never could be an individualist—true, he saw all his athletes as individuals and treated them according to their specific personalities, but in competition, the team was of paramount importance. And under the influence of their coach, the Wolverines placed the same emphasis on team over single gymnast. The only time it could hurt them was when the team was broken up, through the odd system of regionals.

Eight Wolverines qualified, but only five stood a good chance of placing high on their events: the bouncing trio, Erwin, Hamilton and Sanders, in their last hurrah; Mike Henderson on floor; and Rich Blanton on the rings. While Penn State whipped the University of Washington for the national title, Michigan's bouncers moved on to the final, though all of them were competing with nagging injuries. Henderson had finished a "heartbreaking seventh," one place out of qualifying to the finals.

There was more heartbreak waiting. In the finals, Erwin stepped on a spring, forcing him to stop his routine. With that huge deduction, he fell to sixth—and last—place. A first-time champion was crowned in every event.

In the drive for "Six in '66," Newt's squad boasted eight juniors and experienced gymnasts on six of seven events. And a youngster named Wayne Miller, who showed great promise on the trampoline, would gain sophomore status (and therefore, eligibility) in January, just in time for the gymnastics season. In December, Michigan got a glimpse of the future, as Miller and Dave Jacobs, who wouldn't become a sophomore for another year, placed first and third on trampoline in the Midwest Open. And over Christmas break, they topped the podium in a trampoline-only competition in Florida.

Miller originally wanted to be a football player, but like many high schoolers, as a freshman he was cut from the team. The school diving coach alertly put him on a trampoline to distract him, and a love affair was born. In 1963, as a high school junior, he won both the junior and senior national men's titles on trampoline, in addition to the junior men's diving championship. He even invented his own trampoline skill (aptly named the Miller)—a double backflip with a triple twist. And luckily for Newt, the young bouncer held the coach in as high esteem as he held his beloved trampoline.

"Not only is Coach Loken the great promoter that most people know him as, he's one of the greatest coaching coaches in the country," Miller told the *Daily*. Newt put the same boundless energy into both promoting Michigan gymnastics and coaching the gymnasts—clearly, it was paying off in notoriety.

By now, according to the *Daily*, Michigan's yearly Big Ten title was a tradition on par with motherhood, apple pie and democracy. And the Wolverines started the year off right, trouncing Ohio State in the season-opener. A new scoring system was in place—instead of earning points for top placements on events, the top three scores for each team on every event would be added together for the team total.

A subsequent thrashing of Eastern Michigan convinced *Daily* writers that the '66 team was "capable of making the other conference squads look somewhat less agile than Bullwinkle." Even at such an early date, the Wolverines had posted an average score of 8.85. With Newt aiming for a top-notch, 90% hit percentage—where nine of every ten routines would be completed without a major mistake, form break or fall—it was a good place to start.

When the yearly clash with the Illini rolled around in 1966, Michigan had just beaten Iowa, another tough rival. The Illinois-Michigan meet was to be shown on TV in Illinois, and the team was so popular on the Michigan campus that a screen was set up in the IM Building so fans could watch the broadcast in the confines of their home gym. Illinois, always a powerhouse because of the great high school gymnastics teams in the state, possessed an unbeaten record, just like Michigan. But Newt was confident in his boys' ability—that would provide all the luck Michigan would need.

"Depend on the rabbit's foot if you will," he teased a *Daily* writer, offering one of his many and often-used sayings, "but remember, it didn't work for the rabbit."

A crowd of 3,200 packed Illinois' arena the next night for what Charlie Pond would call "the greatest dual meet I've ever seen." Though the Fuller twins went one-two on floor, with Art

Baessler winning side horse and Miller trampoline, Illinois had a tiny .65 lead going into high bar—which it swept. Then the Illini took first on vault, with the Fullers and Miller crashing home just behind. After parallel bars, Michigan had taken the lead by just one tenth. Only a spectacular showing by the rings team, led by event-winner Rich Blanton, secured the 191.20-190.15 victory for Michigan.

Newt could barely contain himself, declaring paradoxically that he'd like to "single out the whole team for the job they did tonight." It was a very Newt thing to say. Michigan wasn't carried by a single individual, but by its collective strength and determination. And Newt wasn't about to miss a chance to emphasize that. But he also maintained a strong respect for his opponents, as well as the overarching appreciation for his sport that had always been part of him.

Like Pete Rose reveling in the classic Game 6 of the 1975 World Series—which his team lost in extra innings on Carlton Fisk's dramatic home run—even with his competitive nature, Newt couldn't help but appreciate the epic battle between the teams. "It was a shame that one team had to lose," he said.

After another classic episode in the Michigan-Illinois rivalry, only one more regular season test remained: Michigan State. Again, the Wolverines would take to the road. Both teams had 6-0 records and had posted scores above 190. Adding fuel to Michigan's fire, George Szypula was already thinking about the postseason, acting as if beating the Wolverines was a given. Newt, on the other hand, warned his boys against getting complacent, urging them to respect their archrivals.

Unfortunately for Michigan, it was Szypula's strategy that seemed to work. The Spartans handed the Wolverines their first loss, snapping a three-year, sixteen-meet win streak. Led by their limping but game star, Phil Curzi, State won five of the seven events and shared in a sixth first place. Now, if the Wolverines hoped to keep their Big Ten streak alive, they'd have to finish at least one place ahead of the Spartans in the conference meet. Once Iowa was factored in, the new formula seemed moot—to win the Big Ten championship, Michigan would have to win the Big Ten meet.

The biggest meet of the season came down to Michigan and Michigan State, once Illinois faltered. In the early afternoon, thanks especially to a dominant performance on trampoline, Michigan built a three-point lead, with high bar, parallel bars and still rings yet to go. In the end, Michigan won the title by two full points.

Ed Gunny of Michigan State maintained stoutly that it didn't matter. "Whether we win or lose isn't important," he said. "We have already had our moment of glory when we beat Michigan last week."

Miller brought home Michigan's only title, with four of his teammates grabbing seconds. Dave Jacobs, who would join him in varsity competition the following year, gave all the credit to Newt.

"We owe this championship to Newt's way of coaching," he said. Rather than focusing on winning, Newt concentrated on improving his gymnasts' proficiency and hit percentage. If they all hit, he knew that would be good enough for victory.

Before the rest of the team headed for regionals, Miller and Jacobs served notice that they were far more than short-lived sensations. Traveling together to the World Trampoline Championships, Miller earned the world title and, along with Jacobs, the world synchronized title.

Two weeks later at regionals in Wheaton, Illinois, Michigan managed a last-minute comeback to grab the third qualifying spot to NCAAs. Though they had trouble getting started, in the evening session the Wolverines roared back to finish less than a point behind second-place Michigan State. Ten of the fifteen Michigan competitors qualified as individuals to nationals, with

Miller winning trampoline and Vander Voort parallel bars. It was the final big highlight of the year.

Michigan finished fifth in the 1966 NCAA championships, held at Penn State, with Southern Illinois adding another title to its collection. Only Miller was able to bring home an event win; Newt wondered if perhaps the pressure had finally gotten to his seemingly impervious boys. It had been a long, arduous season, after all. But once again, Michigan owned the Big Ten title, and it was time to go for seven in '67.

But before the 1967 season could begin, another tragedy struck the Loken family. Always looking for more ways to promote gymnastics, as well as see the latest up-and-comers, Newt conducted numerous gymnastics clinics throughout the state during the summer of 1966. One day in August 1966, while he was away on one of his trips, he left Dorothy and Lani to close up the Huron Valley Swim Club.

At about 9:30 p.m., after closing up, Dorothy and Lani were driving home. They came to an intersection where a car was stationary in the opposite lane, waiting for them to pass so that it could turn onto an adjacent street. Just as the Lokens reached the intersection, a drunk driver rear-ended the stationary car, forcing it into the Lokens' path.

Luckily, Lani was restrained by her seatbelt and only suffered a broken nose. But Dorothy didn't fare as well. With no seatbelt on, Dorothy was seriously injured when her head was propelled through the windshield. She suffered many facial lacerations, requiring over fifty stitches.

Newt rushed to Dorothy's bedside immediately. This was the second time that the Loken family had been severely affected by a car accident. Once again, Newt was faced with the daunting task of dividing his time and energy between the needs of preparing his team for a winning season and the needs of his family.

Chapter 13

Thwarted by Technicalities

For the 1967 season, the team expected to begin competition in the new University Events Building that Athletic Director Fritz Crisler was constructing next to Michigan Stadium. Though the atmosphere in the IM Building's basketball court-cum-gymnastics arena could be thrilling, the space had long been too small. Newt was never one to complain about anything, but a new competition space had to have excited him beyond measure. It would be a huge step up for his team and the sport—they'd really be hitting the big time, competing under the bright lights in front of far more people than could ever hope to fit in the IM Building. It couldn't hurt with recruiting, either.

By the start of the 1966-67 school year, however, the new arena had been under construction for a full calendar year. Finding the site alone had eaten up seven months, and now Crisler was trying to raise an additional $55 million. The project, the *Daily* noted, was costing each student twelve dollars per year in athletic coupons. The crews, in order to have the facility ready for the winter season, planned to ignore such minor details as landscaping, blacktopping the parking lot, finishing two extra locker rooms, a lounge and trophy cases. However, even finding enough manpower soon became a concern, as the workers went on strike; and then one of the 120-ton roof trusses snapped the cable holding it and sliced through the concrete wall below, causing massive damage. A May total-completion date was announced.

Newt, as ever, was consumed by gymnastics. He'd spent the summer of 1966 coaching at the U.S. Olympic Development Clinic at Penn State, alongside Penn State's Gene Wettstone, Temple's Carl Patterson and World Games head coach Abie Grossfeld. It was a coach's dream, and obviously open only to the very best in the coaching ranks. Attendees were a mixture of Pan-Am trainees and World Games gymnasts—and they included Danny Millman.

Millman, eventual author of *The Way of the Peaceful Warrior,* was then just a rising junior and had not yet suffered the injury that would lead to his book. The injury, which seemed career-ending at the time, turned out to be the key to Millman's life after gymnastics. When he couldn't participate in his sport, he met a mysterious teacher he nicknamed Socrates, who helped him learn the life lessons he hadn't been able to absorb as an active gymnast. Millman's experiences, both in book and movie form, have inspired millions.

Millman loved the experience of training under Newt, whose gracious nature he'd noticed when he narrowly beat Newt's protégé, Gary Erwin, in the first World Trampoline Championship in 1964.

"I recall Newt's frequent and enthusiastic reminders to 'Fire up!'" Millman remembered. "And indeed, he did put a fire under us—he was one of those coaches you wanted to please and surprise with a new skill. His enthusiasm was infectious, and his caring and skill obvious."

Millman certainly surprised Newt one day at the clinic. In the mid-sixties, safety equipment wasn't even close to what it is today. At most, it consisted of an extra horsehair mat, perhaps a safety belt and several spotters. The first time a gymnast attempted a trick sans safety belt, the spotters might number six or more.

Millman had been visualizing a full-twisting double flyaway (flip) dismount from high bar for a long time. He hadn't actually practiced it in a physical sense—so when he asked just Newt and Abie Grossfeld, to spot him on his first attempt, you can excuse the coach for assuming Millman wasn't about to throw anything risky. Was Newt ever shocked!

"It worked out well," Millman said, "and I got a secret thrill out of his expression, since he didn't know me or my training style all that well and didn't know what to expect from me as he bravely stood under the bar waiting for whatever might happen."

For his part, Newt's eyes still widen with the memory of his shock. He could barely believe it when, after successfully completing the skill, Millman informed him that he'd never actually done a full-twisting double flyaway before.

Back in Michigan, the highly promising bouncer, Dave Jacobs, was set to be the shining star of the sophomore class. On any other team, he'd immediately have been the No. 1 trampoline man; but any other team didn't have Wayne Miller. Jacobs, in fact, had finished second to Miller by just .05 points at the U.S. World Cup Trials, and both were looking forward to representing their country at the June World Championships in London. Like Newt's first big-time trampoline champion, Tex Buchanan, Jacobs began his bouncing career in Amarillo, Texas. As a high school sophomore, he joined Nard's Trampolining Club, which had already produced a few talented Wolverines. He met former Wolverine Ed Cole at the 1964 National Amateur Athletic Union (NAAU) championships. Cole, at that time, was a graduate student, and quickly took the talented youngster under his wing, serving as his coach starting in 1965.

Between them, Jacobs and Miller held every major trampoline title in the world. Jacobs described their relationship as "the best of friends." While the description may have been generous, as later in their careers their relationship was so fractious that they couldn't practice at the same time, who better to push a world-class trampolinist to his limit than another athlete of his caliber?

Beyond those two, Newt's team was as full of rich characters as ever, including a sophomore named Tim Mousseau. As an eighth grader in Alpena, he'd fallen across the tracks of the New York Central railroad, and a multi-ton carrier crushed his legs at knee level. Despite losing both lower legs, in high school Mousseau participated with great success in gymnastics, winning the Michigan State parallel bar and rings titles as a senior. Newt actively recruited him for the Wolverines. Though he'd always competed as a fully-abled gymnast, Newt knew a bit about using the force of your own personality and staunch determination to succeed in a tough situation. Mousseau's lookout on life—to succeed at what he loved despite his handicap—was undoubtedly very appealing. And with a guy like that in the gym, driving himself to get better every day, the entire team would have a source of inspiration, and maybe a little kick in the pants. When a teammate with no legs is trying his hardest to improve his parallel bars routine, what right has anyone else to slack off the smallest bit?

Obviously, Mousseau's one big problem was dismounts.

"I simply tell [the judges] to judge his performance as they see it, and to credit him with points that are in line with the proficiency of his routine," Newt said.

The seniors were led by the unflappable captain, Gary Vander Voort. Fellow senior Chris Vanden Broek starred with Vander Voort on high bar—which Vanden Broek loved—and side horse—which he professed to despise. Believing himself to be a student first and a gymnast second, he had compiled a 3.6 GPA in the College of Engineering in addition to his solid record as a Wolverine. In 1966, he finished sixth on high bar at Big Tens; in '67, he thought he might have a shot at the event crown.

"One of the reasons I've enjoyed the high bar is that it gives me the feeling of flying," Vanden Broek said. And much of the talented senior's motivation came from his coach.

"The coach's spirit is unbelievable," Vanden Broek told the *Daily*, marveling at Newt's seemingly endless energy. "He is always fired up, and this drive and determination can't help but rub off. … I've never met a guy quite like him."

Vanden Broek, as a senior at Ann Arbor High, won state titles on the high bar, side horse and in the all-around, snagging the last title away from his future teammate and fellow senior, Cliff Chilvers. Chilvers almost ended up a high school dropout as a sophomore. He was ready to quit—that is, until "a friend of mine convinced me to go out for the gymnastics team. Without gymnastics, I probably would have dropped out then." He wasn't sure if he wanted to go to college, but Newt was sure he wanted Chilvers on his team.

"Nobody pushed me, but Coach Loken spurred me on to stay in school," Chilvers said. "He convinced me that Michigan was a good place to go."

The sturdy ring man struggled to get through his classes every year, even as he made impossible feats on rings look easy. But Newt was always there, ready to support Chilvers whenever he needed it.

"Newt has been like a father to me," Chilvers told the *Daily*. "All through the four years I have been here, he has been a source of scholastic and personal advice, which I feel has helped me greatly. If I was having trouble, Newt would understand."

Losing just four gymnasts to graduation and returning seven seniors and five juniors, Newt expected a four-team race in the Big Ten. Illinois, Michigan's old rival, returned all its gymnasts from 1966 and gained a good crop of sophomores; Michigan State was losing only Phil Curzi; and Iowa, quickly replacing Illinois as Michigan's fiercest rival, was tabbed Newt's "team to beat."

Wayne Miller, Newt's established bouncer, had won all six possible titles for American trampolinists: the Midwest Open, Big Ten, NCAA, NAAU, Schuster Cup and of course, the world title. In November, he was invited to an international trampoline meet in Kiel, West Germany—where, unsurprisingly, he won another title. For the second straight year, Miller was named the Southern Amateur Athlete of the Year by the Southern AAU board. He and Jacobs, by wide consensus, were the two best bouncers in the United States. With trampoline as its biggest strength, the team wasn't overly worried about its apparent weakness on parallel bars.

Newt had another new trick up his sleeve as well—a trusty video recorder. He may have been the first gymnastics coach ever to record his charges' routines in order to show them exactly where they were making mistakes. Today, video cameras are familiar sights in nearly every sport. Athletes think nothing of studying themselves repeatedly on a television screen. Newt was one of the first to use video recording to its full advantage, and told the *Daily* it would "lead to a smoother and more precise routine." His was a medical surplus machine.

Michigan had a strong showing at the season-opening Midwest Open in Chicago, with Jacobs taking the trampoline title—the eleventh year in a row a Wolverine had done so. But the team returned from the winter holidays looking mediocre in a win over Indiana. The *Daily*'s story that weekend was written by Daniel Okrent, who would later become the first public editor of the *New York Times*. The writing was great—the meet was not. For each positive, Okrent noted, there was at least one negative and usually more, with the most shocking one coming from Wayne Miller. Miller, the champion of champions, turned in an astonishingly bad performance, missing the center of the trampoline repeatedly and eventually having to stop his routine because he'd bounced too close to the edge. Luckily for Michigan—this would be another year where the conference dual meet record would play a part in determining the Big Ten champion, and Indiana put up little resistance. Next up, though, was Illinois—and with a win against the Illini, Newt would have his hundredth victory as Michigan's head coach.

Illinois' Charlie Pond, of course, believed his team was better in every event, with its top-notch sophomores and seven returning lettermen. In Illinois' "ancient, orange-bricked" Old Men's Gym in front of nine hundred fans, the Wolverines set out to prove him wrong and push their coach to the century mark. The meet turned out to be a classic, a hundredth victory for the ages.

Illinois grabbed the lead at the start with vault, but Michigan quickly reeled off three event wins on floor exercise, side horse and trampoline. Phip and Chip went one-two on floor, putting Michigan up by six tenths; then Baessler and Geddes got second and third on horse to double the lead. Jacobs beat out Miller for trampoline, and Michigan was up by one and a half points.

Dave Weir, one of the *Daily* writers covering the meet, felt the tension in the arena and immediately "added scorekeeping and rooting to his usual duties," later marveling at the excitement which "reached a feverish pitch during the final two events."

Illinois managed to win two of the final three events. On high bar, the Wolverines needed the above-average sets it got from Gary Vander Voort, Mike Sasich and Chris Vanden Broek just to keep an eight-tenth lead. Tim Mousseau was on the bench, having been in a car accident before the season in which he broke his forearm and developed calcium deposits in his elbow. Weir overheard him predict that if his team had the lead going into the last event of the night, rings, it would win. Heading in, the Wolverines were clinging to .125 lead. To give a sense of perspective, what separated the teams was the equivalent of one gymnast bending his knees, or failing to point his toes, on a single skill.

Of the six competitors on still rings, five earned scores above

9.00. Fortunately for Michigan, Rich Kenney and Cliff Chilvers were two of the three tied for first place.

"We are overjoyed to have won this one," a breathless Newt said afterward of the 190.825-190.70 win. "It was a real thriller." Fittingly, he also called it a "fantastic team effort." It was a typical Michigan win, with every gymnast making a key contribution, just the way Newt wanted.

After the Illinois meet, the Wolverines didn't get a crack at top competition again until Wednesday, February 15—nearly a month later. Conference schedule-makers, recognizing the hype that could be generated for the Michigan-Michigan State meet, pushed the combat later in the season to create even more suspense. In the meantime, Michigan rolled over Western Michigan's fledgling team, had a meet with UIC cancelled due to two feet of snow and executed a sloppy victory over Eastern Michigan.

And now Jacobs and Miller were trading places on the injured list with sprained ankles. Just as Jacobs was recovering from his first, single sprain, Miller landed badly on the floor doing a back somersault and ended up in the University Hospital with two sprained ankles. When the Eastern Michigan meet rolled around, Jacobs' ankle wasn't responding to treatment and had to be shot full of cortisone so he'd be ready to take on the Spartans. Miller now seemed questionable for the February 25 meet against powerful Iowa. Without those two, Michigan was losing one to two points off its total before each meet even began. Tim Mousseau provided one of the few bright spots. "[T]he greatest applause of each meet is saved for Tim Mousseau," the *Daily* reported. "There is no one that cannot say good things about him."

Some coaches might have had their hands full keeping their team from falling apart in the face of such injuries to its stars. But Newt was well practiced in the art of infectious optimism. And all his efforts from the time of the Illinois meet were directed at this clash with the Spartans.

By the day of the Michigan State meet, Jacobs was ready to get back in lineup. His partner in crime, Wayne Miller, was not. Both teams were keyed up for the big confrontation, with the Spartans especially angry after absorbing their first conference loss of the season to Illinois.

"Michigan has established a dynasty in Big Ten gymnastics, and they intend to keep it that way," the *Daily* had said back in January, after the Illinois meet. With conference dual-meet records factoring into the Big Ten title, if Michigan lost to the Spartans, it could completely dash the hopes for "Seven in '67." Keep that undefeated record—matched by no other team in the Big Ten at that point—and the conference championship would be theirs to lose.

The two rivals each put on extraordinary performances, both posting scores over 190. Michigan built up a lead after high bar, but Michigan State came back on parallel bars and still rings. And while the Spartans looked consistently solid all night, Michigan suffered shaky routines on vault, side horse and floor. Jacobs, at least, won trampoline with a 9.70; but his team lost 190.80-190.425—less than four tenths of a point. It was Michigan's first home loss in six years and left Jacobs shaking his head and muttering to himself: "Four tenths of a point ..."

And now, after the long wait for the big dual meets, there was no time to rest. The Iowa meet was fast approaching—there would be no weeks-long lead-up to this one. Senior Art Baessler knew it was time for someone to step up.

A Chicago native, Baessler had turned to gymnastics seriously when he was cut from the freshman football team in high school. He'd been interested since he began working out at a YMCA as a five-year-old. Soon, Newt came calling. Baessler said, "Coach Loken's recruiting pitch was so appealing that I could hardly turn him down." Newt would look after him like a second father (this part always appealed to the parents); Baessler would be joining a team with a proven track record of success; he would receive a world-class education; and the road to success would be *fun*. Baessler did turn down a scholarship at Iowa—even though there was none offered at Michigan. From being an all-arounder, Newt had shaped Baessler into a side horse specialist. Baessler loved Michigan, the campus, the town of Ann Arbor—everything.

"After eight years of work and competition," he reflected, "I think all of us seniors will die a little at the end of the season."

So with his team looking glum and the Iowa meet speeding towards them, Baessler gathered his teammates together for a talk.

Slamming his fist on a handy table, he barked, "We want to win this meet against Iowa more than anything. For the seniors on this squad, this next week and a half is the most important period in our gymnastic careers. We've got a streak going in winning the last six Big Ten crowns, and we're not about to let the seventh one get away." He and everyone else knew full well that if Michigan should lose to Iowa, not only would the Wolverines have to finish first at the conference meet, Iowa would have to finish no higher than fourth. The likelihood of that was about as good as a Michigan winter without snow.

Finally, the big day came, and the largest crowd in Michigan gymnastics history squeezed into the big gym at the IM Building. Somehow a Michigan pep band wedged its way in too, ratcheting up the palpable excitement. The rivalry between the Wolverines and Hawkeyes was so tense and heated that Ohio State's presence at the meet was reduced to a mere footnote. (The Buckeyes finished more than thirty points behind Iowa and Michigan.)

Michigan began by sweeping vault and floor exercise, thanks in large part to the Fuller twins (who, naturally, split the event titles). Iowa pulled ahead narrowly on side horse, but Jacobs, Miller, Zadel and Vic Conant on trampoline put Michigan in the lead again. Then it was time to hang on.

At one point, after Vander Voort posted a disappointing 8.55

score on high bar, even Newt's irrepressible optimism took a hit. "Well, there goes the meet," he muttered. Even Newt wasn't immune to the tension. But by the final event, no one was sure what to think. Michigan entered still rings with a tiny lead of .075. The performances from Rich Kenney, Vander Voort and Chilvers were just good enough—by the tiniest of margins.

When Michigan was announced the victor, 188.55-188.525, the gymnasts, pep band and overwrought crowd went ballistic. It was the closest meet in Michigan history, which featured quite a few close contests. Newt, of course, took up temporary residence on Cloud Nine. Once again, his team had pulled together and pulled out the win. Now Michigan and Iowa, the two giants of the Big Ten, had matching 6-1 dual records. The winner of the conference meet would win the Big Ten title (begging the question of why dual meets needed to be factored in at all). And the 1967 Big Tens were in Iowa City.

Sam Bailie, Iowa's head coach, felt his team had the best shot for the title, competing at home. Michigan State and Illinois had to be given a passing glance—it was possible they could tie for the title, under the right circumstances—but everyone's eyes were on Michigan and Iowa. Everyone was expecting another close meet going right down to the wire.

Everyone in the gymnastics world, that is. Apparently, the Iowa campus didn't get the memo. Big Ten team finals began at 11:00 in the morning on a Friday, with little buildup and during classes. Many students thought the competition was only the preliminaries. Whatever the excuse, one *Daily* writer reported an unofficial count of just thirty-seven people watching the two powerhouses duke it out for Big Ten supremacy.

Michigan seemed to be well on its way to that seventh straight title. In the early session, the Wolverines built up a tidy lead. The trampoline squad put on a marvelous showing, with Jacobs, Miller, Conant and Zadel taking four of the top five spots. After a half-hour break so the high bar, still rings and parallel bars could be set up, the gymnasts returned to finish the battle. The Wolverines survived high bar and the puzzlingly low scores they received, hanging on to a two-and-a-half point lead. But on the final two events, "the roof caved in."

In a shocking late surge, Iowa caught and surpassed Michigan on still rings and parallel bars and won the title going away, 187.05-184.87. Michigan's reign over the Big Ten, for now, was over. It was the first time since finally conquering Illinois that Newt's Wolverines had failed to come home with the title. It must have been a crushing feeling, to stand there knowing that the Wolverines would have to hand off the trophy that had lived in Ann Arbor for six years. But Newt didn't have too much time to dwell on Big Tens.

The season wasn't over, and Michigan was still going to the regionals, where a third place finish at least was necessary to push them on to NCAAs. This time, there would be no tiny crowd of thirty-seven people watching. The Mid-East Gymnastics Regional in Wheaton, Illinois, would feature Iowa, Michigan, Michigan State, Illinois and SIU. Carbondale, Illinois, home of the Southern Illinois University Salukis, was crazy for gymnastics. So crazy, in fact, that the team could charge admission and still draw crowds of four thousand people. Many of them would be making the trip to regionals. Newt, once again, was "bubbling over with optimism" and convinced his boys could get into the top three. Big Tens may have been a great disappointment, but no one bounced back faster than Newt.

He was right. Though SIU, the favorite to win it all, won easily, Michigan finished third, with Iowa only breaking the second-place tie on the final event, still rings. Jacobs turned in his best floor exercise showing all year, but the Wolverines ran into trouble on side horse, high bar and parallel bars. No team of Newt's had ever given up in the face of adversity, though, and this wouldn't be the first. Despite the rough patches, Michigan was going to NCAAs. The top teams in the country headed for Carbondale.

The meet was dominated by the three Mid-East teams. Michigan was brilliant, getting comeback performances from gymnasts who'd performed badly at Big Tens and the solid showings it had come to expect from athletes like Jacobs and Miller. Newt never gave up on his athletes, so they never gave up on themselves or their teammates. Vander Voort was tremendous in his final team meet; Fred Rodney rebounded from Big Tens by excelling on vault and then parallel bars, just as Michigan was trying to hold Iowa off. The Wolverines posted the best team scores on trampoline and floor exercise, and at the dinner break, led the entire field.

Eventually, SIU topped the Wolverines with a 189.55, but Michigan came in an excellent second with a 187.40 score, earning a measure of revenge on Iowa by beating out the third-place Hawkeyes by half a point. Jacobs, just a sophomore, earned an NCAA title on trampoline, narrowly beating out his teammate Wayne Miller. To Newt's unbridled glee, on floor exercise, an event Jacobs had only begun doing when Miller sprained his ankles, the sophomore brought home another first-place trophy! It was not only a credit to Jacobs' amazing ability but also to Newt's excellent coaching (though of course, he'd never take the credit). Even losing the Fuller twins, Vander Voort, Vanden Broek, Baessler and Chilvers, the Wolverines looked as though their Big Ten dynasty was merely on a brief hiatus.

Then in the spring of 1967, the NCAA began campaigning to eliminate the trampoline from championship competition. The *Daily* called it a "stinging blow" and noted that if the NCAA's recommendation that the event be stricken from dual meets as well was followed, it "could practically snuff out any Wolverine title plans." Additionally, the NCAA put the "economy rule" into effect—another hindrance for Newt. The rule stated that a coach could use only twelve men in a meet "for reasons of economy." Previously, with the formula of four men competing and three scores counting on each of seven events, one team could conceivably use twenty-eight different gymnasts. While Newt never used that many, his teams up to this point had been structured to succeed with specialists, using eighteen or nineteen men in a meet. That fit with his tendency to give everyone a chance at competing, whenever possible. Now, the premium would be on all-around gymnasts—great for looking toward the Olympics, but terrible for Michigan's prospects.

Also, allegedly in the interests of "economy," the NCAA eliminated the regional competitions of the past two years. Now, only the conference champions and top independents would advance to the national championships. With Iowa and Michigan State losing very little to graduation, Newt admitted that Michigan might end up completely shut out of the biggest postseason meet.

The innovative coach would have to switch up nearly everything he'd been doing. Without trampoline, Michigan would lose the event in which it was most dominant; Newt would have to focus on improving the other six through coaching and recruitment. He'd also have to focus more on recruiting the top all-arounders in the country, instead of trying to draw the best gymnasts on each event. It might produce a more well-rounded group of gymnasts, but at least for a while, the skill level on specific events might drop. And Newt would not be able to give as many athletes the indescribable feeling of competing with the block M on their chests. It had to hurt.

The Rules Committee added an ironic touch. After the

attempt to eliminate trampoline for being "too dangerous" failed—for 1967, at least—the Committee devalued trampoline skills. Therefore, gymnasts would have to do more difficult (and by the Committee's own reasoning, more dangerous) skills to receive the same scores they'd gotten with easier routines in 1967.

Sid Jensen, a talented Canadian sophomore, was the team's only real all-arounder. While he was certainly an excellent competitor—he was the only Canadian gymnast allowed to compete for his country in the pre-Olympics at Mexico City the previous summer—he couldn't do it alone. Fred Rodney was pressed into service on all events, but there were still specialists all over. Wayne Miller, Dave Jacobs and their newest cohort, sophomore "prodigy" George Huntzicker, were arguably the three best bouncers in the world; but with the twelve-man limit, it was unlikely that all three could ever compete at the same time. Completely independent of the limit, they couldn't even practice together. Despite Jacobs' words about him and Miller being best friends, Newt had to juggle the three prickly champions' training times so that only one was in the gym at any given time. As always, he was willing to do whatever it took to help his athletes, and by extension the team, to succeed. When you brought in the very best, you had to be ready to deal with their ultra-competitive personalities.

A local boy, the newcomer Huntzicker wasn't one to mince words or play down his own prowess. About his powerful teammates, Miller and Jacobs, Huntzicker confidently said, "I personally feel that I'm better than either of them." Later, in Tucson, he would back up his brash statement, finishing first while Miller and Jacobs tied for second. Despite the truth of his boasts (as Dizzy Dean said, "It ain't bragging if you can back it up"), they couldn't have helped his relationship with Miller and Jacobs.

"They were pistols, oh boy," Newt remembered of his three champion bouncers. "They literally hated each other because they were competitors. George Huntzicker, Wayne Miller and Dave Jacobs. They couldn't bounce together, because each one was telling the other what was wrong. They'd think the others didn't know what they were talking about, so they asked for private sessions with me. So I had Dave Jacobs in there at 3:00, and then around 4:30 I'd have Wayne Miller come in, and then at night, if I wasn't teaching dancing classes, at 6:00, George Huntzicker would come in."

Ron Rapper was the third up and coming sophomore star. Newt had begun recruiting him as a high school sophomore, after he pulled off a surprise victory in the state parallel bars championship. Rapper had only begun gymnastics the year before, when a gym teacher promised an automatic A to any student who was able to perform a handstand by the end of the semester. A native of Skokie, Illinois, Rapper had the good fortune to be born into the hotbed of high school gymnastics. Once he'd mastered a handstand, the gymnastics coach asked him to try out for the school team. And from the start, despite the widespread emphasis on all-around competition, Rapper was a parallel-bars specialist.

His signature skill became a nearly unbelievable one-armed handstand that started each routine. Most gymnasts, even today when skills previously thought impossible have become commonplace, can't hold a one-bar handstand for very long, much less a one-armed handstand. Newt still remembers Rapper's solidity on the skill with wonder. "You couldn't blow him over!"

Rapper modestly says that the reason he won the state title as a high school sophomore was because the big-name contenders missed their routines, and he didn't. But that title was enough to attract Newt's attention. Newt kept in touch with Rapper, following his progress and sending him newspaper clippings featuring the Michigan team. These letters were Newt's general method of recruiting, keeping a prospective Wolverine in the loop about everything going on with the team. Newt remembers his old rival George Szypula commenting, "Newt, goddamn, you were known as the best damn recruiting coach for writing letters. You wrote letters to the potential gymnasts every year!"

As with so many others, the system worked like a charm on Rapper. By the time he entered his senior year and the recruiting process began in earnest, picking a college wasn't a difficult decision.

"I made the commitment to come to Michigan, and it was one of the better decisions I have ever made in my life," Rapper said later. "I showed up on campus and was enamored with everything about this place."

And upon beginning varsity competition, Rapper crushed all comers on his chosen event. He'd choked once, trying to repeat as state parallel-bars champ as a high school junior; after that, nothing could rattle him. Not as long as all his superstitions were satisfied, anyway.

Every piece of Rapper's uniform had to be put on left-to-right—left pant leg, right pant leg; left sock, right sock. The socks had to be brand new for each meet. And just as the parallel bars rotation began, Rapper had to retreat to the locker room for a Hershey bar with nuts. He didn't watch anyone else compete—both to keep from psyching himself out, and because the habit just seemed to work. When he choked in high school, he'd forgotten his Hershey bar and had to call his parents to rush him a new one. Upon opening the bag they'd brought, he was horrified to find a Mr. Goodbar. (However, Rapper doesn't blame the candy bar snafu for his defeat.)

"In high school, our coach would give us a drink of honey and orange juice for energy before a meet," Rapper remembered. "Somehow, for me that transitioned into a candy bar. So then it became a Hershey bar with nuts."

By the time he got to Michigan, Rapper was buying Hershey bars with nuts by the case—never again would he have to deal with a Mr. Goodbar stand-in.

Newt's emphasis on hitting routines consistently, rather than just winning, could not have been tailored more perfectly to Rapper. Naturally confident, he knew that if he just hit his routine, there were few others that could touch him.

Newt's "family style" was also a big draw. Dave Jacobs often greeted him with a cheery, "Hi, Papa Newt," and Newt considered his boys just an extended part of his family. His wife and children were frequent visitors to the gym as well as spectators at the meets. Lani, now a freshman and a diver at Michigan, often helped her dad out with cheerleading clinics, noting, "It's terrible to have a father whose age is sometimes termed 'over the hill' and be able to wear you out. He can bounce around all day and I'm always exhausted by noon." Christine was now living in New York, after winning a national title with the Michigan water polo team, but Jon and "Newti," at twelve and ten years old, were still at home. Newt called them "little movers"—not much of a surprise, considering their heritage. The two boys often came to the gym to work out with the team, especially focusing on the trampoline. Like father, like sons.

When Jon was ten, Newt took him to the World Trampoline Championships in London, where he had the time of his life spending time with all the competitors. He came away from the experience inspired to take his bouncing even more seriously. This first visit to a foreign country also was the root of Jon's eventual love for travel and learning different languages. (He now lives in China.)

Newt Jr.'s focus on the trampoline would eventually earn him two state high school championships in the event. At Michigan, he naturally joined the trampoline team and competed in the Midwest Open in Chicago, as well as numerous exhibitions. (By then the trampoline team were competing separately from the gymnastics team.) As public interest in the trampoline waned, Newt Jr. joined the acrobatic cheer squad and continued the exhibitions with a new purpose: firing up the fans and rooting for the successful football team. He and former high-school teammate and gymnast, Norm Smit, became co-captains and helped to carry on the senior Newt's cheerleading tradition. Newt Jr. even created a new tradition, introducing end-zone handstand races against an opposing cheer squad member.

While his fellow coaches, like Charlie Pond and George Szypula, were known more for their fiery characters, Newt was known for his smile. Robin Wright, a *Daily* sports writer who would later become a prominent journalist for the *Washington Post*, noted that even in the heat of competition, Newt was "full of smiles and winks, and during a moment of pressure clap[ped] and yell[ed] like one of the fans." Newt's glee, and his accompanying enthusiasm for hard work, rubbed off on his gymnasts, who wanted nothing more than to win titles just for Newt. They'd even given him an award, which read, "To Dr. Newt Loken. Your ability as friend, advisor and coach to motivate individuals will have an everlasting effect upon the lives of all your team members."

Despite all the warm feelings in the gym, the season didn't start off well. After the now-annual drubbing of Marv Johnson's Eastern Michigan team, Michigan absorbed its worst conference loss in years from the Iowa Hawkeyes.

"Our boys were nervous and tight," Newt said afterward. "The routines didn't flow." Clearly the rivalry from the previous year wasn't over. Perhaps the Wolverines wanted to beat the Hawkeyes so badly that they got in their own way.

But the sophomore class provided reason to hope. Their very presence prevented 1968 from becoming a "rebuilding" year, after the loss of seven seniors. Newt even compared Jensen to his former stars Gil Larose and Richard Montpetit. Confidently, Newt said, "Any three of them should be able to win individual Big Ten championships, and they have a good chance of eventually taking an NCAA title." His words would prove prophetic.

Following a sloppy win over the Gophers, the Wolverines headed for East Lansing and Michigan State's packed field house. The Markley Fan Club, the team's most mysterious and rabid supporters, sponsored a bus to take Michigan fans to the meet, and State organizers expected a full house of 2,000. The Spartans boasted an unblemished conference record—and one more loss for the Wolverines would completely devastate their Big Ten title hopes. The Spartans were loaded with talent anyway, but they also had Dave Thor, their big all-arounder, returning from an injury.

"Just the name," Rapper recalled with a smile. "It was *Dave Thor*—you were waiting for the clouds to open up."

Even with Thor back in the lineup, the Spartans couldn't hold off a Michigan upset. The Wolverines knew they had it when they closed on State during pommel horse—the Spartans' best event. Trampoline, naturally, put Michigan ahead for good. On high bar, Coach Szypula had his guys pull out all the stops, performing their hardest tricks, but the gamble ended instead with falls—and a 188.60-187.05 Michigan victory. It was exactly the kind of stunt Newt would never pull; his teams always strove for consistency over flash, and once again, it was working. Finally, the fans could believe Michigan was in the same league as Iowa in the hunt for the conference title.

Now the Wolverines just had to get past Ohio State and Indiana (acknowledged patsies) before their final test, Illinois. Even with "cortisone and substitutes," Michigan managed to best them all. In the Illinois meet, with Jacobs only able to compete thanks to the cortisone shots, both teams posted season-high scores. Meanwhile, Iowa beat Michigan State to preserve its perfect 7-0 record. Now, the Big Ten championships loomed, with all three teams in the running.

In 1968, though, Big Tens were only the start of the drama. Michigan State swept through the conference championships, taking first with a 190.25 score. Michigan came in second, with

Iowa third. Having reversed their conference-record order, all three were declared tied for the Big Ten title. For Michigan State, it was the first title ever; for Michigan, the seventh in eight years; for Iowa, the second straight. In the last few rotations, the State fans cheered on the Wolverines, knowing that if they could push Iowa to third, it would give their own team a share of the title. Dave Jacobs successfully defended his trampoline crown, with Miller and Huntzicker close behind. Rapper snagged top honors on parallel bars. Once the three-way tie was clinched, Newt Loken, George Szypula and Sam Bailie all enjoyed a ride around the field house on their gymnasts' shoulders.

Just a few days later, the euphoria turned to uncertainty. The NCAA refused to allow all three Big Ten champions to attend the national championships—somehow, a single representative would have to be determined. The Big Ten decided a playoff, to be held at a neutral site, would be fairest. Before the season, the coaches had agreed that conference records and championship meet standings would matter equally, so a playoff seemed logical. Newt and Sam Bailie, of course, agreed with this. Feisty Szypula, however, did not. Regardless of the preseason agreement, he believed that by winning the championship meet, his Spartans had earned the right to represent the conference at NCAAs. Under NCAA guidelines, which stated only that the conference meet winner should go to nationals, he was right. But the Big Ten's preseason arrangement negated that.

After Big Ten commissioner Bill Reed announced the March 30 playoff, Szypula responded, "We are not going."

There was no real need to call his bluff. Without competing in the playoff, his team would have no chance at advancing to NCAAs.

"We fully expect Michigan State to attend the gymnastics playoff," Reed said a few days later, after the neutral site, George Williams College in Downer's Grove, Illinois, was determined.

Sure enough, when the big day came, Szypula declared that his boys would compete—under protest, of course, recognizing the great "injustice" to Michigan State.

The playoff, after all that fuss, came up a bit anticlimactic. Iowa, four men deep on every event, led the meet even after trampoline. If Michigan were to take a lead, it would have been on that event. In the end, Michigan State finished behind both its rivals, and Iowa headed off to the NCAAs in Tucson, Arizona.

The Spartan coach had to get in the last word, though.

"When last heard," the *Daily* reported, "Michigan State's George Szypula was screaming about the ring apparatus being deficient and the meet shouldn't count.

"As someone once said, 'If you can't beat 'em, make 'em feel guilty they won.'"

Newt assuredly didn't feel guilty, but he had to have been a bit worn out. Even the years spent trying to best Illinois hadn't been as drama-filled as these past two Big Ten championships.

In Tucson just a week later, over two hundred gymnasts vied for eight individual titles. Newt's top three bouncers, by virtue of their one-two-three finish in Big Tens, advanced to the trampoline competition, where they would compete against Cal's Danny Millman. Millman was completing the brilliant comeback that would eventually jump-start his writing career.

But even Millman's fantastic comeback-from-injury season wasn't enough to best Huntzicker. The sophomore who'd boasted of his prowess at the start of the year knew exactly what he was talking about. For the third straight year, a Michigan sophomore proved himself the best college trampolinist in the country. He was Newt's fifth national trampoline champion in the past six years. Rapper and Jensen tied for third on parallel bars. For such a promising sophomore class, only good fortune could lie ahead.

Chapter 14

The Demise of the Trampoline

Before the 1969 season, the Big Ten put another stumbling block in Michigan's way. The Wolverines were just too dominant at trampoline—so this year, in order to become the Big Ten representative to NCAAs, a team would have to have the best six-event total. It was conceivable that the Big Ten conference champion—the team with the best seven-event (including trampoline) total—might not move on to NCAAs.

Nonetheless, Newt was jovial about his squad. The rookies of the previous year were now juniors, with a full season of college competition under their belts, and graduation had left the roster nearly untouched. Iowa and Michigan State, on the other hand, had lost several seniors. Thanks to Newt's constant renewal by recruiting, now Michigan would add three sophomore all-arounders—Rick McCurdy, Murray Plotkin and Eddie Howard—to the competition squad, bolstering the '68 team's weak spot.

Plotkin's initial experience at Michigan showed just how skilled Newt was at his job. His first day at practice, Plotkin entered the gym and sat down on a stack of mats, watching. Soon, Newt plopped down next to him.

"Have any pet peeves?" the coach asked companionably.

Taken a bit off guard, Plotkin replied that he didn't. Newt began to chatter away, cheerfully detailing a long list of his own small complaints.

"But you know what my biggest pet peeve is?" Newt finally concluded. "Gymnasts coming into my gym not ready to work."

Plotkin left then, and never again entered the little gym in the IM Building unprepared. Later, he marveled at Newt's skill, managing to convey the criticism very effectively, yet without making Plotkin feel bad about himself or humiliated in front of his new teammates. Now, in his sophomore year, Plotkin, along with his two classmates, were ready to contribute in competition.

"At least I can't blame any poor showings this year on lack of depth," Newt said early on. But with trampoline eliminated entirely from NCAAs, predictions of a national title lacked the ring of certainty they might otherwise have had. If trampoline were still counted, a *Daily* writer noted, "The NCAA Championship Meet would have been a formality."

Newt called his 1969 boys "the best [team] I've had in years. … We're solid in nearly every event, and the biggest problem is deciding which performers to use."

This year the NCAA would allow two specialists per event, along with two all-arounders per team, making it possible to use fourteen gymnasts on the six events, instead of twelve on seven. Trampoline would remain an event for the Big Ten regular season, allowing Newt to use, conceivably, sixteen men in a meet. Nonetheless, because of the limitations Newt sometimes still had to go with the athlete who was better at more events, or at a particular event where Michigan was short, rather than choosing each event lineup based on the very best gymnasts on that specific apparatus.

The 1969 Wolverines were captained by bespectacled ring man Rich Kenney. A sculptor in his non-gymnastics life, he was an industrial design major who enjoyed working with free art forms. Kenney was all for anything new. He loved to invent completely new tricks on rings, meet new people and try new things. And always, he strove for perfection.

Kenney was yet another product of the excellent gymnastics programs blanketing the state of Illinois. He'd been in the sport since his freshman year of high school in Villa Park, and said, "Gymnastics is, for me, a scaled down version of life." When the *Daily* wanted to run a story on him in the paper, the team-oriented Kenney told the writer to call Newt beforehand, in case the coach thought the publicity might be detrimental to the rest of the squad.

Newt's unequivocal answer: "Nothing you could print about Rich Kenney could be detrimental to the team."

Chuck Froemming was Kenney's able sidekick on the rings, a gymnast who could compete even with the biggest of distractions.

"He was so cute," Newt said. "He came up to me at a big meet with Illinois or Iowa. He was so good, he always worked last. He said, 'Coach, do you mind if I work first in this dual meet this afternoon?' I said, 'Yes, I suppose it's okay, but why?'

"'Well, my wife is expecting a child, and I'd like to be there when she gives birth. So if I could work the meet and then scoot out of here, off to the maternity ward, and be there...' I said sure. And he did his routine, and it was so stellar. My wife said he was the best ring man she'd ever seen. He'd hang up there and do a slow backward roll to an iron cross and hold it. And the crowd would clap and he'd smile. Then he'd go straight-armed into an L position in the rings. Press handstand, couple of giant swings, then flop down to a Maltese. His body was level to the floor. What a master. He won the event even though he went first!"

In 1969, senior Dave Jacobs was coming off his biggest disappointment—losing out to teammate George Huntzicker in the fight for the World Trampoline Championship. He was also coming back from injury. The previous year, after falling off the trampoline doing a triple flip, his ankle had twisted and given out. Jacobs fell headfirst onto the floor and ended up spending two and a half weeks in the hospital. But nothing could stop Jacobs from getting back on the trampoline.

In high school, he'd quit football because of weak knees and taken up tennis and gymnastics. After becoming the second-best tennis player in the state his sophomore year, he was forced to choose between tennis and trampoline. Jacobs headed for Nard's Trampoline Club and stayed there, bringing a single-minded focus to his sport. When he developed problems keeping his feet together when he bounced, Jacobs began a nightly regimen of taping his feet and thighs together. Now, he still practiced three hours a day, six days a week. And the taping continued, though for different reasons—due to a pulled hamstring, Jacobs had to wrap his left leg in tape all the way to his waist.

To the trampoline champion, Newt was much more than just his coach.

"Newt is probably one of the greatest guys you'll ever meet— he'll do anything for you," Jacobs said fervently, emphasizing Newt's constant philosophy of looking after his boys like a father both inside and outside the gym. "I have the utmost respect for him. There isn't anyone on the team who wouldn't do anything for him, too."

Sid Jensen, now a junior, was also becoming a bigger name. He traveled to Mexico City for the 1968 Olympics in October. As the only male Canadian gymnast, he *was* the men's national team. He called it "paradise for a month." And it might never have happened if not for Newt's unshakeable belief in him.

In a collection of his "Olympic thoughts" that Jensen compiled for the *Daily*, the all-arounder revealed that in his senior year of high school, he "had become despondent about gymnastics and quit the team." But Newt recruited him anyway and proceeded to give him the direction that set him on his successful path.

Though Jensen admitted that at the Olympics, "You become terribly patriotic all of a sudden," he and his Canadian teammates mingled with everyone. They lived with the South Vietnamese athletes, and practiced with the East Germans. All the competitors were in such a cocoon of friendliness that Jensen didn't find out about student demonstrations and unrest related to the Olympics until receiving letters about it from home. And after some thought, he decided he agreed with Tommie Smith and John Carlos' Black Power salute after the 200-meter race.

"They have a bloody good point," Jensen wrote. "I also think it was the best method of protest."

He didn't return from Mexico in time for the start of the season, and actually took the entire fall term off from school.

And by the time Michigan headed for Ypsilanti for a "triangular meet" in early December 1968, the injuries were piling up. Regardless of his health, Jensen couldn't compete in team competitions until he was enrolled in school. George Huntzicker had injured his ankle, and Fred Rodney was still shaken up after a motorcycle accident two weeks earlier. Murray Plotkin's knee injury had put him out for the season. The entire trampoline squad was sitting out the meet. Luckily, weak sisters Eastern Michigan and Kent State were already conceding victory to the Wolverines.

The meet was a snoozer—literally. Dave Jacobs, after winning floor exercise, the first event, fell asleep on the bench and didn't wake up until an hour and a half later. It was a win though, if a sloppy one. Newt didn't seem to mind; Jacobs had done his part, hadn't he?

Over winter break, Newt led his boys south for the National Gymnastics Clinic in Sarasota. This year, Newt would have the honor of coaching the South team in the clinic's biggest event, the North-South meet. Naturally, Newt was excited for the meet and his competitive fires were stoked, thanks to his coaching opponent. His old rival George Szypula had been named the coach of the North team. Conveniently all the Spartans and Wolverines ended up on their own coach's team. How some gymnasts from the state of Michigan could be classified as North and some as South was too trivial for discussion—geography be damned! Years before, Newt had beaten out "Zip" and others in the thirty-five-and-over all-around competition. Now, the rivalry gleefully rekindled, he led his South team to victory.

When the team returned to Ann Arbor following the winter vacation, the string of uninspired wins continued. Against Wisconsin, the Wolverines just had to watch as the Badgers beat themselves. Western Michigan and Minnesota provided little competition. In Minneapolis, to make matters worse, the mat on the floor was so thin that Newt wouldn't let either Rick McCurdy or Dave Jacobs compete on it and risk injuring their already fragile legs.

"It's awfully hard to get up for a meet when you know you've all but won before you begin," Newt admitted. But if anyone could inspire gymnasts to give it their all in a nearly meaningless meet, it was Newt. It was tremendously important to him that Michigan never "mail" a meet in, even if they knew the result was a foregone conclusion. Part of his competitive streak included a deep respect for any opponent.

As February began, everyone expected things to pick up. Finally, the gymnasts would hold their first-ever meet in the "Events Building" (which soon became known as Crisler Arena, named for former Michigan football coach Fritz Crisler). The new arena, which looks vaguely like a UFO perched on a thick pedestal, stood next to Michigan's venerable football stadium, the Big House. And the first men's gymnastics meet within it would feature the Ohio State Buckeyes. The switch from the IM Building was welcome.

"What a venue that was," said Rapper of the new arena. "[The atmosphere was] much better, much better. It was new, it was bright. ... It was more like college. Crisler was the big time for us, most definitely. I loved competing at Crisler."

Though the Buckeyes did not possess a high-powered gymnastics team at the time, no Wolverine or Buckeye has ever let equality of competition (or the lack thereof) dim their intense rivalry.

The meet was billed as a "classic joust," and Ohio State coach James Sweeney predicted that his boys would beat Michigan in at least three events—trampoline, high bar and vault. The *Daily* predicted a possible crowd of 10,000 people.

It turned out to be no contest. The Buckeyes "flopped" on trampoline, while Jacobs led the Wolverines to a 188.20-171.70 win. The victory began an unbelievably long streak—Michigan didn't lose a dual meet at Crisler Arena until seven years later.

The Buckeye bashing set the team on a roll; with Big Tens approaching, Michigan romped over the Spartans and Indiana, posting a 190.825, the best score in the nation that year. For the Olympic events, Michigan had scored 163.025, also tops in the country. In front of over 4,000 people at Crisler, the Wolverines turned in a multitude of stellar performances. Rings, believed at the beginning of the year to be one of the team's weak spots, yielded four 9.00-plus scores.

"We're hitting a terrific momentum towards the Iowa and Big Ten meets," Newt remarked afterward with a grin. By pushing the team to do its best even when, for a particular meet, it wasn't entirely necessary, Newt had his gymnasts hitting their peak at the crucial moment.

The high bar squad, led by senior Mike Sasich, was also a bright spot. According to the *Daily*, Sasich "mesmerize[d] crowds" with his routines, which culminated in a double backflip dismount. And well he should have—Sasich was a daredevil in the best tradition of the event. A decade before, gymnasts had practiced in time to Al Stall's yelps as he experimented with new tricks on high bar; now, Sasich had taken on that mantle.

Four times, Sasich had taken a bad fall from the bar, and four times, he'd been knocked cold. To work high bar, he noted gleefully, was to take your life in your hands.

"Mike loves a tight, pressured meet," Newt said. "He has to be one of the most exciting high bar men that we've ever had at Michigan."

Sasich, naturally, agreed. "I just don't let myself think about getting nervous," he said, as if it wasn't obvious. "The bigger the crowd, the better I'll perform."

While the new football coach, Bo Schembechler, was growling at his players to shave off their facial hair, Newt easily accepted the freewheeling Sasich—who greased his hair and was proud of it. He got married in the middle of the school year, and after a month, declared himself "probably in the best shape of my life."

It was typical of Newt not to react negatively to an athlete like Sasich. Why get a gymnast angry over a little thing like hair? Was Sasich contributing considerably to the team? Yes, indeed he was. Was his hair distracting him or any of his teammates from their athletic goals? No—although it might have if Newt had made a big deal of it. If a gymnast had a good work ethic, got the most out of his talent and acted like a proper teammate, nothing else really mattered. No matter his age, Newt could always relate to his gymnasts and the things that were important to them. It was part of what made him so beloved: he understood what mattered and emphasized it. As long as different hairdos, new clothing styles or getting married didn't interfere with an athlete's performance in school and the gym, there was no reason to kick up a fuss and possibly disturb the team's chemistry.

Sasich grew up in a tough neighborhood in Wisconsin, mixing Puerto Ricans, Mexicans and Texans. His parents sent him to an all-boys school in Milwaukee, where he set a school record in pole vaulting, lettered three times in golf, became the MVP of the track team and, oh yes, captained the gymnastics team. And after four years in Ann Arbor, Sasich couldn't say enough about Newt, who he called "the best gymnastics coach in the nation." Newt was the kind of coach who could make you better on an event where you already excelled, and help you succeed at things you never thought you could do.

"He is one great man," Sasich said. "He can really fire you up for a meet. The coach has helped me in every way possible."

After a tune-up thrashing of the Fighting Illini, the Wolverines were ready for the regular season's biggest test, and final meet: the Iowa Hawkeyes. Both teams had proven their excellence under pressure and were evenly matched in every event.

Over 7,000 fans flooded into Crisler Arena for the big meet, and the Wolverines obliged what one observer called "the most partisan Michigan crowd I have ever seen" by smashing their rivals. The Hawkeyes were unable to best Michigan on any event. Michigan's 192.10 score was the highest in the country, with every counted routine *averaging* a 9.15 score. The Wolverines hit twenty-six of their twenty-seven routines—a tribute to the success of Newt's eternal focus on hit percentage instead of winning. With an unblemished record of 10-0, Michigan had all but clinched a tie for the Big Ten title.

But there was still one important obstacle. At the Big Ten championships, where the conference winner would be decided in Michigan's Crisler Arena, the Wolverines would have to beat out the competition in their biggest meet to date without the benefit of their trampoline score.

Throughout the Big Tens, fans and gymnasts alike had to follow two battles: the one for the Big Ten title, and the one for the best six-event score in prelims. Michigan was a lock to win the conference, but fell into an early hole in the race for the NCAA bid, at one point looking up at Iowa from 2.50 points down.

The Wolverines fell behind on floor exercise, where Huntzicker was injured, and then came the debacle on side horse. In the view of the *Daily* reporter, at least, the entire side horse competition was judged on reputation. "All Iowa had to do," an unidentified gymnast said, "was to walk out on the floor to get a nine-point score." Even Charlie Pond was reportedly suspicious—Iowa was better than Michigan on side horse, unquestionably, but not two full points better.

"The side horse scores really hit us hard," Newt said later. "The 25.30 was one of our lowest scores all year and actually the boys performed quite well. We were very shocked by the scores."

But he and his gymnasts wouldn't give up. Michigan staged a valiant comeback, swamping the field on now-irrelevant trampoline and putting on a spectacular high bar show, where Iowa was only mediocre. But it wasn't enough. Though Michigan qualified first to the team finals, along with Iowa and Illinois, it was Iowa who posted the best six-event score: 161.55 to Michigan's 161.10. Newt was worried his boys might be too depressed to fire up for the finals, knowing that no matter what they did, the Hawkeyes and not the Wolverines were headed for NCAAs in Seattle. It was the reverse of the meets earlier in the season, when no matter what Michigan did, it would win.

The practice paid off. The next day, Michigan sailed to Newt's eighth Big Ten title. Their gutty performance in seeing the competition to the end must have been gratifying for Newt, but knowing that the Big Ten championship wouldn't be enough to get to NCAAs was a bitter pill. Though Newt never complained publicly, it had to rankle him that the title he always worked so hard to prepare his boys to win, and successfully as well, kept being snatched away through rule changes and technicalities.

Senior Dick Richards pulled off a surprise event win on parallel bars, junior Ron Rapper's specialty. Newt has suggested jokingly that it was because Rapper abandoned his usual superstition of eating his Hershey bar with nuts and remaining away from the event until his turn to perform. Rapper stoutly maintains that although he did break tradition and emerge to watch Richards, he did, in fact, eat his candy bar.

"We had a very friendly competitive rivalry." Rapper remembered. "We made each other better. That weekend, he put everything together. I faltered a little bit in the finals, and I didn't lose the championship—Dick won! He won, it was his weekend."

Dave Jacobs, to the surprise of no one, took the trampoline crown, with Huntzicker second. Michigan posted the top team score in five of seven events. None of these happy events changed the fact that Iowa had what the Wolverines had wanted so badly. Michigan had won the Big Ten title, but Iowa had won the six-event competition—and the ticket to NCAA Championships.

"Congratulations on winning the Big Tens," one Iowa gymnast said to Newt. "I'll send you a postcard from Seattle." Newt undoubtedly smiled and remained friendly, but the remark had to hurt. Since he began coaching, Big Tens had always been the jewel of the season. He'd spent years getting Michigan to this point, where winning a title was always within reach. To go through all that, win, and still not get just rewards was patently unfair.

The six Wolverines who'd qualified to nationals spent the next three weeks preparing. Rapper remembers having "the worst practices ever." Richards was on Cloud Nine, gleefully picking up Rapper to go to practice with copies of the *Daily* scattered all over the backseat of his car. All the newspapers featured the same story: Richards as the Big Ten parallel bars champion. The good-natured rivalry continued.

Once NCAAs arrived, though, Rapper got his head on straight and no one could touch him as he breezed to the national title. Jacobs finished second on floor, Chuck Froemming fourth on rings. Big Ten gymnasts won four of the six event titles, and Iowa won the national championship.

Feelings back in Ann Arbor remained bitter. Andy Barbas, the team's main beat writer at the *Daily*, contended that Michigan would have either won NCAAs or come in second to Iowa—only allowing the Big Ten one representative was ludicrous.

"The second best team in the United States won the NCAA Gymnastics Championships last weekend in Seattle," he wrote.

"The best team couldn't make it."

Even Michigan State's George Szypula was upset.

"I used to think the NCAAs were supposed to be among the top teams in the country," he said. "After this past weekend, I see I was wrong." Newt didn't comment—it was completely contrary to his nature to complain bitterly in print—but it's hard to imagine him disagreeing with Barbas and Szypula.

Thus far, the sparkling class of 1970 that Newt had recruited so carefully had experienced three of the toughest years in the recent history of Michigan gymnastics. They'd seen a streak of six straight Big Ten titles broken; they'd lost an NCAA bid in a playoff; and they'd lost a bid on a rule seemingly put in place specifically to trip them up. To see their and their coach's countless hours of hard work constantly thwarted fired them up beyond even what Newt's exhortations could. As their senior year approached, it was time to go out with a bang.

Chapter 15

Two National Titles in One Year

The class of 1970's glorious finish would have to come without trampoline. The phase-out was nearly complete; all that remained was a completely separate NCAA championship for the bouncers, and 1970 would be the final year. Ever so conveniently, the trampoline nationals would be held the same weekend, in the same location as those for gymnastics. Clearly, there was more behind the event's elimination than just "flash" and the element of danger.

Leading Newt's squad was Ron Rapper, who now jokingly considered himself an all-around man—"After all, I'm all around the parallel bars—on top of them, underneath them, next to them." Because he wasn't a true all-arounder, he was entering his final year of competitive gymnastics. There was no space in post-collegiate gymnastics for a one-event man. This year was it. He took his leadership cues from Newt. Newt sent out a yearly newsletter and posted individualized coaching tips on the gym bulletin board daily, making sure his team was on the same page regarding its goals, and how to achieve them through individual improvement and effort. Rapper did the same, with similar effectiveness. Communication was high on his priority list.

One added advantage for his team was that freshmen were now, finally, allowed to compete. The Wolverines expected that the addition of some talented freshmen would help compensate for the loss of six seniors. And with Newt at the helm, Rapper was convinced that his team was set to do big things.

"He's an amazing individual with a knack for communicating," Rapper said of his beloved coach. "He's an inspiration for the whole team. Because of him, we really want to win the national championship this year."

Rapper did remember one "failure" of communication from Newt. One year, the coach contracted the worst possible illness for such a bubbly chatterbox: laryngitis.

"He couldn't talk for a good week," Rapper said with a grin. "So he brought a ten-inch square [magic slate] to the gym. He had to communicate by writing, and he'd get frustrated because he couldn't talk. He'd erase it with the heel of his hand and scribble something else, and we'd say, 'We can't read that, Coach!' Newt without a voice—not a good thing."

Newt's duties as head coach of the cheerleaders continued unabated, though he no longer plucked as many varsity gymnasts from their ranks as in the early days. Now, girls like Newt's daughter Lani had entered the mix. Michigan, the last bastion of all-male cheerleading in the Big Ten, would finally allow female cheerleaders. The group, first selected in 1969, now began cheering at basketball games.

This season, the Wolverines would have their meets in Crisler Arena. And just before the team's first meet, Newt gleefully told the *Daily*, "We have so many fine gymnasts in each event it will be hard to decide who to count." His only worry was his team's lack of experience. Key for Michigan would be its Big Ten regular season record, for this year it would count for half of the conference championship. By posting the best record, Michigan could give itself a little breathing room at Big Tens—if the Wolverines finished second, they could still claim a share of the title.

On January 11, 1970, Michigan notched its first win, a romp over the Wisconsin Badgers, 162.70-150.65. Reaching the 162.00-point level—the top three scores on each of six events counted, making the highest possible score a 180.00—was an indication of an outstanding performance. Newt was especially pleased with the showings from his two all-arounders, Sid Jensen and Rick McCurdy.

"They were competing under tougher conditions than they're used to," Newt told the *Daily* after the meet. "Since the trampoline was eliminated as an event, the all-arounders have to perform in six events in a row. Before, they could rest for ten minutes or so in the middle of the meet during the tramp competition." It was just one more drawback of losing the event that Newt had loved for so long, and inspired so many others to love. But Newt wasn't one to dwell on negatives, ever—and in this situation his team couldn't afford for him to do that. It was a new challenge, and Newt was always up for one of those.

McCurdy, a junior, was the defending Big Ten all-around champ but was still seen as number two to senior Sid Jensen. Despite the championship in 1969, McCurdy believed 1970 would be "much better," with weaker Big Ten competition. He called the team one of the closest he'd been on, with fantastic depth to counter its inexperience.

But the momentum didn't carry into Michigan's next meet. It was supposed to be a cakewalk over Eastern Michigan, which was coached by Marv Johnson, a Michigan captain of years before. Johnson believed his current squad was still a good three or four years away from being able to compete with his old team, and he was right. But even though Michigan won easily, the performance felt like something of a letdown. Sid Jensen was cut back from floor and vault due to stomach flu. And while Eastern Michigan posted its best score of the season—148.10—Michigan had an off night, scoring just 160.25. It was a new kind of team; Newt could no longer afford to ease his freshmen in, when they were expected to compete in their second semester at school. The team's depth, so far was more than making up for its inexperience.

With just one more meet before the opening of the Big Ten season, Michigan needed to get it together. Newt's answer, as usual, was to fire up even more in the gym, putting even more energy into picking the gymnasts up and fine-tuning their routines with expert coaching. And in their final tune-up, a tri-meet against Western Michigan and the University of Illinois-Chicago Circle, the Wolverines finally gelled. Newt planned to divide his squad, using one half against each of the opponents. Newt's boys turned in their finest performance of the young season, routing both teams and scoring a 163.25 against the stronger foe, UICC. Sophomore Dick Kaziny scored a huge 9.40 on side horse, while Ted Marti's 9.15 was enough to claim the high bar title.

Finally, on January 24, Michigan opened its Big Ten season against rival Michigan State—and "outclassed" the Spartans decisively. Jensen and McCurdy turned in banner performances in the all-around, with Jensen averaging better than a 9.00 on each of his events.

"Without those two," captain Ron Rapper told the *Daily* afterward, "this team would not amount to very much."

Michigan's overall team performance was so outstanding that the East Lansing crowd gave the Wolverines a sincere ovation, especially when Rapper showed off his signature trick on parallel bars, balancing on one arm and then pirouetting down. Newt was slightly disturbed by a subpar showing on side horse, but trouble with side horse was becoming something of a tradition. He could deal with that. And he was happy with the performance of his exhibition gymnasts, who were able to get competition experience without the pressure of having their scores count.

Following the meet, Rapper was asked whether Michigan would make the trip to Philadelphia at the end of the season for NCAA championships. As usual, only the Big Ten champions would get a bid to NCAAs.

Rapper's answer was short, sweet and to the point.

"You bet."

Meanwhile, Michigan's three best trampolinists traveled to Memphis for an invitational competition. Freshman Chris Keane finished just behind top bouncer Wayne Miller. Newt, a former trampolinist himself and an avid, lifelong lover of the event, was tremendously pleased. His bouncers seemed to be just as red-hot as the rest of his team.

And the team, heading into its clash with Minnesota, couldn't have been much hotter. The Wolverines were now going for their twenty-sixth consecutive dual meet win.

They not only beat the Gophers, they set a new NCAA record with a 164.45 score. Pat Bird, Minnesota's head coach, was convinced that the Big Ten title would be "no sweat" for Michigan. He'd come a long way from being the assistant coach at Illinois who said Michigan would have to return the trophy after just one year.

Next came the Buckeyes, who rather than being intense rivals, were in 1970 a team in sad shape. The Bucks hadn't gotten a win in three meets, or scored more than 150 points. As expected, Michigan thrashed Ohio State. Or, as the *Daily* observed, the Wolverines "decapitated" their rivals, 164.15-150.90. "The meet would have been just as interesting without [the Buckeyes]," the reporter remarked.

For Newt, it was a "fantastic" performance, a lovely breather before the next weekend's tough test against Indiana State and imposing Southern Illinois on Friday and Indiana on Saturday afternoon. Newt called Indiana State the "stiffest competition to date"—Michigan, Indiana State, and Southern Illinois all regularly scored above 160.

Friday night's showing was subpar—for Michigan, anyway. Most teams would have been thrilled to post a 162.45, especially away from home, but not the Wolverines, who knew they could have done better. Nonetheless, Michigan beat both Indiana State and Southern Illinois in the double dual, even after falling behind following the initial event, floor exercise. The team pulled it together for vault, parallel bars and high bar, with its tremendous depth serving as a key to the victory. Only all-arounder Sid Jensen earned a first place finish, on the parallel bars.

"I was generally pleased with our performance tonight even though we didn't score as well as we have the last couple times out," said Newt afterward. "I feel this was an excellent test of our team for two reasons. One, we were facing top-caliber competition—the best we have faced so far. Two, we were performing before a large crowd away from home." And the Wolverines weren't done yet—with hardly any turnaround time, they took on Indiana. The more challenges Newt could throw at this talented team, the better it would perform.

Despite a season-best performance by the Hoosiers, that Saturday the Wolverines posted a workmanlike 162.55 to beat Indiana. The outcome was never in doubt, with Michigan claiming a commanding lead after the first event. The Wolverines had now stretched their dual meet winning streak to thirty—and their season record was a perfect 10-0.

But much of the campus remained unaware—like today, widespread recognition remained a problem for the team. *Daily* reporter Jerry Clarke rode along on the team's bus and came away nearly as frustrated as the gymnasts themselves with their anonymity. Initially, the column was to focus on trampoline's elimination as an event. With that event, Clarke believed the team would have been unbeatable.

"They may be anyway," he allowed.

Crowds in Ann Arbor, though, remained small and lacked intensity, despite Newt's efforts to explain the sport and make it exciting for them. The team insisted to Clarke "that a larger turnout at the meets could help their performance." Clarke, who had been writing men's gymnastics for over a year, could understand the confusion an outsider might feel at coming to a meet for the first time—after all, he was still learning the sport himself. But he couldn't understand the lack of appreciation for the team's overwhelming skills.

"They are the best in the country," he wrote emphatically, "and want Michigan students to take pride in that fact."

One special group of students did show intense pride in the team—the mysterious Markley Fan Club. The all-female club, whose exact origins can't be pinpointed, was based out of Michigan's Mary Markley Hall, long known for the fun-loving ways of its inhabitants. At nearly all men's gymnastics meets, even on the road, the gymnasts would look up and suddenly see a large banner: "GO BLUE! MARKLEY FAN CLUB SUPPORTS YOU!" They'd often find letters or a box of cookies left by their doors; on Rapper's birthday, he even received a cake. Everything was signed, in proper mysterious fashion, "MFC." In the days before Facebook-stalking, there was only one logical way for the girls to have found out such data as the gymnasts' addresses and birthdays: Newt Loken. (Newt, in proper mysterious form, maintains he has no idea how the girls figured out this information.) The entire team loved the fan club.

"They were instrumental, and enthusiastic," Newt remembered. "Sometimes they'd go to away meets, cheer like crazy, have a banner printed all up. Go Blue and stuff. ... We lived in a time when there was a lot of enthusiasm drummed up by people like them and *The Ann Arbor News* and *The Michigan Daily.* We had support. And we fed on them, encouraged them a little bit after we got to know them. 'It's just great what you kids are doing! Keep doing it!' "

The support from the MFC meant so much to the gymnasts that when the Athletic Department planned a postseason banquet for the team, the athletes asked Newt if he could extend an invitation to the anonymous fans.

"They absolutely deserved to be at this award dinner, because they too played a part in helping us win the championship," Rapper said. "So they came, and it was a group of four, five or six girls that just loved the sport. We had our own, private cheerleaders! It was terrific."

The final home meet of the season loomed ahead, and Clarke compared the clash to the football game of the past November. For the uninitiated, November 22, 1969, is one of the most important dates in Michigan football history. Against Ohio State, the Bo Schembechler-led Wolverines were supposed to lose. Instead, they shocked the world by avenging the previous year's embarrassing defeat. Now, the gymnasts were set to face Illinois, with the Illini playing the part of the underdog. Clarke thought it might end up being the greatest gymnastics meet of all time.

He was wrong, but the Wolverines didn't mind. Rather than Illinois upsetting the heavily favored Michigan, the Wolverines "dazzled" on Senior Night, winning 164.35-158.90. Each senior scored a personal best as the team smashed Illinois' perfect season record, with Rapper posting a 9.60 on parallel bars. The Fighting Illini's venerable head coach, Newt's old friend Charlie Pond, said confidently after the meet, "If they can get by us in the Big Ten

meet, I don't see any way that they will not be NCAA titlists."
Newt, unsurprisingly, was completely delighted.

The team finished up the regular season with a tight victory
over Iowa, which had only lost once previously. The win was
especially crucial because it clinched the regular season title for the
Wolverines. Michigan earned the win even without Huntzicker,
who was away at the World Trampoline Trials in New Orleans.
Michigan's trampolinists continued their journeys as something
of a side note, despite Wayne Miller and Huntzicker finishing
one-two in the qualification trials to represent the United States
in the World Trampoline Meet. Led by Jensen and Rapper,
Michigan earned its thirty-second straight dual meet victory,
and the Big Ten regular season championship.

Now, the team needed to finish first or second in the Big Ten
Championships in order to claim at least a share of the title. And
Michigan had a strong attack everywhere—everywhere, that is,
except for the side horse. Now known as the pommel horse,
routines and requirements have changed. They change constantly,
each year, and every year gymnasts must perform increasingly
difficult routines in order to get the scores to which they are
accustomed. One thing, however, remains the same: For most
teams, it is the weak spot. The event requires a gymnast to support
his full, spinning weight on his hands and wrists as he travels up
and down the horse. Sometimes he must push himself all the way
to a handstand before continuing on his way. Pinpoint balance
and steadiness are required to complete a successful routine—
even the best gymnast in the world can come off on the easiest
skill if his mind wanders for a split-second. Illinois and Iowa
would provide stiff competition—the Hawkeyes, especially, had
their focus on repeating as both Big Ten and NCAA champions.

On Friday, March 10, the Wolverines scored a mediocre (for them) 161.05 in the Big Ten meet. It wasn't a top performance, but it was still enough to claim the Big Ten crown outright, with Iowa finishing a distant second (155.70). In the Friday morning compulsory routines, Michigan's performance was subpar—judging was conservative and none of the teams had performed the tedious compulsories all year. The night, however, went much better. No other school achieved a twenty-seven in any event—a regular occurrence for Michigan. McCurdy, seen as the secondary all-arounder to start the year, won the Big Ten all-around title, with Jensen coming in third. Michigan, as Rapper had predicted, had claimed its place in the NCAA team tournament to be held that April at Philadelphia's Temple University.

Iowa State, coached by Newt's former gymnast, Ed Gagnier, was favored to win in 1970, having scored an astronomical 165.55 in their Big Eight championship performance. The side horse competition would be fierce and probably crucial.

On Thursday, April 2, Michigan's bouncers set the bar for their teammates by repeating as national champions. It was the last year an NCAA championship would be held for trampolinists, and Michigan fittingly went out on top, with Huntzicker besting all comers. The win was bittersweet, not only because it was the last, but because it became something of a side note, even for Michigan.

For the rest of the team, it was the first day of NCAA competition. Newt, as much as he may have wanted to, could not afford any drawn-out celebration of the trampoline title, or long reflection on the events that had led to its demise as a gymnastic apparatus.

None of the first-day scores would count for the team total, but they were vitally important to the Michigan individuals competing for event titles. Rapper, predictably, grabbed the lead in the parallel bars competition with a 9.50 on his compulsory routine.

On Friday, Iowa State, Michigan and Temple qualified through to the team finals, in that order. Temple just barely edged out Southern Illinois. Michigan made up for a subpar beginning with a stellar second half, comfortably ensconced in the runner-up spot going into the finals.

"Today, our object was to qualify [for] tomorrow," Newt told the *Daily*. "Now we'll let it all go, and go all out on every event."

After four events on the final day, Ed Gagnier's Cyclones had taken a huge lead. The Wolverines clawed back, and by the final event, high bar, they were close. Newt's eyes flickered to the scoreboard constantly, as the distance between the two powerhouses shrank to mere tenths. Finally, it came down to Michigan's final performer, Eddie Howard. Iowa State's night was over, and all the Cyclones could do was watch and hope that Michigan wouldn't catch them up. Before Howard's routine, Newt pulled him aside.

"Eddie," he said, "all you need is a 9.40, and we'll win."

"A 9.40?" Howard said incredulously. "Coach, I've never gotten a 9.40 in my life!"

"This time," Newt instructed, his voice full of confidence, "get it."

Howard turned in what Newt remembered as the best routine of the gymnast's life. He dismounted and landed on his feet, his ecstatic teammates swarming him immediately. They weren't just celebrating—they grabbed him in a collective embrace before he even had a chance to take a step. The judges, of course, noticed, and drew Newt aside to ask what was going on. The coach—who knew perfectly well that his boys were preventing the loss of a crucial tenth with their jubilant display—fixed them with a look of pure innocence and surprise.

"They're just excited!" he assured them with his usual wide grin.

Then the scores began to appear. The highest and lowest of the four would be dropped, the middle two averaged for

Howard's final score. First up, a pair of 9.30s. The Wolverines' hearts caught. Then came a 9.50—and another 9.50. Eddie Howard had gotten his 9.40, and Michigan had clinched the championship by just a single tenth, sending the Wolverines into another explosion of joy. Ron Rapper added to the accolades by defending his national parallel bars title.

Asked later if the swarming of Eddie Howard was intentional, Rapper just grinned wickedly and nodded.

"It was phenomenal," Rapper said. "It was an experience that was never duplicated."

In 1970, Ray Gura was a skinny freshman with the good fortune to arrive at Michigan in the first year freshmen were allowed to compete. The experience of winning the national title overwhelmed him.

"It was my first year. I'm not sure I understood how big it was, that only one team wins it every year," Gura remembered. "At that time, there were 180 teams in the country, so most teams never even came close. Most teams never even qualified. And here, we qualified in my freshman year and went on to win it. And … I contributed. So I felt great, although I don't think I understood that it would be something I'd think back on and talk about the rest of my life."

Newt's brilliant weekend wasn't over yet. Upon arriving back at his hotel room, his daughter Lani, called from the national diving championships, where she was competing. Just to be at the championships was a victory for the younger Loken.

Lani had begun showing promise as a diver during her summers at the Huron Valley Swim Club. Michigan diving coach Dick Kimball, one of Newt's former gymnasts, took her under his wing, and she blossomed. After finishing fifth at the 1968 Olympic trials, Lani had gone to visit relatives in Concord, Calif. When she went riding with her two cousins in their new MG, a tire blew out and the car ended up rolling over Lani. Her list of injuries was daunting even to the average person: seven breaks in her back and neck; four broken ribs; a collapsed lung; thirty stitches in the back of her head; multiple facial cuts; two hundred stitches in her right hip; and a deep wound in her torso. For an Olympic-caliber athlete, the prognosis seemed horrific.

But one-and-a-half years later, Lani had fully recovered, and now she was competing in the ten-meter event at the USA Championships. As the meet wound down to her last three dives, Lani's confidence grew. "Wouldn't it be great," she thought, "if I could win this title, and Dad in Philadelphia could win the NCAA gymnastics team title?"

Newt had no idea what had happened until he answered the phone with a bright, "Hi, Lani, how're you doing?"

"How'd you do, Dad?" asked Lani, holding back her own news.

"We won the national championship!" her gleeful father replied.

"You did? Oh, I'm so happy for you!"

"Finally I said, 'And how did you do?'" Newt remembered. "And she said, 'Oh, I won the national title, Dad!' Oh my God, I screamed in the room there to all the gymnasts." Both the national gymnastics title and Lani's diving titles were remarkable accomplishments, huge milestones in Newt's life. To have them both occur on the same day, and be able to share the happiness with his daughter, was nearly unimaginable. The sweetness of the triumph was overwhelming.

When the personal accolades came in, those were for the individual gymnasts. But this victory was for Loken.

"We were the underdogs," Rapper remembers. "We put

everything together that Saturday at Temple, and we beat Iowa State. That thrill of winning the team title was ten times better than me winning a second NCAA [parallel bars] championship, because that was a reflection upon Newt. He could get together a team of young men—find the talent, get us into a cohesive unit, and that was just the best. The absolute best. That really brought the team into the sport, when it's really not a team sport. It was a deserving victory for him. I think that was our goal. We didn't win it for us—we wanted it for him."

Chapter 16

The Early Seventies

At the start of the 1971 season, Newt's office was chock full of clippings and photos commemorating the glorious episodes in his team's history. The coach's seemingly limitless energy was still one of his most obvious qualities, as he could barely sit still for more than a few minutes. He wasn't just coaching his boys, but also teaching physical education and dancing classes and hustling his various books on gymnastics and cheerleading.

Newt had become adept at discovering and recruiting some of the best high school gymnasts in the country, building a Michigan dynasty. Despite his packed schedule, he made time to attend a spate of high school meets, where he met the top up-and-comers in the surrounding states. He also maintained his rich Canadian pipeline, feeding a seemingly endless stream of quality recruits from the north.

Newt's personality was as much of a draw as the success of the Michigan program. He understood how to motivate each of his gymnasts, unfailingly tailoring his coaching to each individual.

"He's not an amateur psychologist," said high-bar man Jim Scully. "He's a professional one."

And unlike many coaches, Newt didn't subscribe to a "Winning Is Everything" philosophy. Instead, he emphasized clean, hit routines. He knew that with the proper focus on the process, results would take care of themselves. His easygoing method produced not only fantastic gymnasts, but men who were almost inevitably successful in their lives after college.

"With Coach Loken, winning is only part of a complex scheme," all-arounder Pete Rogers added. "I don't think winning is his ultimate goal."

Nonetheless, he'd done a lot of winning, and in 1971 the spotlight remained on the defending national and Big Ten champions. Newt's bid to host the NCAA championships—he'd first tried for the sport's biggest competition in 1949—finally got approved, and he spent the year drumming up publicity for the meet. In addition, *The Detroit News*, which sponsored one big Michigan competition each year, chose men's gymnastics NCAAs for 1971. (It didn't hurt that Michigan athletic director Don Canham had a connection on the paper.) Every other day, a huge ad appeared in the paper, encouraging Michiganders to attend the event. Normally, ads like that would have cost $500 each.

"We had a lot of people from Detroit [saying], 'What the hell is gymnastics?'" Newt remembered with a laugh. "They caught on, because *The Detroit News* [had the ads]."

Newt's own promotions, naturally, were a little more flashy. At different intervals before the national championship, Newt gleefully climbed the huge marquee near Crisler Arena for promotional photos. Three hundred sixty five days, three hundred days, two hundred days, one hundred days—one day. Sometimes he'd just sit atop the sign, a good thirty feet up, which counted down each day to the NCAA championships. And at other times, the irrepressible coach would do a V-seat, holding himself on only his hands, with his legs held straight up in front of him to form his body into a V. Like Newt himself, the striking images were impossible to ignore—and no one could help smiling when they saw the pictures. Pure Newt, all the way.

"I was going to do a handstand [on the marquee], and then I thought, that's a thirty-foot drop!" Newt laughed. As the meet drew nearer, other publications picked up the story. The day before NCAAs, *The Ann Arbor News*, which sometimes couldn't even be bothered to print the score of Michigan's meets, ran a huge headline reading, "One Day Left." Of course, the feature photo was of Newt perched on the Crisler marquee.

Newt's inventive promotions ran through the meet itself. A group of girls from Lani's sorority waited at Crisler to welcome the visiting teams and coaches to the arena, which was covered in huge photos of each team. Thanks to one of baseball coach Don Lund's contacts at General Motors, each visiting coach was presented with a brand-new Pontiac to use for the entire weekend.

"We had free Cokes from the Coca-Cola company right in town," Newt said. "And we had free t-shirts. Free, free, free, for everybody on the team. I had a whole crew [of people] for every judge, and we had half a dozen judges."

Newt's sons, Jon and Newt Jr., even climbed up into Crisler's rafters to hang a special surprise for their dad. When Newt returned from a foray into Detroit, where he was promoting the meet, he discovered a big GO BLUE sign newly hung next to Iowa's team banner.

"Who the hell did that?" Newt asked Don Canham.

"Your two boys, Jon and Newt," the Athletic Director replied happily.

"They climbed up there with no life belts!" Newt remembered with undimmed wonder. "All they had was a cable." They were clearly their father's sons.

Some teams arrived a week before the competition—many were coming off two- to three-week breaks. Two or three squads would practice at once in Crisler, getting used to the equipment and trying to create the feel of the competition.

"If you're going to talk about preparation say something about Coach Loken," one gymnast told *The Michigan Daily*. "He's the one running around like a chicken with his head cut off, trying to make this championship a success. So far he's done a great job."

Newt's hard work paid off, as his NCAAs drew a record 25,000 people over three days.

"We filled up all the blue seats, and that means you're over 5,000," Newt remembered. "Then you creep up into the yellow seats—oh gee!"

It didn't make it into the record books, though—Newt only charged a dollar admission, and to be counted, he needed to charge five.

The only thing that didn't go perfectly was his own team's performance. Despite losing Sid Jensen and Ron Rapper to graduation, the Wolverines had been highly favored entering the competition, having won NCAAs the year before and yet another Big Ten championship in 1971. But compulsory routines on the first day went badly, and the team ended up fifth in the preliminaries. Only the top three teams would advance to the team finals. Newt was "dejected," according to the *Daily*, as he watched Iowa State, Southern Illinois and Penn State move on. Iowa State became the eventual champion, which held a measure of satisfaction for Newt—the Cyclones' head coach, Ed Gagnier, was one of his former gymnasts. Only Dick Kaziny of his current team advanced to individual finals, placing fourth on pommel horse.

Newt was recognized as the Coach of the Year, possibly due in part to his incredible efforts to make NCAAs such a rousing success, in addition to his outstanding coaching abilities. But even then, he felt he'd let down the team somewhat. He felt his showbiz side might have taken over more than usual, taking some of his attention away from the day-to-day business of coaching. If Newt had had a few assistant coaches, as all gymnastics coaches do now, it might have been different; but in 1971, Newt was still largely handling all the duties himself. In addition to promoting NCAAs tirelessly, he was coaching every day in the gym, sometimes adjusting or lengthening his schedule there to accommodate various gymnasts, teaching classes, recruiting, dealing with travel arrangements and other bureaucratic duties, and of course spending time with his family. Even if Newt's energy seemed boundless, there was a limit to the hours in the day. And Newt felt he could have spent more of them with his team, rather than promoting.

He and all his gymnasts remained tremendously disappointed. They'd wanted so badly to do well in front of their home fans—quite a normal occurrence for most teams—and not only had they turned in a subpar performance, but Iowa State had been almost as perplexed over their own tremendous show.

"The other teams were very good too," Newt said, "but it was still a downer. Any time any sport has a dynasty, it's because they buy into the image of being a winner. Jeez, that was a downer."

Heading into 1972, Newt decided to implement a three-phased program. First, he would replace his lost seniors, most notably Rick McCurdy, Eddie Howard and Mike Gluck. Then, the Wolverines would win the dual meets leading up to the Big Ten finals. And finally, they'd control the Big Ten weekend. Easy enough, right?

It seemed to be. The Wolverines ran their dual-meet win streak to forty-four with a win over Georgia Southern in mid-January, then to forty five in a meet against Chicago Circle and Eastern Michigan.

Then they ran into Iowa.

Michigan's old nemesis edged the Wolverines out 160.70-160.45. In a bittersweet achievement, Newt's boys had broken the 160-point mark—it just wasn't enough. The University of Iowa Fieldhouse was packed with rabid fans, who only got louder when the meet came down to high bar, the final event. Michigan had been ahead by over a point. But on high bar, Iowa scored nothing lower than a nine, while Michigan could manage nothing above that mark.

"I don't think [the streak] meant anything until it stopped," Gura said. "Michigan had such a strong tradition, they were so good, that it was just assumed that we would win. ... After we lost it, it was like someone hit you on the head with a two-by-four. It was like, 'This is how it feels to lose.' None of us had lost a meet before."

Michigan had little time to mourn the end of the four-year-old streak. A clash with Minnesota approached, along with a convocation of Michigan gymnasts from the past twenty-five years, all coming to town to honor Newt's twenty-fifth anniversary with the team. Like most such events, attendees must have felt contradicting emotions, that time had both flown and kept going forever. A quarter century at Michigan. Newt had brought the team from a fledgling enterprise to a recognized powerhouse, expected each year to contend for the conference title and even NCAA crown. And he had affected countless lives for the better. All the old Wolverines were returning to celebrate their collective past, and to thank the man who had helped them so much.

With the Gophers putting up their best team in a decade, Michigan's current Wolverines rose to the occasion, thumping the Gophers in a 164.90-160.55 win. This time, high bar was the site of Michigan's biggest triumph, with Ted Marti posting a huge 9.55 score. Newt's boys were back on track.

They went on a roll. First the Wolverines beat the "orangutangs (sic) of Ohio State" in what a few *Daily* writers called "the armpit of the nation." Then they trounced a banged-up Indiana squad. Newt was happy and confident.

"With Michigan State and Illinois coming up next weekend," he told the *Daily*, "the boys are going to be feeling like old pros by the time we get to Champaign."

It was a weekend of double action: a meet against the tough Spartans on Friday night in familiar Crisler Arena, then a tilt with the Illini in Champaign on Saturday. With his best friend, Ted Marti, turning in subpar performances, junior all-arounder Ray Gura picked up the slack. Gura beat Spartan all-arounder Randy Bellhorn for the first time ever in his home gym, leading the Wolverines to a win with his "sparkling performance." The next day, in front of an Illinois crowd "still hyper-active from the basketball game," the Wolverines and Gura were hyperactive themselves. After taking the lead on floor exercise, Michigan just kept building, eventually winning by almost twenty points. Now, it was finally time for Big Tens. Michigan knew Iowa would be its toughest opponent, and the fight between the two rivals came down to the wire. And despite the fact that Michigan had outscored Iowa in optionals and finals, the lead the Hawkeyes had built through the compulsories held off the Wolverines' comeback by six tenths of a point. Having been here before, Newt was philosophical.

"I guess we've won our share of the close ones," he said, perhaps thinking back to the 1970 NCAA title. "Maybe things are just balancing out."

Ray Gura, who won the floor and vault titles, wasn't so easygoing. Named the captain for the 1973 season, the senior was sick of watching Michigan's tradition of pummeling its opponents fade away. Though he'd been able to compete as a freshman—part of the first class able to do so—the 1970 national title had been built on other gymnasts' work. Gura and his classmates wanted a championship of their own and a return to national glory for Michigan.

A native of Cleveland, Ohio, Gura started his gymnastics career at an American Turners Club, attracted by the promise of a trampoline to bounce on. By the end of high school, the Wolverines and Buckeyes were both after Gura, but for the gymnast, it wasn't a very tough decision.

"Michigan was a much better team," Gura remembered. "Ohio State was last in the Big Ten at the time. Not a factor in the national picture. And academically, Michigan was superior. I visited and there was just a whole attitude difference. Ohio State, it seemed almost a recreational sport, even though it was varsity. Michigan was a whole different ballgame as far as intensity, ambition, expectation level, the whole thing."

For Gura and his teammates, the feeling of losing was still fresh. And they were determined not to feel it again.

The 1973 edition of the Wolverines had lost Ted Marti and Dick Kaziny, but Newt had hit the recruiting trail hard. His freshman class was chock-full of talent, featuring future standouts Bob Darden (who would later succeed Newt as Michigan's head coach), Richard Bigras, Pierre LeClerc and Joe Neuenswander. The year's schedule pitted the young Wolverines against Southern Illinois, Iowa, Minnesota and powerful Penn State.

"To be great, you must meet the great," Newt explained. Like many successful people who'd grown up in the Depression, Newt firmly believed in earning success. If you won every meet but never faced a challenging opponent, your record didn't mean very much. It was almost like lying.

Unlike coaches today, Newt did his recruiting largely alone. Despite this, he'd established pipelines in Illinois, the hotbed of high school gymnastics, and in Canadian clubs around Montreal. Newt somehow found time to keep the coaches updated with a mailing list and go to numerous high school meets, all while responding to letters of inquiry from the gymnasts themselves. Newt offered scholarships on the basis of talent, then financial need, often giving out partials that made Michigan more affordable. Once the boys arrived, whether recruits or walk-ons, practice began immediately. The gym was open from 2:00-7:00 seven days a week, but Newt encouraged his regulars to skip at least one day per week. In addition to learning Olympic compulsories, the new gymnasts built and improved on their high school routines, using them as a basis for growth. Newt wrote daily notes and suggestions to his gymnasts, trying to help them fix small flaws in their routines. He posted these above the water fountain for the athletes to see as they came in.

Neuenswander, Newt's new ring man, came from the same North Farmington high school as Terry Boys and Rupert Hansen. Until ninth grade, when he took up gymnastics, he was a wrestler—giving him the perfect body type for a ring man. As he improved, he gave much of the credit to Monty Falb, his older teammate, who showed him better, stronger techniques for swinging skills and holding strength positions like a Maltese or planche. He and Newt got along famously as well.

Falb, like Newt, saw himself as something of an entertainer— "We wouldn't get up in front of all those people and do the things we do if we weren't," he told the *Daily*. Without Newt, he didn't think he could have gotten through collegiate gymnastics.

"He treats everyone as an individual and tries to get to know everyone as a friend," Falb said of his coach.

Michigan's top ring man just had to be careful not to perform too much on instinct. Where Neuenswander could allow his mind to go blank during routines, if Falb followed suit, his body became too loose, his movements too sloppy. On rings, though, he said, he didn't have time to worry.

Michigan certainly didn't look great at the start. After a mediocre showing at the Midwest Open, the team headed for the crowded, chaotic Windy City Invitational. All six events would be running simultaneously, with two teams on each and a whistle to signal the end of a rotation. According to the *Daily*, the meet "developed into a major catastrophe," with Michigan finishing sixth of sixteen teams.

In January, the team finally made its home debut against Ohio State, and freshmen Neuenswander and Darden served notice that they had arrived. Gura, as usual, won the all-around, with Terry Boys and Ward Black providing their usual excellent performances on floor. The redheaded Darden posted a 9.15 on rings, with Neuenswander just barely beating him with a 9.20. They were ready to contribute not in their sophomore year, but now.

And their first big test leapt upon them when the Salukis of Southern Illinois rode into town. Gura had injured his ankle against Ohio State, and was questionable for the meet. The youngsters would face the defending national champions with their captain not at full strength.

"I had hurt my ankle the week before, during warmups," Gura said. "I competed, no big deal, but after the meet it ballooned up." He took it easy on the ankle before the Southern Illinois meet, then hoped for the best.

Michigan took a slim lead early and hung on for dear life. Ward Black's floor routine got the team rolling.

"Ward definitely gave us a lift with his great show," Newt said afterward. "He set the pace and the other men picked it up."

The Wolverines lost the rings event, but already the combination of Monty Falb and Neuenswander was proving "devastating," as the pair posted a 9.40 and 9.30. And Gura, ever the consummate captain, provided just the shot of inspiration his teammates needed.

He'd sat out the floor rotation, and no one expected him to vault. But he'd told Newt he was ready, if he were needed. "If you think you can do it, do it," said the coach, all optimistic belief. Gura walked to the end of the vault runway, ready to go.

"Showing no signs of his injury, the gutty senior flew through the air and was swarmed at the middle of the floor by a fired-up bunch of Michigan Wolverines," the *Daily* reported. The crowd of over 1,500 went crazy, and Gura got a 9.30—a counting score. We can safely assume that Newt was going a little crazy, too. Clearly, his boys would run through walls for their coach and their teammates.

"I didn't think a whole lot of it," Gura said, "but one of my teammates, I think it was Ward Black, commented that the way I was running down the vault [runway], how slow it was, he didn't think I was even going to get over the horse. ... With the adrenaline and pressure of the moment, I didn't realize it but someone else said I wasn't running very hard. I couldn't really run, and yet I did a vault."

The Wolverines were sloppy on parallel bars, but against the best high bar team in the nation, Michigan put the meet away. After that, even Michigan's losses were impressive, and those were very few. The loss to Penn State drew a crowd of over 6,000 to Rec Hall, and saw both teams shatter the 160-point barrier. All-arounder Jean Gagnon began to come into his own, with some Canadian experts saying he had "the potential to be the top gymnast in North America."

As the end of March neared, the Wolverines headed for Bloomington and Big Tens. Again, they didn't start well. Compulsories went badly and Michigan had to claw its way back, pulling into third halfway through the optionals, with Minnesota and Iowa in first and second. During the floor exercise, Terry Boys sprained his ankle (he still managed to finish), but the ring men carried the day, along with Gura, who was leading the all-around competition.

And on the second day of competition, the Wolverines made it all the way back to the top. Michigan compiled a 317.60 score, with Minnesota and Iowa dropping back to tie for second with

316.85. Newt and Murray Plotkin, now his assistant coach, were in disbelief as they calculated the final scores. Maybe they hadn't exhausted their share of "close ones" after all. Newt's steady philosophy of hitting clean sets, and letting the wins take care of themselves, had been validated once again.

As one *Daily* writer said, "In the three final pressure packed events, everyone from diminutive dynamo Pierre LeClerc to the steady Gura hit their routines as though they were charged by some divine spirit." Ward Black called the atmosphere "hellish;" Falb spoke of a "natural high;" Gura said only, "Beautiful, just beautiful."

Years later, he had much more to say about one of the sweetest moments of his gymnastics career.

"I won the all-around, and I remember when they read off the names to get your medal, I was so excited, we were so happy about the team, it was like I didn't want to be bothered," Gura remembered. "I went up and got the award, but I just wanted to get back down off the podium and be with the team. ... It was redemption, individually and the team."

"We came into today's events really psyched up, and more than anything else, I think that helped us to pull it out," Newt said. No matter how many titles his team won, it never got old—he was already planning the team celebration. Newt would likely never take credit, but it was because of him that so many young men became not a group of individuals, but a team, fighting for a collective triumph. Newt would individualize training programs as much as his athletes required—but it was all in the service of the greater group, and the Wolverines never lost sight of that.

After the drama of the championship, Newt took a full twelve-man squad to NCAAs in Eugene, Oregon—including Terry Boys. Gura was a finalist for the Nissen-Emery Award, the Heisman of men's gymnastics. The Wolverines moved into second after a solid round of compulsories on the first day, but dropped to fourth on the second day—and out of the finals.

Even so, the Wolverines were the talk of the crowd. Everyone had heard of their comeback to win the Big Ten title, and "it became clear that the majority of the heretofore non-partisan fans were now pulling for Michigan to pull one more upset." Through the whirlwind season, Newt's youngsters had become veterans. And Newt had already put up a sign at the team hotel: "Only 365 days until the 1974 gymnastics meet at Penn State." Always looking ahead, Newt never allowed himself to sit back and get complacently satisfied. There was always another goal for him and the gymnasts to aim for.

The *Daily* was a little more inclined to dwell on the season just past—and the unexpected success, which it laid at Newt's feet.

"The signs by Loken and the letters and telegrams of encouragement that were posted at Michigan's team hotel perhaps best exemplify the unity that helped Michigan get so far this season," wrote columnist Rich Stuck. "Every one of them had the word TEAM on it. Without that and a fellow named Newt Loken, the Michigan gymnastics team would never have reached the height it did."

Chapter 17

Newt's Last Big Ten Title

After the emotional 1973 season, Newt threw himself into preparing the Wolverines for another dogfight for the Big Ten. Now, Indiana had joined Iowa and Michigan at the top of the conference—and this year, Michigan would host the season opening Big Ten Invite in January. The Wolverines expected to be weak on pommel horse, as often was the case, but strong on rings, where they'd be led by captain Monty Falb and Joe Neuenswander. The vault team would be another high point, its top performers— Richard Bigras, J.P. Bouchard, Jean Gagnon and Pierre LeClerc— provided ample evidence that Newt's pipeline to Canada was still alive and well.

After a disappointing fifth-place finish at the Windy City Invitational and a narrow win over "much-improved" Ohio State, the Wolverines returned to Ann Arbor for the Big Ten Invite.

And the Wolverines proved they'd once again be a force to be reckoned with. In the compulsories, they placed at least one man in the top three of every event, with Gagnon, Bruce Medd and LeClerc sweeping the top three all-around spots. For Saturday's competition, optionals would begin at 10:30 in the morning, with finals that evening. Each coach was allowed to pick one automatic qualifier to each event, who would be joined by the top four gymnasts (by average of the optional and compulsory routines) in that apparatus.

Saturday proved to be another all-Michigan day, with Wolverines winning all but one event. LeClerc, Medd and Gagnon again went one-two-three in an all-around sweep. Randy Sakamoto won floor, Jerry Poynton pommel horse, LeClerc the vault, Gagnon the parallel bars and Medd the high bar. But it wasn't the time to get cocky. Iowa, Michigan's main rival, hadn't participated, and the next weekend, Michigan was set to face the still-powerful Salukis of Southern Illinois.

Newt watched his boys coast to a 160.10-156.45 victory, with Jean Gagnon leading the way. He notched a career high of 52.05 in his all-around win.

"He's really been coming into his own," Newt remarked afterward. His carefully nurtured Canadian pipeline had yielded another star.

A "spunky French-Canadian from Montreal," Gagnon had been a gymnast for eight years. He'd loved the atmosphere of the 1973 team, whose success surprised even him.

"The guys started to work seriously," Gagnon said. "There was a feeling of togetherness in the gym."

But despite dreams of making the Canadian Olympic team in 1976, Gagnon didn't see himself as much of a competitor, preferring to adopt gymnastics as his life philosophy.

"I'm not a competitor," Gagnon said. "It is an artistic sport. It's almost like getting into yoga and meditation."

He'd spent the summer in Ottawa, putting on exhibitions with the Chinese national teams. He got so close with one of the Chinese gymnasts that they even exchanged clothes. His experience with the highly talented team convinced him that with proper facilities and motivation, gymnastics could be just as big in North America.

To Gagnon, Newt's joy in coaching was a key to the team's

success. With Newt in charge, the sport never lost any of its sparkle for any of his athletes, as it sometimes can in the pressurized grind of college sports. Newt would never allow gymnastics to be anything but the most fun activity in the world.

"Newt understands there is a generation gap and adjusts himself to it," Gagnon said. "The coach is a real nice guy; I hope people learn from him."

Though Gagnon's emergence was encouraging, Newt was still concerned about Iowa, Michigan's biggest challenge—while Michigan had been averaging scores in the low 160s, the Hawkeyes had been averaging 164s. And the Hawkeyes would have the added advantage hosting Big Tens.

The Wolverines' next meet, a win over "clumsy" Minnesota, made a believer of Gopher head coach and legend Fred Roethlisberger.

"Michigan was much stronger than us," Roethlisberger told the *Daily*. "I think they're even better than last year."

Michigan won a "mini" Big Ten, beating out Illinois and Indiana in a two-day tri-meet. Then the Wolverines rolled over their old enemy, Michigan State. Now, finally, the two biggest tests of the regular season were upon them: Iowa and unbeaten Penn State.

To Newt's delight, the Wolverines pulled off a narrow upset of the Hawkeyes, winning 161.10-160.80. And pommel horse, which Newt had earlier called the team's "Achilles tendon," proved to be the key event, with Poynton and Rupert Hansen leading the way.

"The guys were really fired up for this one," Newt said. "There were some tremendous performances by the gang, especially the specialists."

A week later, the Nittany Lion juggernaut that had finished second in the 1973 NCAAs arrived in Ann Arbor. Penn State scored in the 163-164 range regularly, and Michigan's main man,

Gagnon, was nursing a severely swollen thumb. Bouchard was out completely, with an injured tendon in his left foot.

The meet, as advertised, was tense and exciting. Penn State took a narrow lead after floor exercise, but looked "lackadaisical" on pommel horse, where Michigan jumped ahead on a top-notch routine by Poynton. The Wolverines padded their tiny lead with wins on the still rings and vault. But with Gagnon scratched for the final three events, Penn State began to close the gap. The Nittany Lions inched closer on parallel bars, and even beat Michigan for the top total on high bar. But it wasn't enough.

Michigan had earned its second upset in two weeks, beating Penn State by almost a full point. Legendary head coach Gene Wettstone was a little bitter, but Newt couldn't contain himself, bubbling over to reporters about the show his boys had just put on.

"Wow, it was just wonderful," he enthused. "[Randy] Sakamoto was just tremendous. Pierre [LeClerc] and Bruce [Medd] had great evenings. [Jerry] Poynton was absolutely wonderful and the ring team came through again. The vaulting was out of sight and the three high bar men sailed through to a great finish."

Michigan's dual meet record for the year was now a perfect 7-0. The Big Ten championship seemed destined to remain in Ann Arbor.

But Bouchard, it was now clear, wouldn't be able to compete on anything but vault. Worse, Gagnon was nearly incapacitated by his jammed thumb. The Wolverines headed for Iowa City with two of their top performers at less than one hundred percent. Bouchard managed to win the vault title; Bob Darden and Carey Culbertson tied for the high bar championship; and Falb came in second on rings. But it wasn't enough to topple Iowa. Michigan finished a bitter second.

The Hawkeyes had punched their ticket to the NCAA championships. Michigan waited and watched the results of the other conference championships, hoping to slip through a loophole in the rules into the biggest meet of the season.

The NCAA had declared that not only did a school have to win its conference championship in order to attend NCAA Championships, but it also had to score at least 300 points over the two-day competition in doing so. Michigan had posted a 322.20 total at Big Tens; if Air Force, the likely winner of the Western Independent Conference, couldn't manage a 300, the Wolverines would be the best of the second-place teams.

On the last Sunday in March, Newt's boys gathered at West Quad director Leon West's house for the annual team dinner. It was even more of a celebration than usual, because the news had finally come in that Air Force had only scored a 297. Michigan was going to the NCAA Championships in State College! Sure, the Wolverines would be handicapped by the near-month of waiting around to see if they'd be going, and by the loss of Falb to bicep surgery, but just to be invited was a victory in itself.

"Loken declined to make a flat out prediction on the meet's outcome, but the wry smile and wink that accompanied his opinion seemed to indicate that the gymnastics genius knew more than he disclosed," the *Daily* reported.

" 'Anything can happen in a two-day meet,' he said.

"We certainly hope so, Mr. Loken. We certainly do."

At any rate, it was sure to be an unforgettable experience. Penn State, known for its excellent gymnastics crowds, had already sold out Rec Hall. The little arena would be rocking.

Michigan headed for State College without Bouchard or Falb. After the compulsories, where the Wolverines had major pommel horse trouble, they sat in seventh place of eight teams. A rally in the final three events had proved too little, too late. Iowa State, Cal and Arizona State qualified to team finals after the optionals, with Michigan in last place. The Wolverines didn't even send an individual finalist into the third day of competition. It was a rough, disappointing end to what could have been a season for the ages; but even though the Wolverines hadn't made the most of their chance, at least they'd gotten it. Newt had to be satisfied with that.

The boys would get a second chance at glory in 1975 though, only losing Bouchard and Falb to graduation. In addition to the '74 stalwarts, Newt added new recruits Harley Danner, a Michigan state high school all-around champion; Bob Creek, a quality high bar man; and Dave Keeshin, Bruce's younger brother. He also welcomed a transfer from Alpena Junior College, a rings specialist with a puffy afro named Kurt Golder. Golder would never forget the chance Newt took in bringing him to Ann Arbor, or the opportunities he received because of it. Twenty years later, Newt would be instrumental in bringing Golder back to the University of Michigan—this time, as a head coach.

Newt continued heading the football cheerleading squad, and a new wrinkle entered the equation for 1974-75—girls. Female cheerleaders had been a fixture at basketball games for several years by then, but now they would be on the hallowed Michigan football field.

The *Daily* wailed that the "sacred tradition of all-male football cheerleaders is being threatened," noting sullenly that at least the squads would be kept completely separate (the girls would remain exclusively with the band). And only the male cheerleaders would be allowed to perform the traditional backflips off the wall at the Big House. Newt, of course, took the news with the same philosophical equanimity with which he would greet the newly formed women's gymnastics team a year later.

"[Athletic Director] Don Canham had a daughter, Claire," Newt said. "She was on the pom-pom squad at the high school, and she was coming to Michigan. So he thought, 'Well, we have pom-pom girls.' He just decided, and he talked to the Board in Control [of Intercollegiate Athletics] about having pom-pom girls on the field. Won't interfere with the men's gym cheer squad, because they've got to do their backflips off the wall and all that jazz. … At first it was a mild setback, you think you can't handle it, macho, all that, but it worked out very good."

It was like the change of tumbling to floor exercise, or the demise of trampoline—maybe at the beginning, it was upsetting. But after a while, it wasn't so bad any more. Newt was never one to be a stick-in-the-mud, dwelling on how much better things were in the past. And he had seen what his own daughters were capable of, especially with Lani's diving championship. Newt certainly wasn't going to stand in the way of college women gaining opportunities.

As Newt's gymnasts headed into their season, they had already absorbed several injuries. Co-captain Carey Culbertson, Jean Gagnon and Randy Sakamoto were all sidelined with, respectively, a broken wrist, severe shoulder tendonitis and an ankle injury. And, once again, there was a new rule in place: instead of counting the top three scores of five competing gymnasts on each event, in 1975, the top four scores would count, bumping desirable team totals to around 200. Depth would be more important, especially where all-arounders were concerned. Without two quality all-arounders, it would be very difficult for a team to succeed.

Michigan, fortunately, had just such depth. Co-captain Bruce Keeshin would lead the all-arounders, and to complete the pair, Newt could choose from Bruce Medd, Jean Gagnon, Richard Bigras, Bob Darden, Harley Danner, John Udell and Sam Roberts. And their season wouldn't truly start until after the Windy City Invitational and Michigan's winter holiday.

But when Michigan hosted the Big Ten Invitational to open the season in January, the injured list hadn't improved. Nonetheless, the Wolverines dominated their competition in front of 2,000 Crisler fans. Michigan took home the most individual honors "with machine-like consistency," placing at least two gymnasts in the top three of every event. The only event a Wolverine didn't win was still rings—and Golder and Neuenswander were hot on the heels of Indiana's champ, Jack Malmedhal, in second and third.

"We're gradually pulling everything together," Newt said afterward. "If we keep progressing like this, our team performance will be much better in another month."

In just a week, though, the Wolverines faced one of their toughest tests of the season, a meet with the Louisiana State Tigers. The Tigers had consistently scored above 200, and Michigan was still missing Gagnon and Culbertson. For the first time since 1973, the Wolverines lost a dual meet. Though they kept up with LSU on every event but pommel horse and parallel bars, where they were badly outscored, the Wolverines didn't notch a single apparatus win. Over 4,500 fans—a record crowd for LSU—attended the meet.

But one of the best-remembered parts of the trip came not in the arena, but on the corner of Bourbon and Toulouse in New Orleans, just an hour's drive from Baton Rouge. Newt set his boys loose in the city, instructing them to be back on the corner by nine o' clock. Newt's wanderings didn't take him far from the street corner. Soon a young boy had set up shop there, tap dancing and passing around a hat to his impressed observers. Newt, nudged by his inner showman, just couldn't resist.

Approaching the boy, he said, "I'll match you for steps. You do a step, and I'll match it. Then I'll do a step and you'll match it." And they were off.

"So we watched each other's feet and he'd do a step and I'd almost duplicate it, and then I'd do a step and he'd do it better than ever," Newt remembered. "We did that for about a half an hour. And when I looked up, jeez, there was a big crowd! Big crowd standing around watching us perform! That was a compliment. And within the crowd I saw some of the team. I said, 'Hey guys, after this next step, pass a hat and let's get out of here!' So they passed a hat and didn't get anything. But they had a million laughs about it afterward."

It was typical Newt. How many other coaches would have even thought of challenging a kid to a tap-dancing contest? It made his gymnasts love him even more.

Michigan's toughest Big Ten dual of the year, against Minnesota in Minneapolis, came just after the seven-point loss to the Tigers. "They always seem to psych up for us," Newt noted, "and with the Gymnastic Alumni Day attracting many of the old charges plus the expected large crowd, it will be one heck of a meet."

For Michigan, it certainly was. With its best team score of the season, Michigan thrashed the Gophers, 209.40-205.15, winning every event and sweeping the high bar. The only thing that didn't go perfectly for the Wolverines was Bruce Keeshin losing the all-around competition to Jeff LaFleur.

While the gymnasts were rolling over Ohio State and Indiana, ominous rumblings began emanating from the Athletic Department. More and more people were pushing for women's sports—and women's athletic scholarships.

"No," Athletic Director Don Canham asserted, "We are not going to offer women's scholarships at Michigan. At present we award twenty to non-revenue sports and next year it'll be eighteen. Pretty soon we won't be able to give any to men." Though he wasn't entirely correct, he was closer to the truth than many people thought then.

But the gymnastics team wasn't taking much notice. They just continued to win. When the big clash with Iowa, the defending Big Ten champions, arrived on February 21, Newt had 199 career wins. No coach in collegiate gymnastics had ever reached the two hundred milestone; legendary Penn State coach Gene Wettstone was the closest, with 194, but had coached for ten years longer than Newt when he achieved that mark. Ever the consummate coach, Newt maintained it was just another meet.

"The number isn't as important as the reflection that it represents many fine and talented young men who have passed through our gym," Newt said, as always deflecting the credit to the athletes. "It has been my pleasure associating with all of them."

Rupert Hansen assured *Daily* reporters that the gymnasts weren't taking the milestone lightly.

"We're really firing up for this one," he said. "We've all been looking forward to the two hundredth, and we want to do the job for Newt."

The Wolverines put on an inspired performance, erupting for a season-high 215 points to Iowa's 205. A sullen Iowa head coach Neil Schmidt admitted, "It was a helluva meet. I'm really happy for Newt and his team. They all finally hit." Newt couldn't contain his glee at the team's performance—especially not when his boys threw him a surprise party following the meet. Newt even received a telegram congratulating him on his 200th win from President Gerald Ford, another Michigan man (who had been prompted by Newt's captain, Jerry Poynton). Newt was well known before, but this was truly *national* recognition.

"I was most impressed by the letter I received from your team members," wrote President Ford in the telegram. "Your record certainly attests to your coaching ability, but their very obvious respect for you speaks highly of the warmth and affection you inspire as a leader."

"Everybody thought it was great," Newt remembered. "It was certainly posted on the bulletin board. It was a high spot, to hear from the President of the United States of America about gymnastics."

Unfortunately for Michigan, there was one more meet left: a showdown with top-ranked Indiana State, which finished the

Wolverines' season with a defeat. Newt described his team as "sufficiently humbled," and busily set about scheduling challenges for the break before Big Ten championships. Michigan was heavily favored, and Pierre LeClerc declared himself "positive Michigan will win."

Michigan, Iowa and Minnesota were slated to be the contenders among the eight Big Ten squads. After the opening day of competition, it seemed that Iowa and Minnesota had already conceded the title to Michigan. Already, their focus had shifted to individual event titles. They were on to something. Halfway through the optional routines, the Wolverines were up on their nearest rivals, the Gophers, by nearly twenty points. In front of a crowd of 2,000 people, many of the Wolverines improved on their best scores of the season. Minnesota coach Fred Roethlisberger could only admire the show.

"Michigan is just great," he said. "They're the only team that could compete at the nationals."

On the final day, 6,000 people came to watch Michigan dominate its competition. The team had four first-place finishers, and swept the top three in floor and high bar. Harley Danner became the first freshman ever to win the all-around title.

Newt couldn't fit enough superlatives into his sentences.

"This was a fantastic performance by the guys," he gushed afterward. "I'm tremendously elated with the super job of our team." He was the first Big Ten coach ever to win twelve conference titles, calling his latest one the "best ever." No coach yet has matched Loken's mark—and it's unlikely anyone ever will.

After the elation of Big Tens, the NCAA Championships were a bit of a letdown, with Michigan getting bumped from the team finals. Three Wolverines earned All-America status: Joe Neuenswander on rings, Richard Bigras on vault and Bob Creek on high bar, as Cal took home the team title. No one knew that Loken's dynasty had finally come to an end.

Chapter 18

Title IX Arrives

Barely eight hours after the end of the 1975 season, Newt was looking forward to the 1976 season. But he, and the rest of the Michigan Athletic Department, had a new challenge to face. Title IX, an act that required public institutions to provide equal educational opportunities to both men and women, went into effect on July 21, 1975. That requirement extended to sports—and though there was no way the coaches and administrators could have known the effect it would have on their programs, they were already worried. Over the next few decades, many of their fears proved to be well founded, especially concerning men's gymnastics.

"Who's got the money?" Athletic Director Don Canham asked rhetorically in the *Daily*. At the time, Michigan and Ohio State were the only self-supporting athletic departments in the Big Ten—and even those two were seriously worried. "We haven't got enough money here at Michigan or anywhere else to add sports and staffs. We're doing just the opposite. … There's no possibility we could match the women's scholarships with our men's scholarships. If we were forced to do that we'd drop the men's scholarships, that's all. We just can't do it."

Canham described exactly what would happen after Title IX was reinforced with gender equality laws.

"If you add a women's program, where does the money come from? If it comes at the expense of the men's program, you're going to have fewer sports," Canham said. "Sports that don't bring in revenue are going to have to be dropped because you can't drop your money-making sports."

Title IX's full effect wouldn't be felt for many more years—but for the 1976 season, Michigan finally added a women's gymnastics team. Newt coached the team, naturally, with assistants Bruce Keeshin and Linda Morton, the coach of the "highly successful Ann Arbor YWCA" gym team. Though he had to split time between the teams for much of the school year, Newt and his gymnasts don't remember the men's team getting neglected. At the time, it's doubtful that members of such a highly successful program would have worried about the possible effects of a brand-new women's team and the larger ripples from Title IX itself. The women's team, interestingly, held its practices in the Sports Coliseum—the building that, starting in 2003, would house the Newt Loken Men's Gymnastics Training Center. Newt had coached girls before, and shown himself adept at it even with the different events—just four instead of six, with balance beam and the uneven bars in addition to floor exercise and vault.

"That was a toughie," Newt remembered. "I would finish my men, and … around six o' clock, I'd take my yogurt, walk over to the women's gym, which is now the men's gym, and I'd coach these half a dozen girls that didn't know much about competition. And we'd try to teach them things on the balance beam, back handsprings, handstands, and so on. We found that the girls have a tendency to want to be spotted. They come up from a girls' club where everyone is treasured as a student, because they come back the next day and [the clubs] get some revenue from their parents. So they grew up under the philosophy of spotting. And I would say to them, 'Why don't you just pull a crash mat over here and land on that?' And they'd say, 'Oh no, we can't do that.' 'But my boys do it all the time.' 'Spot me, spot me.' So I'd spot them. After a week or two or more, I'd come home, and my wife would have a hot tub of water and a couple aspirin and a Coke or maybe a beer. I'd get in that hot tub and have to rest my body. I really needed it. … We placed ninth in the Big Ten, ninth out of ten. Wasn't last, but it was almost last. And then the next year we got a lady coach [named Anne Cornell], so I backed off."

The women's team has since claimed nineteen Big Ten team titles, with seventeen coming under current head coach Bev Plocki. Michigan is one of the few schools today to boast elite squads in both men's and women's gymnastics—there are only 17 varsity men's teams left in the country.

Newt's 1976 men's team was strongly favored to win another Big Ten championship. Despite the loss of Jean Gagnon, Bruce Keeshin and Bruce Medd, the core of the team was still solid. Much would depend on the incoming freshmen, which included Canadian Nigel Rothwell, a protégé of former Michigan gymnast Nino Marion, and parallel-bars whiz John Corritore, a finalist in the Illinois State championships.

Thanks to donations from former gymnasts, in the fall of 1975 Newt was able to purchase a new videotape system— the innovative coach was one of the first in gymnastics to use videotape to help his athletes improve their routines. He and the gymnasts jokingly referred to it as "Hal," like the computer in the movie *2001: A Space Odyssey.* The Wolverines used it two or three times a week during workouts and filmed every one of their competitions for later observations. The near-instant feedback proved invaluable as an aid to Newt's already formidable coaching skills. A skill could be slowed down, repeated over and over, whatever it took to show (rather than tell) the gymnast exactly what he needed to change.

Newt's new assistant coach spent the year learning about the other side of his sport and came away even more in awe of the coach than he had been previously. "I was *very* impressed by how well Coach could remain in control of a very complicated situation," Ray Gura wrote in his journal of the season after the Big Ten Invitational in early February. "For example, during the meet he was doing the following things, at the same time: 1) spotting, 2) coaching, 3) watching the judging, 4) keeping track of the line-up, etc. He managed to keep ahead of all these things, and watch some of the other teams too." Newt's new assistant was consistently impressed with the coach's ability to solve every problem in the quickest, most efficient way possible.

Gura made his own significant contributions as well. In 1971, he'd trained in Japan with best friend and teammate Ted Marti, and the two Wolverines had brought back the idea of the *Gashuku*, an intensive training camp. Prior to the 1976 season, Gura organized a Gashuku that would involve the specialists for the first time.

"The objectives of the program fall into two general headings," Gura wrote. "Gymnastic Improvement—increase in skills, strength, endurance, etc. [and] Team Feelings—a closer feeling of team spirit and friendship." This incarnation of the Gashuku was "like six Gashukus going on at the same time" because of the specialists' participation. Newt's usual enthusiasm was evident as he handed out Michigan Gashuku '75 t-shirts to all his gymnasts. The pommel horse men, especially, took the idea to heart and maintained great intensity throughout the week.

While the women struggled through their first season, understandably having a hard time matching scores against the more established teams, the men's team enjoyed its usual domination. Newt's boys showed nearly unbeatable consistency on every event. According to Gura, most of Michigan's troubles in the regular season came when deciding whom to leave out of the starting lineup. From the very beginning, Newt had far more talented gymnasts than competition slots. "I think that the worst part of his job is telling guys that they didn't make the team," Gura noted.

Though the decisions regarding the all-around, parallel bars and rings lineups were difficult, no event cost the coaches more sleep than high bar. On high bar, Michigan had three former Big Ten champions: Bob Darden, Carey Culbertson and Bob Creek.

"Two of them tied one year, and that's how we got three," Gura said. "We could only use two of them [in a given meet]. So we were going to have a Big Ten horizontal bar champion sitting on the bench. And you know no other team had one. ... It was just a credit to how deep we were and how good Michigan was at the time, that we would be forced to put a Big Ten defending champion on the bench because we didn't have room for him in the lineup."

Creek proved to be, in every sense of the word, the scholar-athlete. He remained with the team for five years; in 1979, his final year, he was a graduate student in chemical engineering, maintaining a 3.6 GPA while balancing eighteen hours a week of practice with his studies. To top it off, he won another Big Ten high bar championship and placed third on the event at NCAAs. For the ever-busy Creek, the team *was* his social life. A gymnast since the seventh grade, he set high standards for himself and usually met them. His relationship with Newt was marked by mutual affection.

"Coach Loken is a real person who doesn't deny that he has strengths or weaknesses," Creek told the *Daily*. "Everyone loves him because he shows personal interest. He's more interested in the growth of the individual than winning, although [winning] is our goal."

That goal received a minor but shocking setback on February 14, 1976, when something happened that no one had ever seen before: Michigan lost a dual meet in Crisler Arena. Since 1968, when the Wolverines first started competing at Crisler, they'd never lost a home dual. But in front of about 1,500 fans, Michigan narrowly fell to Indiana State. The Cyclones were led by a future Olympian, the incomparable Kurt Thomas. The Wolverines edged out the Cyclones on floor exercise, thanks in part to a "smooth and artistic performance" by Randy Sakamoto. Jerry Poynton stole the show on pommel horse with a 9.40, but Indiana State won the event. Michigan pulled ahead on rings with strong performances from Joe Neuenswander, Pierre LeClerc and Scott Ponto, but after that, it was all Indiana State.

Two weeks later, Michigan's two gymnastics teams hosted their first double dual at Crisler. It would be the girls' first home meet ever, and their final dual of the season. For the men, it was all about celebrating the careers of the seven seniors, as well as Newt's birthday; Indiana wasn't expected to put up much of a fight. On Newt's 57th birthday, he guided both his teams to wins before 2,500 fans, with the men crushing the Hoosiers 211.50-192.80 and the women coming back to beat Eastern Michigan, 78.45-74.95. Afterward, his boys surprised him with a party, celebrating his already long and storied career.

According to Ray Gura's journal, Jerry Poynton took care of all the arrangements. The men's and women's teams, along with friends, parents and other guests gathered in the Victors Room at Crisler Arena for apple cider and cake. Pierre LeClerc presented Newt with two tickets to the Resurrection Jazz Band concert and a gift dinner at the Gandy Dancer, a favorite Ann Arbor restaurant, for him and Dorothy. Clearly, the men's and women's teams didn't feel they were in competition with each other, a warm relationship that still exists today. They didn't compete against each other—they competed *for* Michigan, and they competed for Newt.

Heading into Big Tens, however, everything started to fall

apart. On March 14, the coaches began to fear an outbreak of chicken pox on the team—two of the members of the Georgia Southern team, against whom Michigan had had a meet in early March, had come down with it. "The incubation period is from 7-20 days," Gura wrote on March 14. "We won't be sure until Big Ten time. This could be disastrous." Then on March 19, Harley Danner reinjured his knee doing a full twist on floor exercise. Pierre LeClerc pulled his groin the Monday before the meet, but decided to compete through it. Chuck Stillerman's grandfather had a heart attack.

"We leave for Big Tens tomorrow," Gura wrote on March 23. "Today was a pretty good day ... but there is still a strange, sad, blah atmosphere in the gym. I can't believe how many things have gone wrong in the last 4-5 days. We were going so good, and we were so prepared, and then about a week ago the roof fell in."

Though Michigan was still favored—Gura thought they could pull out the victory—the picture wasn't as rosy. And after the first day of competition, Minnesota had taken a commanding lead. "We still have three events to go," Newt said, trying to keep up his optimism, "but it looks pretty bleak." Without sophomore sensation Danner, the team was faltering—and the final three events were Minnesota's strongest. On Saturday, led by all-around brothers Tim and Jeff LaFleur, the Gophers captured their first Big Ten title since 1949.

"The seniors are very disappointed," Newt said afterward. "We were up against a team that was just super this weekend. ... We missed that third all-around man. We missed Harley Danner." Winning had never been the be-all, end-all for Newt, but he felt the disappointment of his athletes keenly. He knew what it would have meant for his seniors to go out with another conference championship, and how much it hurt to know that the title could have been theirs easily, with a healthy Danner.

The loss clearly haunted his team. Even heading into NCAAs,

Jerry Poynton was still thinking about the team's failure at Big Tens. With nine competitors, Michigan had the most individuals at the national championships; and Minnesota, with Tim LaFleur now injured, looked as if it couldn't make a run for the title.

"I still haven't been able to get the Big Ten meet out of my mind," he told the *Daily*. "If we would've only had Danner we could've come [to Philadelphia] and won [NCAAs]."

Bob Darden put on the finest Wolverine showing at NCAAs, earning a second-place finish on high bar. Penn State took home the team title. As had happened for so many years before Newt's dynasty was established, Newt was left with an off season wondering what could have been … if only.

Chapter 19

The Late Seventies

As Newt entered his thirtieth year at the University of Michigan, he had a tough rebuilding job ahead. He'd lost seven seniors from the 1976 team and had big holes to fill, especially in the all-around. Harley Danner was still out with his knee injury, but sophomore Nigel Rothwell appeared ready to step into the lead all-around position. Though the rules had changed slightly, allowing four all-arounders and two specialists to compete on every event under the six-up, four-count system that continues today, all-arounders were still key to a successful team.

"The purpose [of the rule change] was to promote the all-around without losing sight of the specialist program," Newt told the *Daily*, no doubt with a bit of relief. Despite all the emphasis on all-arounders, Newt had never stopped encouraging and recruiting his outstanding specialists.

As usual, Newt had a few specialists who were second-to-none in the conference: co-captains Scott Ponto and Chuck Stillerman on the rings and pommel horse, respectively. Stillerman had also taken second place on the floor exercise at the NAAU championships, delighting crowds with his double backflip.

As a pre-med student, Stillerman had managed to balance a demanding course load with gymnastics practice for four years.

Now a senior, he counted his relationship with Newt as far more important than any of his accomplishments, which included two Big Ten floor titles.

When he was a high school senior, Stillerman broke his leg in a motorcycle accident, putting his gymnastics career in jeopardy. "Most universities would have taken away my scholarship, at least until I proved myself again," Stillerman told the *Daily*. "But not Coach Loken. He stuck by me and had faith." Stillerman considered Newt not only his coach but his counselor and friend. To Newt, serving as a father figure was one of his paramount functions.

Other specialists included senior Kurt Golder on the rings, senior Doug Shokes on the parallel bars and junior Bob Creek on the high bar. And after a year of splitting time between his boys and the newly formed women's gymnastics team, Newt would be back with the men exclusively. The women's team hired a full time head coach named Anne Cornell, who had coached the championship women's gymnastics team at Ann Arbor Huron High School for the past two years. Ray Gura had moved on, but Newt would have coaching help from both Bob Darden and Jerry Poynton.

Before the season even began, the gymnasts would witness two significant campus events, one exciting and one melancholy. In December 1976, the Soviet gymnasts, who had "dazzled" at the Montreal Olympics, would perform at Crisler Arena. The Soviet men had taken silver, the women gold. At the same time, plans for demolishing the eighty-two-year-old Waterman Gymnasium to make room for an addition to the Chemistry Building kicked into gear.

According to the administration, the Waterman-Barbour gym complex was more expensive to renovate and refurbish than to demolish. A two-thousand signature petition to save the historic buildings was "brushed off," according to the *Daily*, the buildings were closed to keep them out of sight and out of mind. By the end of the school year, the first place on campus where Newt had taught the art of tumbling and gymnastics was gone. In April, about five hundred people were allowed to rummage through and purchase the assorted objects still in the building.

"They just don't build spaces like this anymore," said architect Richard Neumann wistfully.

Among the memorabilia were light switches, Venetian blinds, mirrors, basketball hoops—and a trampoline.

The Soviet visit, despite the still-frosty relations between the USSR and the United States, was a highlight of the year. On December 7, twenty-one world-class Soviet gymnasts arrived in Ann Arbor, nineteen of whom had been world or Olympic team members. They were on a ten-city U.S. tour, part of a program sponsored by the U.S. Gymnastics Federation. The Michigan gymnasts welcomed the Soviets with an enormous sign, which said Welcome Soviet Gymnasts in Russian lettering.

"I'm tremendously excited," Newt said, to no one's surprise. "Ann Arbor is a super gymnastics town, and they're going to get what they deserve: the best show on earth."

No one wanted to miss this: 13,600 fans flooded Crisler Arena until it was standing-room only as the Soviets put on breathtaking demonstrations of artistic, acrobatic and rhythmic gymnastics. Sometimes, they even used each other's bodies as pieces of apparatus.

"They radiated a mastery of their art form of gymnastics," Newt said afterward, inspired even more than ever to aim for perfection with his own gymnasts.

When the regular season began for his boys, though, they didn't show the same sort of mastery. A new set of Olympic compulsories had been handed down, and Newt wasn't the only coach who thought they might be over the top. After an invitational meet, former Michigan gymnast Jim Brown, now the Indiana head coach, remarked, "These routines are too hard for college gymnasts."

Michigan got its first look at conference favorite Minnesota in mid-January. On Gopher Alumni Day, with many of Newt's old teammates in attendance, Minnesota soundly beat the Wolverines, taking first in four of the six events and placing four gymnasts in the top five in the all-arounders. Nigel Rothwell took first on vault, with Ponto and Golder going one-two on still rings. "They're going to be hard to beat in the conference championships," Newt said afterward.

The following weekend, Michigan, finally back to full health, got back in the win column with a double dual against the Spartans. Over eight hundred people struggled through a blizzard to watch the meet, in which the Wolverines, to Newt's evident delight, broke the 200.00-point barrier. His boys went on to squeak out a narrow win by just one tenth over Indiana, 207.10-207.00. Down by .15 going into high bar, the final event, Doug Zahour and Bob Creek came through with clutch routines to pull Michigan into the lead.

In the Big Ten Quadrangular meet against Iowa, Ohio State and Wisconsin, Michigan would face a crucial test. The team passed with flying colors. It was the last Crisler meet for the four seniors, but Michigan's winning effort was led by the standout all-around sophomore, Nigel Rothwell, who won the all-around competition. The Wolverines took home scads of titles: Rothwell in the all-around and on the floor, Chuck Ventura on the pommel horse, Ponto on the rings (Golder was second), John Corritore on the parallel bars and Bob Creek on the high bar.

But for the seniors, it was bittersweet. "It seems like yesterday I walked in here as a freshman," Ponto said, "and here it is my last meet."

Chuck Stillerman had come in early to work out and bumped into his senior friend on the wrestling team, who was also competing for his last time. "We saw each other," he said, "and the tears came to the eyes."

"It's such a special thing, competing at Crisler," Kurt Golder remembered. "And my time as an athlete at Michigan was so special to me that it was a sad [thing], when the meet was over."

Golder's story was distinctive among the rest of his teammates—among most gymnasts competing for top college teams. Golder had caught the gymnastics bug from his older brother and an older cousin. "I knew right away, after just watching a couple of practices, that that's what I wanted to do," Golder said. But after high school, where he was an admitted "goof-off," Golder didn't have the grades to get into a four-year college. He spent two years at Alpena Junior College in his hometown, serving as an assistant coach for the Alpena High School gymnastics team on the side.

Golder had already met Newt once before when he attended a coaching seminar in Traverse City led by Mas Watanabe, the legendary gymnastics coach renowned for his technical expertise. Newt came to the same seminar, but had no idea that Golder could be a strong addition to his team. Seeing Golder's puffy afro and bushy black mustache, Newt thought Golder had already graduated from college. In fact, Golder wasn't even twenty yet. Upon learning that Golder still had years of eligibility left, Newt gave him an application to Michigan. And as they say, the rest is history. Golder became a strong ring man for Newt's teams in the mid-70s, and in 1997, returned to Ann Arbor as the head coach of the men's gymnastics team.

And Golder loved few things more than competitions at Crisler Arena.

"I loved competing there because of the energy that the team had and the adrenaline that was flowing through my veins," Golder said. "We always dominated."

Following that year's final meet at Crisler, the Wolverines would face Indiana State as a "warm-up" to Big Ten Championships. "The timing for the meet is perfect," Newt said before he and his team left for the Hoosier State. "A powerhouse like Indiana State will serve as excellent preparation for the Big Ten meet."

But the Kurt Thomas-led Sycamores were too much for the Wolverines, who scored a season high and still lost by ten points.

"He was spectacular," Golder said of Kurt Thomas. "He never missed a routine, and ... he had a real unique flashy skill on each event. ... It was great to be on the same competitive floor as him."

The team stayed in Ann Arbor as a group over spring break to prepare for Big Tens. Co-captain Scott Ponto asserted that he wasn't worried about either injuries or the layoff before the big meet.

"You gotta be cocky," he told the *Daily*. "You have to know that you'll come through, otherwise you won't."

Golder believed he'd learned his lesson in 1976 about peaking too early and that he was now in his best condition ever. All year, he'd worried about putting together his perfect routine; now, the hard work seemed about to pay off. In a statement that he'd repeat in various forms as a head coach, he told the *Daily*, "You have to go for broke, no doubt about it. Playing it cautious is the key to an 8.00 score. There's no second chance."

Despite all their preparation, things seemed to have come full circle for the Wolverines. At Big Tens, Michigan came in third behind champion Minnesota and second-place Illinois—the same order of finish as the Wolverines' first-ever conference meet. Chuck Ventura won the pommel horse title; five Wolverines went on to NCAAs, where John Corritore came in second on parallel bars to the sublime Kurt Thomas.

Corritore had entered Michigan as a parallel bars specialist, but as a freshman, assistant coach Ray Gura had noted he was a "timid" gymnast.

"He is very hesitant and frightened to try new moves," Gura wrote. "However he is sincere and serious about improving."

He was serious all right. Corritore sometimes daydreamed so

vividly about gymnastics that he'd get an adrenaline rush. For him, though, the group atmosphere of general practice wasn't as helpful to him as one-on-one instruction. Newt, of course, was always available—"If it'll produce a champion," he said, "I'll give them all the individual attention they want."

Corritore and Newt would meet at the gym at noon every day, with the coach perching on the spotting platform and munching a peanut butter and jelly sandwich as the gymnast practiced his routines. With no one else in the gym, Corritore could concentrate on his gymnastics with no distractions—and have Newt's undivided attention.

But Corritore wasn't an exception; in fact, he was the rule. Gura remembered Newt making time for individual instruction during his career as well.

"He'd work one-on-one with me on the skills I was having trouble with," Gura said. "I think that went on, one way or another, almost all four years. And probably with about four other individuals, who were probably not even aware that he was doing that [with several other gymnasts]. ... It was a tribute to him. Of course, it made the team better, which is what he was trying to do. But there was no clock that he'd time in and out on. He'd do as much as he had to."

At NCAAs, John Corritore had put all his instruction from Newt into action. As he swept through his routine, the national title seemed within his grasp. The crowd in Arizona began screaming his name. But he still had one more lesson to learn.

"He was up there and swinging like crazy," Newt remembered. "Near the end of his routine, he said to himself, 'You know, John? I am going to win the national title.' And then he missed. He missed! Missed his routine. Balked on a handstand. He came back and afterwards he said on the way home, 'Coach, I was telling myself I won the title before I won it. And you've often told us that you aren't done with your routine until you're back on the players' bench. Then you're done, not before.' So the next year, he made a pledge to himself: 'I'm not going to talk to myself on the damn parallel bars until I'm finished.'"

And in 1978, it all finally came together for Corritore. After a tremendous regular season and a Big Ten parallel bars title, he came into event finals at NCAAs tied with Long Beach State's Yoichi Tomita for the lead. The little voice in his head was silent through his routine. This year, there would be no balking, no silly mistakes.

"John knew he had to have a 9.70, and by God, he did it!" Newt exulted afterward. Newt would never take credit for an athlete's success, but Corritore's championship was a testament to Newt's positive, all-in style of coaching. Today, the parallel bars area in the Newt Loken Gymnastics Training Center is named for Corritore.

Chapter 20

Renaissance Man

In addition to his life's work of coaching the Michigan men's gymnastics team, Newt always kept up a full schedule of extra-curriculars. Having earned his doctorate in the School of Education, he not only taught classes in physical education and gymnastics (where, early in his career, he often found some candidates for his teams) but also classes in a variety of dancing styles. Coaching his team remained priority number one, but in order to support his family, extra jobs were necessary.

"I don't know how [Dorothy] survived," Newt said of his wife, who worked as a nurse for many years. "I was always doing something. Square-dance calling, cheerleading clinics." Daughters Chris and Lani worked many of Newt's cheerleading clinics, demonstrating and teaching cheers as well as selling many of Newt's cheerleading books. "It made a buck," Newt said of his activities outside coaching. "It seemed like money was the important thing with us, because my salary was so minimum. ... The philosophy was [at] Michigan, what you do is you coach, but you get a job on the side to support. My job was physical education. I was teaching full-time in phys ed. ... In the meantime, you convert some of this energy over here towards coaching, more and more and more, recruiting and all that stuff, it became a big full-time job for me versus phys ed."

Nonetheless, his non-gymnastics activities continued. He especially loved golf and skiing, and encouraged his children in a variety of sports. He was a fitness director at Camp Michikewa in Cheboygan, Michigan, where Dorothy was the camp nurse. Newt taught cheerleading camps and clinics, along with heading the Michigan cheerleading squad. One of his notable cheerleading ventures was the Smith-Walbridge cheerleading camps, coaching alongside Lawrence "Herkie" Herkimer.

"He made many wonderful contacts [there]," Newt's daughter Lani said. "Herkie eventually asked him to leave the U of M and join Herkie in creating a new cheerleading organization, the National Cheerleaders' Association. Dad decided that his heart was at the U of M and turned the offer down. Herkie's business made him a multi-millionaire."

Newt wasn't about money; he cared about all the people he touched. And not all those people were at the University of Michigan.

For twelve years, Newt was the director of the Huron Valley Swim Club. Lani remembered the summers there as a wonderful time. In preparation for the club's opening each Memorial Day, Dorothy lovingly coaxed each flowerbed of pink petunias into full bloom. The Loken children spent the majority of every summer day there, playing in the water, soaking up the sun, and participating in the swimming and diving competitions. As the girls grew older, they became part of the Huron Valley Swim Club lifeguarding crew. And there was nothing as enjoyable as the line-dancing (led by Newt, naturally) in the evenings in front of the clubhouse, to the tune of Don Ho's "Tiny Bubbles." The swim club provided the perfect opportunity to blend work and family.

"When I visit Ann Arbor, I still run into former Huron Valley Swim Club people (some were very, very young when we were there)," Lani said. "They all remember their wonderful times and beloved Newt Loken."

And aside from gymnastics, one of the things Newt was best known for was heading the trampoline float in the Hudson's Thanksgiving Day Parade in Detroit for fifty years. Early in Newt's association with Michigan, the J. L. Hudson promotions department called, attracted by the trampoline act that was becoming well known. Now they wanted Newt to bounce on a trampoline float in the parade. First, the trampoline was Newt's; after a few years, Hudson's decided to invest in its own trampoline. The float was one of the most popular in the parade. Newt fondly remembers seeing grown-up children from the early years, coming back to see the parade with their own children, and sometimes even grandchildren.

"Every Thanksgiving, we'd hope that the weather wasn't too cold," Newt said. "Fifty years I bounced in that, and then I turned it over to [former gymnast and diver] Dick Kimball. He's still got it. They dropped it for a few years, but I think there were some fans … that wrote to the company and said, 'You should have the trampoline back!' It was the only live float."

Jim Hayslett, one of Newt's boys in the late fifties, remembered being roped into performing in the parade when he was just a sophomore.

One day in November, Newt had called Hayslett into his office. "Hayslett," he said, "you're not going home for Thanksgiving this year."

"Coach, I want to go home," the gymnast protested.

"You can, but you can't go home until after the parade," Newt compromised. Hayslett had no idea what he was talking about— the Hudson's Parade in Detroit. That year, Newt took Hayslett and five others to Detroit, where they found an enormous float designed like a chunk of Swiss cheese, with a trampoline hidden deep in the middle.

"There [was] a big cat head coming out of the front of the float, with paws and the tongue coming out," Hayslett remembered.

"We've got six of us dressed as mice—we had mice suits—jumping off this cat's tongue onto the cheese and doing flips."

Back in Ann Arbor after the parade, Newt presented each of his boys with $25 for their fine performance. The next year, Hayslett gleefully dressed up in long pajamas along with several of his teammates and spent the parade bouncing on a trampoline recessed inside a four-poster bed float. "That was typical of what he was doing," Hayslett remembered with a grin. Newt later received an honorary citation for being such a longtime participant in the Hudson's Parade festivities.

On September 23, 1975, Ray Gura and Newt Loken ate lunch together in the Delta Restaurant. Newt had just come from an Athletic Department coaches' meeting, and the news wasn't good. The Big Ten had just accepted new NCAA recruiting and scholarship restrictions; now, gymnastics scholarships would be cut to a maximum of seven full-rides per team. Only four recruits would be allowed paid visits.

"We have come full-circle," Newt told Gura. "We started as a club sport, and we are approaching club sport status again."

Gura, who didn't believe college sports should have become so big in the first place, was not upset by the new restrictions. But their potential effect on Newt and his program was sobering.

"For a coach like Newt Loken," he wrote, "It signals the end of an era. Since starting at the University of Michigan almost thirty years ago he has seen the program grow to a point of national prominence. And now, a group of athletic directors (for money reasons) make some changes that will definitely de-emphasize the gymnastics program. The program that took him almost thirty years to develop."

If Newt felt bitter about the changes, he never showed it. His overarching goals—to instill a love for gymnastics and an excellent work ethic in his athletes—were still eminently possible. But it was then that Gura, who became a boys' coach in Cleveland, Ohio, knew that he didn't want to coach at a university. And Newt had to have felt at least somewhat saddened that the sport he had devoted his life to, especially at Michigan, would not be so prominent in the future.

In the late '70s and early '80s, Michigan slipped from its traditional position at the top of the Big Ten heap. Once, the big names in men's gymnastics coaching had been Loken, Pond and Szypula; now, new and younger coaches like Fred Roethlisberger were taking over and reinvigorating the storied programs. And after the 1975 and 1976 seasons, Newt had lost a huge core of talent.

"We didn't quite replace them with the same caliber guys," Kurt Golder remembered. "We were then in second and third in the Big Ten, and that was it. We never really got it back until I came back [to coach Michigan in 1997]."

For years, Newt had had strong pipelines flowing from the top gyms in Canada and the powerhouse high school programs in Chicago. But Newt's recruiting style was very low profile, and the new breed of coach was more aggressive than in the past. Before, Newt's enthusiasm could outlast anyone else's—he was the exception. Now, irrepressible energy like Newt's was practically part of the job description. The other programs had caught on, and wanted to do what Michigan had done.

"There were a lot of coaches in Newt's time ... who could not maintain that enthusiasm year after year," Ray Gura said. "So I think they lose that competitive edge. I think a number of those guys retired toward the end of Newt's career and new guys came in who were more aggressive, recruiting-wise or more aggressive coaching-wise. ... I think just as Newt's tenure was coming to an end, a lot of new, fresh coaches were coming on the scene and out-recruited him."

Newt still had some standout gymnasts in those last few years. Darrell Yee, a star rings specialist and eventual team captain, arrived in 1978 and went on to win three Big Ten titles in the event. Newt's enthusiasm remained an attractive recruiting tool.

"Although I was also interested in Michigan State, I chose Michigan even though I was impressed with both coaches and their programs," Yee remembered. "Newt was a big factor because of his contagious enthusiasm for the sport and life. He really sold his program well and the rich history of Michigan gymnastics."

Above the gym entrance, Newt had hung a sign in Chinese, which his daughter Chris had sent him. It translated to: "If you labor humbly with diligent care, you will barely fall short of perfection." The motto fit Newt's entire career—his long, uncomplaining hours in the gym coaching, his humility and joy in his team's accomplishments, and the many accolades he amassed. (He did enjoy telling people that the sign meant, "Watch out for falling bricks.") Yee never forgot that sign, applying its message to his whole career—especially after one of his first meets freshman year. On one hand, Yee thought he'd done a good job. Newt, on the other hand, was visibly upset.

"My form was lacking, with bent legs and feet apart at times," Yee remembered. "He really got on my case about that. But that was a good early lesson for me. After that incident I never wanted him upset at me again over bad form during the competitions."

Following Newt's lesson, Yee hardly ever gave anyone a chance to be displeased with his performance—or to win a rings title. From his sophomore year on, he was a sure bet at the Big Ten Championships.

"After I won the third title I remember breathing a huge sigh of relief while on the podium receiving the award because I was under so much pressure," Yee said. "I think I got lucky winning the first one in my sophomore year. I think I earned the title in my junior and senior year! If I had to rank one as the sweetest, I would say the third and last one. Newt was so supportive and happy for me. I am so glad I was able to share the experience with a coach that I both admired and looked up to my entire college career."

One teammate that especially stood out to Yee was all-arounder Nigel Rothwell. "[He was] definitely the leader of the team and most popular," Yee said.

Rothwell, a protégé of former Michigan gymnast Nino Marion, contributed not only to Michigan but also to the Canadian National team in the late 1970s, competing year-round. The only international competitor on Michigan's team by 1979, Rothwell competed in England, France, Yugoslavia, Romania, Japan and China, where there could be up to 20,000 people in the crowd. Not surprisingly, Newt told the *Daily* "Nigel enjoys performing and radiates a pleasant disposition. The judges like to watch him."

"Ask Nigel Rothwell about gymnastics," the *Daily* noted, "and he'll turn on a 300-watt grin that just never burns out."

Rothwell's love for his sport was unabashed. He remembered forgetting what he was doing on floor exercise at Big Tens in his sophomore year; since then, he had gained a much stronger focus

"For me it's fun," he told the *Daily*. "I get fired up, and I just have a really good time."

By the 1979-80 school year, expectations for Newt's team had fallen from their heyday. Now, most fans expected to be entertained, even if Michigan wasn't winning much. At entertaining, of course, few people could top Newt. He had always felt that getting the crowd excited about gymnastics was a large part of his program's success, and poured almost as much energy and verve into that as into coaching.

In September, Newt revealed the "ultimate promotion"—he was bringing in the Korean National Team for an exhibition on

October 28 at Crisler Arena. He'd scheduled the best competition possible for his boys in the regular season, hoping for gradual improvement and maybe a spark from the new freshman twins, Kevin and Mike McKee of Toledo. The competition would start with an informal contest against the visiting Koreans.

On the first stop of their Great Lakes Tour, the Koreans easily beat Michigan's men's and women's gymnastics teams. But afterward, both coaches "couldn't contain their pleasure over their own team's (sic) performances." Darrell Yee provided the Wolverines with their only outright individual win on rings, the one event that Michigan won as a team.

"Super stimulating," said Newt after the meet, his excitement unabated. "I was elated over our winning rings."

Three other Wolverines besides Yee tied for first with Koreans—senior Dorian Deaver on pommel horse, freshman Kevin McKee on vault and sophomore Marshall Garfield on the parallel bars.

Next up on the schedule was York University in Toronto, a team that featured three members of the Canadian national squad. The Wolverines lost by only 1.50 points—a much better performance than the nearly twelve-point loss to the Koreans.

But the early moral victories didn't forecast a successful season. Even with an exciting upset of Indiana State at the end of the year, the Wolverines didn't make NCAA Championships; no Big Ten team did. And the following season wasn't much better. Losing suddenly became the norm for Michigan, a hard fall for a team that had for so long piled up wins like clockwork.

The Wolverines got back on track somewhat, winning more than they lost in 1982, but still finishing fifth in the Big Ten, once again out of the NCAA team picture. Newt, now decidedly a part of the old guard in gymnastics coaching and thinking of spending more time with his beloved Dorothy, didn't tell anyone that he was contemplating retirement.

Chapter 21

1983—Newt's Last Season

On August 1, 1982, the letter came, as it always did. Newt always sent out a welcoming preseason letter to his gymnasts just before they returned to Ann Arbor. He'd summarize the events of the summer, emphasize any achievements (especially academic ones), and generally try to get his boys fired up for the coming season.

This year, it read:

And so summer is swiftly coming to a close with your well deserved break near completion and the commencement of school just over the horizon. For many of you, it'll be the climax of your four years at Michigan and for others it'll be just the start of your great years ahead. Regardless, I am sure it'll be a good one since you seem to have a knack of making it so. ...

Once again I must compliment you on your academic prowess as evidenced by those marvelous transcripts that passed my desk. With all those 3.0's (and better) we must be the most studious team on campus. If we can't win a Big Ten Gym title we're surely a winning academic team—proud of you!

> *Can't believe how we constantly come up with a better schedule each year in spite of this being our thirty-sixth year of Michigan Gymnastics. … By season's end we should be ol' pros & completely ready for the Big Tens and NCAA's. Have a place for all your names on The Wall so work on it—especially our departing seniors since it's their last chance.*

Nowhere did Newt mention that this was the last preseason letter he'd send out. Nowhere did he hint that this was to be his last season. As always, he was thinking of his gymnasts first. He knew that to announce his impending retirement before the season even began would take the focus off his team and place it squarely on himself, making the competitions more of a farewell tour than just another one in the long line of years. No one knew except for Newt, Dorothy, and the Loken kids, but the end of his coaching career was approaching. He wanted, like most hardworking men, the freedom to spend more time with his family, not just Dorothy but the four talented, Michigan-graduated children he'd helped raise and who were now scattered across the country.

"I thought I wouldn't work on any of those angles," Newt said. "I'd just wait until after the Big Ten meet, then announce it. I told Fritz Crisler and Don Canham, 'If you will, don't say anything to anybody until after I've announced it.' At one time, [Canham] had an alumni gathering and said, 'Coach Loken, he's actually thinking about retiring. Let's try and keep him around.' Joking, kind of humorous. I just felt I'd like to go slam-bang until the end. The only one who knew about it was Newti, and he came all the way across the country from Colorado in a train [to see my last Big Tens]."

In a fairy tale, Newt's career would culminate with a thirteenth Big Ten title and third national championship. But it wasn't to be. The dynasties of the sixties and seventies had gone; and other schools had caught up to Michigan, especially with the demise of the trampoline as a gymnastic event. The ever-shifting rules had been modified yet again—now each team would send up five men on each event, and every score would count. More than ever, one mistake could sink a team. Newt, along with his old friend George Szypula, who was now coaching at Michigan State, fought the rule change but were thwarted. As always, however, Newt was unfailingly optimistic about his team's chances, and his enjoyment of his final season as coach wouldn't be dimmed by a won-lost record. Newt's relationships with people, not his wins on the competition floor, were always what mattered most.

Now, the Wolverines were led by Milan Stanovich, who Newt felt led by example.

"A captain can be good more so by his actions than his words," Newt said. "This year, he has done a good job leading the team by example with his organized workouts and meet performances." Unlike in past years, however, the team lacked depth of talent. Newt hoped to alleviate that somewhat by adding a South African gymnast, Gavin Meyerowitz, to the mix, but depth problems and injuries continued to plague the team throughout the year. Now it was Michigan who could post its highest score of the season, as weaker teams had once done against the Wolverines, and still be "outclassed." Defending national champion Nebraska rolled into Ann Arbor at the end of January in 1983, having won four NCAA championships in a row. Newt told the *Daily* that "it could be neck and neck if the pommel horse goes really well," but even with a fine performance on the apparatus, the Cornhuskers, along with Ohio State, soundly beat Michigan, which finally broke the 270-point mark. Michigan's top gymnasts, like Stanovich, Dino Manus and the curly-haired McKee twins, Mike and Kevin, could match up with any in the nation.

Mike and Kevin McKee were identical twins, who, Newt said, had "talent coming out of their ears." He'd known them nearly their whole lives (basically making them typical Michigan recruits)—growing up in Toledo, they'd begun coming to Ann Arbor to practice with Newt since they were seven years old. Their coach, Neil Goldbey, always brought his best tumblers to Ann Arbor to see Newt.

"They had the bounce, the lift, the energy, and most importantly, the aerial sense," Newt said. "I treasured the day I could get 'em up here as legitimate Michigan gymnasts."

The twins felt the same—"I always wanted to go to Michigan," said Kevin.

Both contributed on floor and vault, while Kevin, who often tended to outshine his brother, was also in the high bar lineup. Newt said Kevin's double backflip floor mount was "high enough to walk under." So many years later, even as his own career was about to end, Newt couldn't believe these little McKees who he'd watched grow up were about to graduate from the University of Michigan.

Dino Manus was another top senior from whom Newt was expecting big things. Manus had found the perfect coach in Newt, who eagerly allowed Manus to put his academics first—along with competing as a varsity gymnast, he was trying to get into medical school. Occasionally, he even had to miss practice. Some coaches might have resented it or even forbidden it. But Newt's support was constant, whether Manus' endeavors took him into or out of the gym.

"He let me have both gymnastics and medical school," Manus told the *Daily* gratefully. "And he's so cute—he looks like Mr. Magoo."

But just before the Michigan State meet, Manus injured himself during practice on the parallel bars, opening the injury floodgates. At the meet, Meyerowitz knocked out his kneecap falling off the pommel horse. Michigan only had four men to compete on rings. By the end of the competition, captain Stanovich's ankle was beginning to bother him. The Spartans walked all over their old rivals, but afterward Szypula wasn't shy about barking out his contempt for the new, no-cushion scoring.

"The rules are stupid," he said unequivocally. "But they're still the rules."

Newt, as usual, tried to focus on the bright side of the meet. Despite the loss, his boys had won five of the six event titles.

A few weeks later, without Manus or Meyerowitz, the team traveled to UCLA and Houston for spring break. As a squad, the Wolverines fared badly due to the absence of two top gymnasts; but Kevin McKee took first on the high bar at the UCLA Invitational, and senior Rick Kaufmann won the still rings at Houston. Now Big Tens were coming up—Newt's last chance at a title, though none of his boys yet knew it. With the injuries to Manus and Meyerowitz still lingering, Michigan wasn't even thought to be a contender.

Despite his pain, Manus managed to compete and even excel, earning fifth place on high bar. As a team, however, Michigan barely escaped the cellar, finishing fifth as Illinois and Ohio State tied for the championship. Six gymnasts made it to event finals, bringing home seven awards. Mike McKee topped his brother and won the floor title, and Dave Miller, an Ann Arbor native, turned in a surprising second place finish on the parallel bars.

Because the Wolverines hadn't won Big Tens, only individuals—Stanovich, Manus, the McKees and Kaufmann—would compete for titles at the national championships. With team competition over for the season, Newt finally broke the news of his retirement to everyone on March 17. And not only his gymnasts were affected; when the notice was posted on the cheerleading squad's bulletin board, the co-captain of the team, Bob Seymour, was "pretty floored."

"There's no way that gymnastics will ever be able to give back to Newt Loken what he's given to gymnastics," said Manus.

"[He's] not just a great coach," freshman Rich Landman said. "He almost adopted you when you came on the team."

Newt was floored too when he saw the emotions that came pouring from his gymnasts.

"Some of my gymnasts came into my office and ... they'd sit there and almost cry," Newt remembered. "It really affected me. I saw this and I thought, 'I'm just a guy passing through. I happened to have a job and they kept me on the job for thirty-eight years. Two years before that, a teacher's assistant. ... I'm very thankful for the employment and I hope I did all right.' I don't cry because it ended but [smile] because it happened. The greatest thing in the world. I could have been in phys ed at some grade school. Who am I to be Michigan? All the Minneapolis friends up there, they think Michigan is so great. But it happened."

No one but Newt himself would put his years of accomplishment at Michigan so modestly.

A group of Newt's former gymnasts, Ward Black, David Seely and Rich Kenney, flew back to Ann Arbor as soon as they heard the announcement. The weather in Michigan was cold and unwelcoming—making it that much nicer to step into the gym.

"Inside it was warm, rich with the smell of hardwood and leather," Black wrote afterward. "And there was Coach Loken, a big smiling bear of a man, holding out his hand and radiating a warmth of his own. We walked toward his office past a long gym wall covered with plaques, medals, and photographs of Michigan gymnasts from the present and past. Amidst all these totems of athletic achievement was a large banner that read 'THE WALL OF CHAMPIONS.' These were champions whose skill, muscle, desire, and drive had all been molded by one man, a man who would soon be leaving this place and this sport behind. But Newt

Loken's spirit and inspiration will always beam like a beacon through those names and faces on the wall."

All those Michigan men, whose lives Newt had touched, are his enduring legacy.

In his usual unassuming way, Newt had waited until the end of the year to announce his retirement, preventing a big celebration.

"I think he was sorry about it," daughter Lani said later. "Not that he felt that he needed a big celebration, but that it would have been a wonderful time to bring so many people back to Ann Arbor and share with them."

Newt may not have gotten his farewell night in 1983, but that didn't stop his family or the Michigan Athletic Department. During the 1983 football season, the Michigan marching band spelled out "NEWT" on the field during halftime to honor the longtime coach. And quietly, Lani and her siblings were gathering the heartfelt letters of thanks for Newt's memory book—and donations for a trip to Norway for him and Dorothy. For years he had enjoyed interjecting a hearty "Uff da!" into everyday conversation—a Norwegian expression that Newt could work into almost any situation. He had long wanted to visit the country of his heritage.

"The response was more than I could have ever imagined," Lani said. "Within the week, I received beautiful letters with $100 checks in them. All together, his friends contributed over $5,000 to their trip to Norway. ... [Later Newt] stayed up all night reading the letters, as tears were flowing from his eyes. The next day he was almost speechless. He was so appreciative of the kind thoughts of all the people who had written."

Newt sent out a heartfelt thank-you note to his many gymnasts, colleagues and friends on August 5, 1983.

"I have just returned from a week in Eugene, Oregon visiting my daughter, Lani, and her family and at that time she showed me the stack of letters which have arrived at her residence," Newt wrote. "Until then I had not seen any of them so obviously it was quite overwhelming reading all of your beautiful letters." Of course, he couldn't resist a plug for his beloved team. Having popped into the gym repeatedly all summer, he reported that "they're looking good and with the super group of incoming recruits it should be a banner year of gymnastics under Coach Bob Darden's tutelage!"

Chapter 22

Life After Coaching

In the fall of 1983 Newt and Dorothy made their long-awaited trip to Europe. They stopped first in Germany, where their son, Jon, was studying. He had been instrumental in helping them find Newt's ancestral village in Hallingdal, Norway. They also traveled to Sweden, where Dorothy's maternal ancestors had lived before immigrating to the Midwest in the late 1800s.

But after thirty-six years immersed in Michigan sports, there was no way Newt could remove himself completely. Following his trip with Dorothy, he was back in the gym. He could never leave.

Now, one of his former gymnasts and assistant coaches, Bob Darden, took over head coaching duties. The old traditions continued, and Newt was always an honored guest at practice—and at meets. He still hadn't missed one since he took the reins of the team in 1948. He also never missed a Homecoming football game. The cheerleader to end all cheerleaders just couldn't stay away. Until the early 2000s, Newt continued his yearly bounce around the field at the Big House, leading cheers and bringing a smile to every fan's face.

"You may not know the name, but you know the man," a Michigan magazine said of Newt. "Remember your last Homecoming game?

"The alumni cheerleaders jump up on the wall in front of the stands to lead some cheers. 'Gimme a long cheer,' shouts an impish-looking fellow wearing a crushed-down navy hat, its front brim turned up to reveal a maize block 'M'.

"'Yea-a-a-a,' he draws his hands apart, stretching out the crowd's responding cheer.

"'Gimme a short cheer,' he grins, 'Ye-' and he abruptly cuts it off.

"'Gimme a loud cheer,' he braces himself for the ensuing roar.

"'Gimme a silent cheer,' his mouth opens wide but there is no sound. The puckish grin returns, followed by a leprechaun's giggle, and he jumps off the wall to repeat the performance for the next section."

Rich Dopp, a Michigan gymnast from 1991-1995, warmly remembered the performances in 2007, a few years after they'd finally ended.

"It may sound a little dorky, but it just makes me want to go, 'Meechigan! Meechigan! Rah, rah!'"

Unfortunately for Darden, the red-headed high-bar man's success in competition didn't translate to success coaching his old team. In thirteen years, he compiled only two winning seasons, never finishing higher than fifth in the Big Ten. None of his teams made the NCAA team finals.

"He was a smooth, elegant worker, a good competitor," Kurt Golder remembered. "As for why he wasn't as successful as a coach as he was as a gymnast, it's really hard for me to say because I wasn't there all the time. ... A big percentage of it is getting the good athletes. A really good coach can take a walk-on athlete or a mediocre athlete and develop him into a champion, but you can't do that year-in and year-out. He probably wasn't getting enough of the top echelon recruits, the blue-chip recruits."

As Darden's coaching career drew to its close, the Athletic Department announced it was dropping the men's gymnastics program. Though Darden may not have had much success as a coach, he enjoyed strong support from the gymnastics community. He and assistant coach Mike Milidonis easily riled up the friends and alumni of the gymnastics team and fought the cut with a fact-finding and letter-writing campaign, discrediting every reason the Athletic Department gave for why the program needed to go.

Darden managed to keep the fight going even when his team was deprived of its scholarships. And when a new Athletic Director, Joe Roberson, took over, one look at the massive gymnastics turmoil he'd inherited prompted the obvious question: Why was the University trying to drop a program with such strong and obvious support? Roberson promptly reinstated the program and began searching for a new coach to bring it back to prominence.

The top three candidates were Mark Williams, who later became the head coach of national powerhouse Oklahoma; Mike Burns, a future Michigan assistant coach and Minnesota head coach; and Kurt Golder.

Golder's first job out of college was as an assistant coach for the Michigan women's gymnastics team, and he lived quite close to where the men's practice facility, the Newt Loken Gymnastics Training Center, stands today. After that, he took a job coaching at Ann Arbor Huron High School, finally departing Ann Arbor in 1977.

Before the 1991-92 season, Golder fielded assistant coaching job offers from the University of Iowa and another school. Iowa seemed as though it was meant to be for Golder. As he tried to decide between the two offers, the movie *Field of Dreams* popped onto his TV in the hotel.

"Is this heaven?" Shoeless Joe asked, standing on the grass of the magical field.

"No," replied Ray Kinsella. "It's Iowa."

For Golder, it was a perfect sign. He took the Iowa job, planning to stay indefinitely.

In 1996, the Michigan head coaching job opened up. But Golder wasn't jumping at the chance. He was content at Iowa, the pay was the same as the Michigan job, and the cost of living was much less. That would have been the end of it—except the phone calls from Newt just wouldn't stop. The coach had lost none of his dogged persistence.

Urgings from his old coach were nothing to take lightly. Newt was instrumental in bringing Golder back to Michigan.

"He gave me my big opportunity," said Golder. Newt, he acknowledged, could recruit anyone he wanted when Golder was looking at Michigan. Yet Newt gave Golder, who had to attend junior college in preparation for the university, a shot at the team. "He took me and gave me a scholarship, and gave me an opportunity to get a Big Ten education and a Michigan education, where otherwise I would have had to settle for a lot less."

Finally, Golder agreed to interview for the Michigan job. From Newt, he'd learned to be the first one in the gym and the last to leave—in other words, if you were going to do something, you'd better do it right. Golder threw himself full-force into the interview process—and got the position.

"Some of the administrators, the assistant administrators … were of the spirit that, if we're going to keep [the gymnastics program], let's do it right," Golder said. "One of the conditions I made was I wouldn't even consider the job if they wouldn't give me the full NCAA allotment of scholarships. When they hired me, that's when they put the scholarships back in place. Then it went from very poor or hardly any support in the department, to very good support, and that's the way it's been since I've been here."

He's been the head coach ever since, winning three Big Ten titles and two national championships, one in 1999 and one in

2010. And he made sure that Newt was present for that first championship, won at the University of Nebraska.

"We took him out to the competition with us, and he was sitting at the head table," Golder remembered. "Bart Conner made the comment, 'Here's Coach Loken from the Michigan Wolverines. He is looked upon by everybody in the gymnastics world [like] John Wooden of basketball.' ... Very similar to the Bo Schembechler of football."

Throughout his life, one of Newt's favorite pastimes was to "circulate." No day was complete without some amount of socializing. In the Athletic Department, they even began calling him "Scooter," because of his trait of scooting here and there between offices, relishing the opportunity to visit with coaches, administrators, secretaries and others.

Following his retirement, with his days no longer filled with teaching and coaching, Newt turned "circulating" into a true profession. Now, he could circulate as he wanted. Typically, he'd start at his favorite doughnut shop, where he'd buy a cup of coffee and a doughnut, then chat up the gals behind the counter. From there he had a choice of countless places in town—after all, everyone knew and loved him. He'd always make sure to visit with his former associates in the Athletic Department, and Monday afternoons would always find him at the gym, eagerly watching the gymnasts practice their routines.

Newt also got tremendous enjoyment out of being with his grandchildren, Todd and Tucker Loken-Dahle and Kaj and Kari Loken-Kim. He often took them on "Mystery Rides," during which they'd go from one place to another, never disclosing the next location. With no particular schedule, he made sure they were places the kids would enjoy. They might start at the bowling alley for forty-five minutes, then go to McDonald's for an Egg McMuffin, then to the golf driving range, and then to see a movie. Of course, one of his favorite places to take the grandkids was

Chuck-E-Cheese. Swimming also became a regular part of his life after his retirement, and he often took his grandchildren along. Nearly every day, he would head to the warmest pool in town to swim some lengths and work out with the flotation devices.

In Newt's later years, he often took trips down Memory Lane—sometimes literally. If just thinking about the good old days wasn't enough, he'd revisit the places he loved—Mt. Pleasant, Caberfae Lodge, Mackinac Island, Petoskey, Traverse City—to reminisce. He loved not just the University of Michigan and Ann Arbor, but the entire state. He and Dorothy always tried to head north several times a year to visit their beloved Michigan countryside in their recreational vehicle (nicknamed "The Hollie").

In 2003, the men's gymnastics team moved out of their beloved but cramped quarters in the Intramural Sports Building and into a new practice facility in the Sports Coliseum. To put it kindly, the small IM gym had been overly cozy, with events constantly overlapping. To vault, a gymnast had to start in the hallway. Now, the team had its own space, dedicated only to men's gymnastics, full of any equipment the gymnasts could want. Like Newt, the new gym exuded warmth (quite literally, in the summer). Looking past the Coliseum's unassuming exterior, the gymnasts found not just an excellent practice facility, but a welcoming home away from home.

Their new gym's name? The Newt Loken Gymnastics Training Center. The Wall of Champions was recreated, bigger and better (and longer!). It's still the highlight of a gymnast's Michigan career to know that his name is on the Wall, with all the other Wolverine greats of the past sixty years. Everyone wants to win the Newt Loken Award, given at every home meet for the best performance of the night.

And every gymnast, from the Darden through the Golder eras, has known and loved Newt. Until moving to Oregon after the 2010 season to be closer to two of his children, the father of Michigan men's gymnastics was a regular presence at practice, especially during the competition season. In fact, he didn't miss a home meet for over sixty years.

Michigan head coach Kurt Golder lined up his team of twenty-four gymnasts in the Newt Loken Gymnastics Training Center on March 16, 2008. On most Mondays like this one, Newt would already be seated in his chair by the gym's door, waiting eagerly for the start of practice. Today, because the team had gotten the previous weekend off, Newt decided to stay home. There were few things he enjoyed more than rehashing the most recent meet with the Wolverines. But his absence played right into Golder's plans.

"This Saturday, against Ohio State, we're going to honor Newt for sixty years of perfect attendance at home meets," Golder announced as the boys grinned. Then he explained what he wanted them to do.

"The announcer is going to read off the plaque on the PA system, and when he says, 'Newt Loken,' I want you all to bow."

A smattering of giggles broke out. Junior Scott Bregman, on crutches, wondered exactly what he was supposed to do about this whole bowing thing. Golder demonstrated, going down on one knee with a hand over his heart, as if he was being knighted. It was difficult to keep a straight face as the boys practiced kneeling and bowing in perfect unison—or at least something close.

Finally, the big night arrived. Newt had no idea what was planned, or why Dorothy had suddenly decided that tonight, she'd accompany him to the meet. Bob Willoughby picked them up as usual—driving at night had become too dangerous for

Newt—and brought them to Cliff Keen Arena, where the air was thick with gleeful anticipation. A good portion of the crowd knew of the upcoming ceremony, and the Wolverines hadn't beaten the hated Buckeyes head-to-head since 2004. This was an important evening in more ways than one.

Two cushioned folding chairs stood in their usual place of honor, near the floor exercise, for Newt and his guest to sit. No stairs for the coach to climb, and no hard benches to deal with. Newt's entrances were never conspicuous, but always, it seemed as though a happy glow would pass into the crowd. Almost simultaneously, all the gymnasts, parents and serious fans in the arena would realize Newt had arrived, and one by one, admirers would make their way to his chair. On this night, nearly all his visitors had mischievous smiles on their faces—"I know something you don't!" Newt, even with Dorothy as his unusual guest, suspected nothing.

With the meet's start just minutes away, the Michigan and Ohio State gymnasts were introduced, lining up on the floor facing Newt's chairs, as always. Then Bob Willoughby rose with Michigan assistant coach Scott Vetere (an honorary member of "Newt's boys"), leading the coach out on the floor. Kurt Golder, along with his assistant coach Xiao Yuan, Ohio State head coach Miles Avery and Big Ten Network cameras, waited at the edge, Golder holding the plaque.

"Tonight," intoned the public address announcer, "we will recognize Dr. Newt Loken's perfect attendance record for sixty consecutive years at men's gymnastics home competitions." Along with the Michigan gymnasts, the crowd stood and applauded— and suddenly, in near-perfect unison, the Wolverines knelt with hands over hearts, grinning up at the father of their program.

"For me, it was great," Golder said afterward, grinning as much over Newt's ceremony as his team's big win over their archrivals. "I've had a rapport with Newt for over thirty years,